Mastering T-SQL: A Comprehensive Guide to SQL Server Programming

Preface

Data is at the heart of every modern organization, and the ability to effectively query, manipulate, and manage that data is a crucial skill for developers, analysts, and database administrators alike. T-SQL, the powerful extension of SQL (Structured Query Language) for Microsoft SQL Server, has become an indispensable tool for these tasks. Whether you're building complex queries, optimizing performance, or implementing advanced data processing logic, mastering T-SQL can set you apart as a database professional.

"Mastering T-SQL: A Comprehensive Guide to SQL Server Programming" is designed to be your go-to resource for learning and mastering T-SQL, no matter where you are in your journey. From the basics of querying a database to advanced topics like dynamic SQL and performance tuning, this book provides a structured and practical approach to T-SQL programming.

Why This Book?

This book is more than a collection of syntax and examples. It's a carefully crafted guide that emphasizes both the "how" and the "why" of T-SQL programming. By the time you finish, you'll not only know how to write effective T-SQL scripts but also understand the underlying principles that make your scripts efficient, secure, and maintainable.

Who Is This Book For?

This book is written for:

- **Beginners**: If you're new to T-SQL, this book will walk you through the fundamentals in a clear and approachable way.
- **Intermediate Users**: If you already have some experience with SQL, this book will deepen your knowledge and introduce advanced concepts that you can immediately apply.
- **Advanced Users**: If you're a seasoned professional, this book will serve as a reference guide and provide insights into optimization techniques and advanced use cases.

What Will You Learn?

Through this book, you will:

- Understand the basics of querying and managing data with T-SQL.
- Learn how to write efficient and maintainable code.
- Explore advanced topics like stored procedures, triggers, and error handling.
- Master performance tuning, indexing, and query optimization.
- Work with modern data formats like XML and JSON.
- Develop the skills to handle real-world scenarios and large-scale data systems.

How Is This Book Structured?

The book is divided into five parts to guide you through the learning process:

1. **Getting Started with T-SQL**: Learn the basics of T-SQL and set up your environment.
2. **Core T-SQL Features**: Build a solid foundation with essential T-SQL skills, including joins, subqueries, and functions.
3. **Advanced Programming with T-SQL**: Dive into advanced concepts like dynamic SQL, transactions, and triggers.
4. **Optimization and Best Practices**: Focus on performance tuning, indexing, and secure coding practices.
5. **Advanced Topics and Case Studies**: Apply your knowledge to real-world scenarios and explore specialized techniques.

What Makes This Book Unique?

- **Practical Examples**: Each chapter is filled with hands-on exercises and real-world examples to reinforce learning.
- **Focus on Best Practices**: Emphasis is placed on writing secure, efficient, and maintainable T-SQL code.
- **Comprehensive Coverage**: The book spans a wide range of topics, ensuring you're prepared for any T-SQL challenge.
- **Accessible Language**: Complex concepts are explained in plain language, making the book accessible to all readers.

Acknowledgments

This book would not have been possible without the support and feedback of the vibrant SQL Server community. Special thanks go to database professionals, mentors, and colleagues who shared their insights and experiences, inspiring many of the examples and solutions presented in this book.

Final Words

As you work through the chapters of this book, you'll discover not only how to use T-SQL but also how to think like a database professional. Whether you're building reports, automating tasks, or tackling enterprise-level challenges, the knowledge you gain here will empower you to excel in your role.

Let's embark on this journey together and unlock the full potential of T-SQL!

Happy learning,

BOSCO-IT CONSULTING

Table of Contents

Part	Chapter	Topics Covered
Part 1: Getting Started with T-SQL	**Chapter 1: Introduction to T-SQL**	What is T-SQL? T-SQL vs Standard SQL T-SQL use cases Overview of SQL Server Management Studio (SSMS)
	Chapter 2: Setting Up the Environment	Installing SQL Server and SSMS Connecting to a database instance Creating your first database
	Chapter 3: Basics of SQL	Overview of SQL commands: DDL, DML, and DCL Writing your first SELECT statement Filtering data with WHERE Sorting data with ORDER BY
Part 2: Core T-SQL Features	**Chapter 4: Data Types and Variables**	Overview of T-SQL data types Declaring and using variables Type conversions and casting

	Chapter 5: Functions in T-SQL	Scalar functions Aggregate functions String manipulation functions Date and time functions
	Chapter 6: Joins and Subqueries	Types of joins: INNER, OUTER, CROSS Writing efficient joins Subqueries and correlated subqueries Common Table Expressions (CTEs)
	Chapter 7: Advanced Query Techniques	Grouping and aggregation HAVING vs WHERE clauses Window functions (ROW_NUMBER, RANK, etc.) PIVOT and UNPIVOT
Part 3: Advanced Programming with T-SQL	**Chapter 8: Stored Procedures and User-Defined Functions**	Creating stored procedures Parameterized queries User-defined scalar and table-valued functions
	Chapter 9: Error Handling and Transactions	TRY...CATCH for error handling BEGIN TRANSACTION and COMMIT/ROLLBACK Managing nested transactions
	Chapter 10: Triggers and Events	What are triggers? DML triggers: AFTER and INSTEAD OF Audit logging with triggers
	Chapter 11: Working with XML and JSON	Generating and parsing XML in T-SQL Querying JSON data in SQL Server Practical use cases of XML and JSON in T-SQL

Part 4: Optimization and Best Practices	**Chapter 12: Indexing and Performance Tuning**	Types of indexes: clustered and non-clustered Query execution plans Identifying and resolving slow queries
	Chapter 13: Security and Permissions	Granting and revoking permissions Securing sensitive data Using roles and users for access control
	Chapter 14: Best Practices for T-SQL Development	Writing readable and maintainable code Avoiding common pitfalls Tips for debugging T-SQL scripts
Part 5: Advanced Topics and Case Studies	**Chapter 15: Dynamic SQL**	When and how to use dynamic SQL Risks and mitigations (SQL injection) Practical examples of dynamic SQL
	Chapter 16: Working with Large Datasets	Bulk operations with BULK INSERT Partitioning tables and queries Working with temp tables and table variables
	Chapter 17: Real-World Applications	Building a reporting system with T-SQL Data validation and cleanup with T-SQL Automating tasks with scheduled jobs and SQL Agent
Appendices	**Appendix A**	T-SQL Reserved Keywords

Appendix B   Common Error Codes and
                          Troubleshooting

Appendix C   Glossary of Terms

Part 1: Getting Started with T-SQL

Chapter 1: Introduction to T-SQL

What is T-SQL?

Transact-SQL, commonly known as T-SQL, is Microsoft's proprietary extension to the standard SQL (Structured Query Language) used in SQL Server and Azure SQL Database. T-SQL enhances the capabilities of standard SQL by adding a rich set of procedural programming constructs, making it a powerful language for developing complex database applications.

T-SQL serves as both a data manipulation language (DML) and a data definition language (DDL), allowing users to not only query and modify data but also create and manage database objects. It provides a comprehensive set of tools for:

1. Data retrieval and manipulation
2. Database schema creation and modification
3. Stored procedure and function development
4. Transaction management
5. Error handling and flow control

T-SQL's origins can be traced back to the 1980s when Sybase developed it for their relational database management system. Microsoft later acquired a license to use Sybase's codebase, which became the foundation for SQL Server. Over the years,

Microsoft has significantly enhanced T-SQL, adding numerous features and capabilities that make it a robust and versatile language for database programming.

Key features of T-SQL include:

- **Extended functionality**: T-SQL includes additional commands and clauses not found in standard SQL, providing more control over data manipulation and database management.
- **Procedural programming**: Unlike standard SQL, which is primarily declarative, T-SQL allows for procedural programming with constructs like variables, loops, and conditional statements.
- **Integration with SQL Server**: T-SQL is tightly integrated with SQL Server, allowing developers to leverage the full power of the database engine and its features.
- **Advanced querying capabilities**: T-SQL offers sophisticated querying techniques, including common table expressions (CTEs), window functions, and pivoting/unpivoting operations.
- **Security features**: T-SQL provides robust security mechanisms, including user-defined roles, permissions, and encryption.

Understanding T-SQL is crucial for anyone working with SQL Server or Azure SQL Database, as it forms the foundation for interacting with these database systems effectively.

T-SQL vs Standard SQL

While T-SQL is based on standard SQL, it includes several extensions and modifications that set it apart. Understanding these differences is essential for developers transitioning from other database systems or those aiming to write portable SQL code.

Similarities:

1. **Basic syntax**: Both T-SQL and standard SQL share common syntax for basic operations like SELECT, INSERT, UPDATE, and DELETE.
2. **Data types**: Many core data types are the same or similar between T-SQL and standard SQL.
3. **Join operations**: Basic join operations (INNER, LEFT, RIGHT, FULL) are consistent across both languages.
4. **Aggregate functions**: Common aggregate functions like SUM, AVG, COUNT are present in both.

Key Differences:

1. **Procedural programming constructs**:

- T-SQL includes IF...ELSE statements, WHILE loops, and other control-of-flow elements not present in standard SQL.
- Example:

```
IF EXISTS (SELECT 1 FROM Customers WHERE CustomerID = 1)
BEGIN
    PRINT 'Customer found'
END
ELSE
BEGIN
    PRINT 'Customer not found'
```

```
END
```

2. **Top and Offset-Fetch**:

- T-SQL uses TOP for limiting result sets, while standard SQL typically uses LIMIT.
- T-SQL Example:

```
SELECT TOP 10 * FROM Products ORDER BY Price DESC
```

- Standard SQL Example:

```
SELECT * FROM Products ORDER BY Price DESC LIMIT 10
```

3. **Date and time functions**:

- T-SQL has its own set of date and time functions, which differ from standard SQL.
- T-SQL Example:

```
SELECT DATEADD(day, 7, GETDATE()) AS OneWeekFromNow
```

4. **String concatenation**:

- T-SQL uses the '+' operator for string concatenation, while standard SQL typically uses '||'.
- T-SQL Example:

```
SELECT FirstName + ' ' + LastName AS FullName FROM
Employees
```

- Standard SQL Example:

```
SELECT FirstName || ' ' || LastName AS FullName FROM
Employees
```

5. Common Table Expressions (CTEs):

- While CTEs are part of the SQL standard, T-SQL's implementation includes additional features like recursive CTEs.
- T-SQL Recursive CTE Example:

```
WITH EmployeeHierarchy AS (
    SELECT EmployeeID, ManagerID, FirstName, 0 AS Level
    FROM Employees
    WHERE ManagerID IS NULL
    UNION ALL
    SELECT e.EmployeeID, e.ManagerID, e.FirstName,
eh.Level + 1
    FROM Employees e
    INNER JOIN EmployeeHierarchy eh ON e.ManagerID =
eh.EmployeeID
)
SELECT * FROM EmployeeHierarchy
```

6. Error handling:

- T-SQL uses TRY...CATCH blocks for error handling, which is not part of standard SQL.
- Example:

```
BEGIN TRY
    -- Code that might cause an error
    INSERT INTO Customers (CustomerID, Name) VALUES (1,
'John Doe')
END TRY
BEGIN CATCH
    PRINT 'An error occurred: ' + ERROR_MESSAGE()
```

```
END CATCH
```

7. **Temporary tables**:

- T-SQL allows for the creation of local and global temporary tables using '#' and '##' prefixes, respectively.
- Example:

```
CREATE TABLE #TempCustomers (
    CustomerID INT,
    Name NVARCHAR(100)
)
```

8. **Identity columns**:

- T-SQL uses the IDENTITY property for auto-incrementing columns, while standard SQL typically uses AUTO_INCREMENT or SERIAL.
- T-SQL Example:

```
CREATE TABLE Products (
    ProductID INT IDENTITY(1,1) PRIMARY KEY,
    ProductName NVARCHAR(100)
)
```

9. **Pivot and Unpivot operations**:

- T-SQL provides PIVOT and UNPIVOT operators for transforming row data into column data and vice versa.
- Example:

```
SELECT *
FROM (SELECT Category, ProductName, Price FROM Products)
AS SourceTable
```

```
PIVOT (
    AVG(Price)
    FOR Category IN ([Electronics], [Clothing], [Books])
) AS PivotTable
```

10. **Window functions**:

- While window functions are part of the SQL standard, T-SQL's implementation and syntax may differ slightly.
- T-SQL Example:

```
SELECT
    ProductName,
    Price,
    ROW_NUMBER() OVER (ORDER BY Price DESC) AS PriceRank
FROM Products
```

Understanding these differences is crucial for writing efficient and portable SQL code, especially when working across different database systems or migrating between platforms.

T-SQL Use Cases

T-SQL's versatility and power make it suitable for a wide range of database-related tasks and applications. Here are some common use cases for T-SQL:

1. **Data Retrieval and Reporting**:

- Complex queries for business intelligence and reporting
- Ad-hoc data analysis
- Generation of dynamic reports

Example:

```
SELECT
    c.CustomerName,
    COUNT(o.OrderID) AS TotalOrders,
    SUM(od.Quantity * p.Price) AS TotalRevenue
FROM Customers c
LEFT JOIN Orders o ON c.CustomerID = o.CustomerID
LEFT JOIN OrderDetails od ON o.OrderID = od.OrderID
LEFT JOIN Products p ON od.ProductID = p.ProductID
GROUP BY c.CustomerName
HAVING COUNT(o.OrderID) > 5
ORDER BY TotalRevenue DESC
```

2. **Data Manipulation and Management**:

- Bulk data updates and deletions

- Data cleansing and normalization

- Merging data from multiple sources

Example:

```
-- Update product prices with a 10% increase for a specific
category
UPDATE Products
SET Price = Price * 1.10
WHERE CategoryID = 5

-- Delete old order records
DELETE FROM Orders
WHERE OrderDate < DATEADD(year, -5, GETDATE())
```

3. **Database Administration**:

- Managing database objects (tables, views, indexes, etc.)

- Implementing security measures and access control

- Monitoring database performance

Example:

```sql
-- Create a new table
CREATE TABLE Employees (
    EmployeeID INT PRIMARY KEY,
    FirstName NVARCHAR(50),
    LastName NVARCHAR(50),
    HireDate DATE
)

-- Create an index for improved query performance
CREATE NONCLUSTERED INDEX IX_Employees_LastName
ON Employees (LastName)

-- Grant select permission to a role
GRANT SELECT ON Employees TO [HR_Role]
```

4. **Stored Procedure Development**:

- Encapsulating complex business logic

- Improving performance by reducing network traffic

- Enhancing security by controlling data access

Example:

```sql
CREATE PROCEDURE usp_GetTopCustomers
    @TopN INT,
    @StartDate DATE,
    @EndDate DATE
AS
BEGIN
    SELECT TOP (@TopN)
        c.CustomerName,
        SUM(od.Quantity * p.Price) AS TotalPurchases
    FROM Customers c
    JOIN Orders o ON c.CustomerID = o.CustomerID
```

```sql
    JOIN OrderDetails od ON o.OrderID = od.OrderID
    JOIN Products p ON od.ProductID = p.ProductID
    WHERE o.OrderDate BETWEEN @StartDate AND @EndDate
    GROUP BY c.CustomerName
    ORDER BY TotalPurchases DESC
END
```

5. **ETL (Extract, Transform, Load) Processes**:

- Data warehousing operations
- Integrating data from multiple sources
- Performing complex data transformations

Example:

```sql
-- Extract data from source tables
WITH SourceData AS (
    SELECT
        c.CustomerID,
        c.CustomerName,
        o.OrderDate,
        p.ProductName,
        od.Quantity,
        p.Price
    FROM Customers c
    JOIN Orders o ON c.CustomerID = o.CustomerID
    JOIN OrderDetails od ON o.OrderID = od.OrderID
    JOIN Products p ON od.ProductID = p.ProductID
)
-- Transform and load into a fact table
INSERT INTO FactSales (CustomerID, OrderDate, ProductName,
Quantity, Revenue)
SELECT
    CustomerID,
    OrderDate,
    ProductName,
    Quantity,
    Quantity * Price AS Revenue
```

```
FROM SourceData
```

6. **Transaction Management**:

- Ensuring data integrity in multi-step operations
- Implementing complex business rules
- Handling concurrent data access

Example:

```
BEGIN TRANSACTION

BEGIN TRY
    -- Deduct inventory
    UPDATE Inventory
    SET Quantity = Quantity - @OrderQuantity
    WHERE ProductID = @ProductID

    -- Create order
    INSERT INTO Orders (CustomerID, OrderDate, TotalAmount)
    VALUES (@CustomerID, GETDATE(), @TotalAmount)

    -- Get the new OrderID
    DECLARE @NewOrderID INT = SCOPE_IDENTITY()

    -- Add order details
    INSERT INTO OrderDetails (OrderID, ProductID, Quantity,
Price)
    VALUES (@NewOrderID, @ProductID, @OrderQuantity,
@ProductPrice)

    COMMIT TRANSACTION
END TRY
BEGIN CATCH
    ROLLBACK TRANSACTION
    -- Log error or raise an exception
END CATCH
```

7. **Data Analysis and Business Intelligence**:

- Creating and managing data warehouses
- Implementing OLAP (Online Analytical Processing) solutions
- Developing complex analytical queries

Example:

```sql
WITH SalesData AS (
    SELECT
        YEAR(OrderDate) AS SalesYear,
        MONTH(OrderDate) AS SalesMonth,
        ProductID,
        SUM(Quantity * Price) AS Revenue
    FROM Orders o
    JOIN OrderDetails od ON o.OrderID = od.OrderID
    GROUP BY YEAR(OrderDate), MONTH(OrderDate), ProductID
)
SELECT
    SalesYear,
    SalesMonth,
    ProductID,
    Revenue,
    AVG(Revenue) OVER (
        PARTITION BY ProductID
        ORDER BY SalesYear, SalesMonth
        ROWS BETWEEN 2 PRECEDING AND CURRENT ROW
    ) AS MovingAvgRevenue
FROM SalesData
ORDER BY ProductID, SalesYear, SalesMonth
```

8. **Application Development**:

- Backend data access layer for applications
- Implementing business logic in the database

- Creating and managing database-driven web applications

Example:

```
CREATE PROCEDURE usp_CreateUser
    @Username NVARCHAR(50),
    @Email NVARCHAR(100),
    @Password NVARCHAR(100)
AS
BEGIN
    IF EXISTS (SELECT 1 FROM Users WHERE Username = @Username OR
Email = @Email)
    BEGIN
        RAISERROR('Username or email already exists', 16, 1)
        RETURN
    END

    INSERT INTO Users (Username, Email, PasswordHash,
CreatedDate)
    VALUES (@Username, @Email, HASHBYTES('SHA2_256', @Password),
GETDATE())

    SELECT SCOPE_IDENTITY() AS NewUserID
END
```

9. **Data Archiving and Purging**:

- Implementing data retention policies
- Archiving historical data
- Maintaining database performance by managing data volume

Example:

```
-- Archive old orders
INSERT INTO ArchivedOrders (OrderID, CustomerID, OrderDate,
TotalAmount)
SELECT OrderID, CustomerID, OrderDate, TotalAmount
FROM Orders
```

```
WHERE OrderDate < DATEADD(year, -5, GETDATE())

-- Delete archived orders from the main table
DELETE FROM Orders
WHERE OrderID IN (SELECT OrderID FROM ArchivedOrders)
```

10. **Performance Tuning and Optimization**:

- Writing efficient queries

- Creating and managing indexes

- Analyzing and improving query execution plans

    Example:

```
-- Create a covering index for a frequently used query
CREATE NONCLUSTERED INDEX IX_Orders_CustomerDate
ON Orders (CustomerID, OrderDate)
INCLUDE (TotalAmount)

-- Analyze query performance
SET STATISTICS IO ON
SET STATISTICS TIME ON

-- Run the query
SELECT CustomerID, SUM(TotalAmount) AS TotalRevenue
FROM Orders
WHERE OrderDate >= DATEADD(month, -6, GETDATE())
GROUP BY CustomerID

-- Review the statistics output
SET STATISTICS IO OFF
SET STATISTICS TIME OFF
```

These use cases demonstrate the versatility and power of T-SQL in handling a wide range of database-related tasks, from simple data retrieval to complex analytical processing and application development.

Overview of SQL Server Management Studio (SSMS)

SQL Server Management Studio (SSMS) is a powerful integrated environment for managing and interacting with SQL Server databases. It provides a comprehensive set of tools for database administrators, developers, and data analysts to configure, manage, and develop all components of SQL Server.

Key Features of SSMS:

1. **Object Explorer**:

   - Hierarchical view of all database objects
   - Easy navigation through servers, databases, tables, views, stored procedures, etc.
   - Context-sensitive right-click menus for quick actions

2. **Query Editor**:

   - Advanced T-SQL editing capabilities with syntax highlighting and IntelliSense
   - Multiple query windows for working on different scripts simultaneously
   - Execution plan visualization for query performance analysis

3. **Solution Explorer**:

   - Project management for database development

- Version control integration
- Script organization and management

4. **Template Explorer**:

- Pre-built T-SQL templates for common tasks
- Custom template creation and management

5. **Database Diagrams**:

- Visual representation of database schema
- Drag-and-drop interface for creating and modifying tables and relationships

6. **Activity Monitor**:

- Real-time monitoring of database processes and resource usage
- Identification of long-running queries and blocking issues

7. **Execution Plan Analysis**:

- Graphical and XML showplan for query execution analysis
- Performance statistics and optimization suggestions

8. **Data Import and Export Wizards**:

- Easy-to-use interfaces for transferring data between SQL Server and various data sources

- Support for flat files, Excel, and other database systems

9. **Backup and Restore Capabilities**:

- GUI-based tools for database backup and restore operations
- Scheduling and automation of backup tasks

10. **Security Management**:

- User and role management interfaces
- Permission assignment and auditing tools

11. **Replication Tools**:

- Configuration and management of database replication
- Monitoring of replication status and performance

12. **Maintenance Plans**:

- Creation and scheduling of database maintenance tasks
- Performance optimization and integrity checks

Working with SSMS:

1. **Connecting to a Database**:

- Launch SSMS and use the "Connect to Server" dialog

- Enter server name, authentication method, and credentials
- Select the database you want to work with

2. **Writing and Executing Queries**:

- Open a new query window (Ctrl+N)
- Write your T-SQL query
- Use F5 or the "Execute" button to run the query
- View results in the Results pane

Example:

```
USE AdventureWorks2019;
GO

SELECT TOP 10 ProductID, Name, ListPrice
FROM Production.Product
ORDER BY ListPrice DESC;
```

3. **Creating Database Objects**:

- Use Object Explorer to navigate to the desired location
- Right-click and select "New" to create tables, views, stored procedures, etc.
- Alternatively, use T-SQL scripts in the Query Editor

Example (Creating a table):

```
CREATE TABLE dbo.Employees (
    EmployeeID INT PRIMARY KEY IDENTITY(1,1),
    FirstName NVARCHAR(50),
    LastName NVARCHAR(50),
    HireDate DATE,
    Department NVARCHAR(50)
```

```
);
```

4. **Modifying Data**:

- Use the Query Editor to write INSERT, UPDATE, or DELETE statements
- For small datasets, you can use the table editor by right-clicking on a table and selecting "Edit Top 200 Rows"

Example:

```
INSERT INTO dbo.Employees (FirstName, LastName, HireDate,
Department)
VALUES ('John', 'Doe', '2023-01-15', 'IT');

UPDATE dbo.Employees
SET Department = 'Human Resources'
WHERE EmployeeID = 1;

DELETE FROM dbo.Employees
WHERE EmployeeID = 2;
```

5. **Viewing Execution Plans**:

- Enable "Include Actual Execution Plan" (Ctrl+M) before running a query
- Analyze the graphical plan to identify performance bottlenecks

6. **Managing Index**:

- Use Object Explorer to view existing indexes
- Right-click on a table and select "Design" to add or modify indexes
- Use the Index Tuning Advisor for index recommendations

7. **Backup and Restore**:

- Right-click on a database in Object Explorer
- Select "Tasks" > "Back Up..." or "Restore" > "Database..."
- Follow the wizard to complete the operation

8. **Generating Scripts**:

- Right-click on a database or object in Object Explorer
- Select "Script as" > "CREATE To" > "New Query Editor Window"
- Modify the generated script as needed

9. **Using Templates**:

- Open Template Explorer (View > Template Explorer)
- Double-click a template to open it in a new query window
- Customize the template for your specific needs

10. **Profiler and Extended Events**:

- Use SQL Server Profiler (Tools > SQL Server Profiler) for tracing database events
- Configure Extended Events sessions for more advanced monitoring and troubleshooting

SSMS is an essential tool for anyone working with SQL Server databases. Its rich feature set and intuitive interface make it possible to perform a wide range of database management and development tasks efficiently. As you become more familiar with SSMS, you'll discover numerous shortcuts and advanced features that can significantly enhance your productivity when working with T-SQL and SQL Server databases.

Chapter 2: Setting Up the Environment

Installing SQL Server and SSMS

Setting up your SQL Server environment is the first crucial step in your journey to mastering T-SQL. This process involves installing two primary components: SQL Server itself and SQL Server Management Studio (SSMS). Let's dive into the details of each installation and explore why they are essential for your database development journey.

SQL Server Installation

SQL Server is Microsoft's relational database management system (RDBMS). It's the core engine that stores and manages your data, processes queries, and handles transactions. Here's a step-by-step guide to installing SQL Server:

1. **Download the Installer**: Visit the official Microsoft website and download the SQL Server installer. You'll find different editions available, including Developer, Express, and Enterprise. For learning purposes, the Developer edition is recommended as it's free and includes all the features of the Enterprise edition.

2. **Run the Installer**: Once downloaded, run the SQL Server Installation Center. This will launch a wizard that guides you through the installation process.

3. **Choose Installation Type**: Select "New SQL Server stand-alone installation or add features to an existing installation."

4. **Select Features**: Choose the features you want to install. At a minimum, you'll need the Database Engine Services. Other features like Analysis Services, Reporting Services, and Integration Services can be added based on your needs.

5. **Instance Configuration**: Decide whether to use the default instance or create a named instance. For beginners, the default instance is usually sufficient.

6. **Server Configuration**: Set up the SQL Server services and configure their startup types. The SQL Server Database Engine service is essential and should be set to automatic startup.

7. **Database Engine Configuration**: Choose the authentication mode (Windows Authentication or Mixed Mode) and add any necessary administrators.

8. **Complete Installation**: Review your choices and click "Install" to begin the installation process.

During the installation, you'll encounter several important decisions:

- **Edition Selection**: As mentioned, the Developer edition is ideal for learning and non-production environments. It's free and includes all Enterprise edition features.

- **Instance Name**: This is how you'll refer to your SQL Server installation. The default instance is simply referred to by the server name, while named instances are referred to as `servername\instancename`.

- **Authentication Mode**: Windows Authentication uses your Windows login credentials, while Mixed Mode allows for both Windows Authentication and SQL Server Authentication (username and password specific to SQL Server).
- **Data Directories**: These determine where your database files, log files, and backup files will be stored by default.

SQL Server Management Studio (SSMS) Installation

SSMS is a powerful integrated environment for managing and interacting with your SQL Server instances. It provides a graphical interface for administrative tasks and a robust query editor for writing and executing T-SQL code. Here's how to install SSMS:

1. **Download SSMS**: Visit the Microsoft SQL Server Management Studio download page and get the latest version of SSMS.
2. **Run the Installer**: Launch the downloaded file to start the installation process.
3. **Accept License Terms**: Read and accept the license agreement.
4. **Choose Install Location**: Select where you want SSMS to be installed on your system.
5. **Begin Installation**: Click "Install" to start the process.
6. **Complete Installation**: Once finished, you can launch SSMS from the Start menu.

SSMS is a separate download from SQL Server itself, which allows Microsoft to update it more frequently with new features and improvements.

Key features of SSMS include:

- **Object Explorer**: A tree view of all database objects, making it easy to navigate your databases.
- **Query Editor**: A powerful environment for writing, testing, and optimizing T-SQL code.
- **Execution Plan Viewer**: A visual representation of how SQL Server executes your queries, crucial for performance tuning.
- **IntelliSense**: Auto-completion and syntax highlighting to help you write T-SQL more efficiently.
- **Integration with Source Control**: Allows you to version control your database objects and scripts.

Connecting to a Database Instance

Once you have SQL Server and SSMS installed, the next step is to connect to your database instance. This process establishes a link between SSMS and your SQL Server, allowing you to interact with your databases. Here's a detailed guide on how to connect:

1. **Launch SSMS**: Open SQL Server Management Studio from your Start menu or desktop shortcut.
2. **Connect to Server Dialog**: When SSMS opens, you'll be presented with the "Connect to Server" dialog box.
3. **Server Type**: Ensure "Database Engine" is selected in the "Server type" dropdown.
4. **Server Name**: Enter the name of your SQL Server instance. If you're connecting to a local default instance, you can use "." or "(local)" or

your computer name. For a named instance, use "computernameinstan-cename".

5. **Authentication**: Choose your authentication method:

- **Windows Authentication**: Uses your current Windows login creden-tials. This is the default and most secure option for domain-joined com-puters.
- **SQL Server Authentication**: Requires a SQL Server-specific username and password. This option needs to be enabled during SQL Server in-stallation and is often used in non-domain environments.

6. **Connect**: Click the "Connect" button to establish the connection.

Once connected, you'll see your server listed in the Object Explorer pane on the left side of SSMS.

Understanding Connection Properties

When connecting to a database instance, there are several important properties to be aware of:

- **Connection Encryption**: By default, SSMS attempts to encrypt the con-nection to SQL Server. This can be modified in the connection proper-ties.
- **Network Protocol**: SQL Server can communicate over various protocols like TCP/IP, Named Pipes, or Shared Memory. TCP/IP is the most com-mon for network connections.

- **Port Number**: By default, SQL Server listens on port 1433. If your instance uses a different port, you'll need to specify it in the server name (e.g., "servername,portnumber").
- **Connection Timeout**: This determines how long SSMS will attempt to connect before giving up. The default is 15 seconds but can be adjusted for slow network connections.

Troubleshooting Connection Issues

If you encounter problems connecting to your SQL Server instance, consider these common issues and solutions:

1. **SQL Server Service Not Running**: Ensure the SQL Server service is started in Windows Services.
2. **Firewall Blocking**: Check if the Windows Firewall or any antivirus software is blocking the connection.
3. **Network Connectivity**: Verify network connectivity between your client machine and the SQL Server.
4. **Incorrect Server Name**: Double-check the server name, especially for named instances or non-default ports.
5. **Authentication Issues**: Ensure you're using the correct authentication method and credentials.

Creating Your First Database

With a successful connection established, you're ready to create your first database. A database in SQL Server is a collection of tables, views, stored procedures, and other objects that are related to a specific application or business function. Here's how to create a new database using SSMS:

Using the Graphical Interface

1. **Navigate in Object Explorer**: In SSMS's Object Explorer, right-click on the "Databases" folder.
2. **New Database**: Select "New Database" from the context menu.
3. **Database Name**: In the "New Database" dialog, enter a name for your database.
4. **Set Options**: You can set various options for your database, including:

   - Initial size of data and log files
   - Autogrowth settings
   - File locations
   - Collation (character set and sort order)

5. **Create**: Click "OK" to create the database.

Using T-SQL

Alternatively, you can create a database using T-SQL, which gives you more control and is the method you'll often use in scripts or automated processes. Here's a basic example:

```
CREATE DATABASE MyFirstDatabase
ON PRIMARY
(
    NAME = MyFirstDatabase_Data,
```

```
    FILENAME = 'C:\Program Files\Microsoft SQL
Server\MSSQL15.SQLEXPRESS\MSSQL\DATA\MyFirstDatabase.mdf',
    SIZE = 8MB,
    MAXSIZE = UNLIMITED,
    FILEGROWTH = 65536KB
)
LOG ON
(
    NAME = MyFirstDatabase_Log,
    FILENAME = 'C:\Program Files\Microsoft SQL
Server\MSSQL15.SQLEXPRESS\MSSQL\DATA\MyFirstDatabase_log.ldf',
    SIZE = 8MB,
    MAXSIZE = 2048GB,
    FILEGROWTH = 65536KB
)
```

This script creates a database named "MyFirstDatabase" with specific settings for the data and log files. Let's break down the components:

- `ON PRIMARY`: Specifies the primary filegroup, which contains the primary data file.
- `NAME`: Logical name for the file within SQL Server.
- `FILENAME`: Physical path where the file will be stored.
- `SIZE`: Initial size of the file.
- `MAXSIZE`: Maximum size the file can grow to (UNLIMITED for data file).
- `FILEGROWTH`: Amount by which the file grows when more space is needed.

The `LOG ON` section specifies similar settings for the transaction log file.

Understanding Database Files

Every SQL Server database consists of at least two files:

1. **Data File (.mdf)**: Contains the actual data and objects like tables, views, and stored procedures.
2. **Log File (.ldf)**: Stores the transaction log information used for recovery purposes.

Larger databases may have multiple data files and filegroups for better performance and manageability.

Database Options

When creating a database, you can set various options to control its behavior:

- **Recovery Model**: Determines how transactions are logged, affecting the database's recoverability and backup strategy. Options include Simple, Full, and Bulk-Logged.
- **Compatibility Level**: Sets the SQL Server version compatibility, which can affect the behavior of certain T-SQL statements and functions.
- **Collation**: Defines the character set and sort order for the database. This affects how string comparisons and sorting are performed.
- **Auto Close**: Determines whether the database shuts down cleanly and frees resources after the last user exits.
- **Auto Shrink**: Controls whether the database files are automatically shrunk during periodic checks for unused space.
- **Auto Create Statistics**: Enables or disables automatic creation of statistics on columns used in queries.
- **Auto Update Statistics**: Controls whether existing statistics are automatically updated when they become out-of-date.

These options can be set during database creation or modified later using the `ALTER DATABASE` statement.

Best Practices for Database Creation

When creating databases, consider these best practices:

1. **Naming Conventions**: Use clear, consistent naming conventions for databases and files.
2. **File Placement**: Place data and log files on separate physical drives for better performance and easier recovery.
3. **Initial Size**: Set an appropriate initial size to avoid frequent auto-growth events.
4. **Growth Settings**: Configure sensible auto-growth settings to balance performance and space utilization.
5. **Recovery Model**: Choose the appropriate recovery model based on your backup and recovery requirements.
6. **Security**: Plan your security model, including logins, users, and permissions, before creating the database.
7. **Documentation**: Document your database design, including the purpose of the database, its structure, and any specific configuration choices.

Exploring Your New Database

After creating your database, it's time to explore and understand its structure. SSMS provides several tools to help you navigate and manage your new database:

Object Explorer

The Object Explorer in SSMS provides a hierarchical view of all objects in your database. Expand your newly created database to see folders for:

- Tables
- Views
- Programmability (which includes Stored Procedures, Functions, etc.)
- Security
- Storage

Each of these folders can be expanded to view and manage the specific objects they contain.

System Databases

In addition to your new database, you'll notice several system databases:

- **master**: Tracks all system-level information for an instance of SQL Server.
- **model**: Serves as the template for all databases created on the instance.
- **msdb**: Used by SQL Server Agent for scheduling alerts and jobs.
- **tempdb**: Holds temporary objects and intermediate result sets.

Understanding these system databases is crucial as you delve deeper into SQL Server administration.

Querying System Views

SQL Server provides a wealth of system views that allow you to query metadata about your databases and server. For example, to view information about all databases on the server:

```
SELECT name, database_id, create_date
FROM sys.databases;
```

To see details about the files in your new database:

```
USE MyFirstDatabase;
GO

SELECT name, physical_name, size, max_size, growth
FROM sys.database_files;
```

These queries introduce you to some basic T-SQL syntax and the concept of system views, which will be invaluable as you continue your SQL Server journey.

Conclusion

Setting up your SQL Server environment is a crucial first step in your T-SQL learning journey. By installing SQL Server and SSMS, connecting to your database instance, and creating your first database, you've laid the foundation for all the exciting database development work to come.

As you progress, you'll build on this foundation, learning to create and manage tables, write complex queries, optimize performance, and much more. Remember, the key to mastering T-SQL is practice and exploration. Don't hesitate to experiment with different settings, create multiple databases, and explore the various features SQL Server and SSMS offer.

In the next chapters, we'll dive deeper into T-SQL syntax, database design principles, and advanced SQL Server features. Each new concept will build upon the environment you've set up here, allowing you to immediately put your new knowledge into practice.

Chapter 3: Basics of SQL

Overview of SQL Commands: DDL, DML, and DCL

SQL (Structured Query Language) is a standardized language used for managing and manipulating relational databases. It provides a set of commands that can be categorized into three main types: DDL, DML, and DCL. Understanding these categories is crucial for effective database management and querying.

Data Definition Language (DDL)

DDL commands are used to define, modify, and remove database objects such as tables, indexes, and views. These commands directly affect the structure of the database.

Key DDL commands include:

1. CREATE: Used to create new database objects.

Example: `CREATE TABLE Employees (EmployeeID INT, FirstName VARCHAR(50), LastName VARCHAR(50));`

2. ALTER: Used to modify existing database objects.

Example: `ALTER TABLE Employees ADD Email VARCHAR(100);`

3. DROP: Used to remove existing database objects.

Example: `DROP TABLE Employees;`

4. TRUNCATE: Used to remove all data from a table while keeping its structure intact.

Example: `TRUNCATE TABLE Employees;`

5. RENAME: Used to rename an existing database object.

Example: `RENAME TABLE Employees TO Staff;`

DDL commands are essential for database administrators and developers who need to set up and maintain the database schema. They provide the foundation for organizing data and ensuring data integrity through constraints and relationships.

Data Manipulation Language (DML)

DML commands are used to manipulate data within database objects. These commands allow users to insert, retrieve, update, and delete data from tables.

Key DML commands include:

1. SELECT: Used to retrieve data from one or more tables.

Example: `SELECT FirstName, LastName FROM Employees;`

2. INSERT: Used to add new records into a table.

Example: `INSERT INTO Employees (FirstName, LastName) VALUES ('John', 'Doe');`

3. UPDATE: Used to modify existing records in a table.

Example: `UPDATE Employees SET Email = 'john.doe@example.com' WHERE EmployeeID = 1;`

4. DELETE: Used to remove records from a table.

Example: `DELETE FROM Employees WHERE EmployeeID = 1;`

DML commands are the most frequently used SQL commands in day-to-day database operations. They allow users to interact with the data stored in the database, perform data analysis, and maintain data accuracy.

Data Control Language (DCL)

DCL commands are used to control access to data within the database. These commands deal with user permissions and security aspects of the database.

Key DCL commands include:

1. GRANT: Used to give specific privileges to database users.

Example: `GRANT SELECT, INSERT ON Employees TO user1;`

2. REVOKE: Used to remove specific privileges from database users.

Example: `REVOKE INSERT ON Employees FROM user1;`

3. DENY: Used to explicitly deny specific privileges to users.

Example: `DENY DELETE ON Employees TO user1;`

DCL commands are crucial for database administrators to manage security and access control within the database system. They ensure that users have appropriate permissions to perform their required tasks while maintaining data security and integrity.

Understanding the differences between DDL, DML, and DCL commands is essential for effective database management and querying. Each category serves a specific purpose in the database ecosystem, and mastering all three types of commands will enable you to work with databases more efficiently and securely.

Writing Your First SELECT Statement

The SELECT statement is one of the most fundamental and frequently used SQL commands. It allows you to retrieve data from one or more tables in a database. Understanding how to write effective SELECT statements is crucial for data analysis, reporting, and application development.

Basic SELECT Statement Structure

The basic structure of a SELECT statement is as follows:

```
SELECT column1, column2, ...
FROM table_name;
```

- SELECT: Specifies which columns you want to retrieve data from.
- FROM: Specifies the table or tables from which to retrieve the data.

Let's break down the components of a SELECT statement:

1. SELECT Clause:

- Lists the columns you want to retrieve.
- Use an asterisk (*) to select all columns: `SELECT *`
- You can also use expressions or functions in the SELECT clause.

2. FROM Clause:

- Specifies the table or tables from which to retrieve the data.
- If selecting from multiple tables, you'll need to use JOINs (covered in later chapters).

Examples of Basic SELECT Statements

1. Selecting all columns from a table:

```
SELECT *
FROM Employees;
```

2. Selecting specific columns from a table:

```
SELECT FirstName, LastName, Email
FROM Employees;
```

3. Using expressions in the SELECT clause:

```
SELECT FirstName, LastName, Salary, Salary * 1.1 AS
IncreasedSalary
FROM Employees;
```

4. Using functions in the SELECT clause:

```
SELECT FirstName, LastName, UPPER(Email) AS UppercaseEmail
FROM Employees;
```

Column Aliases

Column aliases allow you to give a temporary name to a column or expression in the result set. This is useful for improving readability or when working with expressions or functions.

Syntax:

```
SELECT column_name AS alias_name
FROM table_name;
```

Examples:

1. Simple alias:

```
SELECT FirstName AS GivenName, LastName AS Surname
FROM Employees;
```

2. Alias with spaces (requires quotes):

```
SELECT FirstName AS "Given Name", LastName AS "Family Name"
FROM Employees;
```

3. Alias for an expression:

```
SELECT FirstName, LastName, Salary * 12 AS "Annual Salary"
FROM Employees;
```

Removing Duplicates with DISTINCT

The DISTINCT keyword is used to remove duplicate rows from the result set. It's placed immediately after the SELECT keyword.

Syntax:

```
SELECT DISTINCT column1, column2, ...
FROM table_name;
```

Examples:

1. Selecting distinct values from a single column:

```
SELECT DISTINCT Department
FROM Employees;
```

2. Selecting distinct combinations of multiple columns:

```
SELECT DISTINCT Department, JobTitle
FROM Employees;
```

Combining Columns with Concatenation

In SQL Server, you can use the + operator or the CONCAT() function to combine values from multiple columns or with literal strings.

Examples:

1. Using the + operator:

```
SELECT FirstName + ' ' + LastName AS FullName
FROM Employees;
```

2. Using the CONCAT() function:

```
SELECT CONCAT(FirstName, ' ', LastName) AS FullName
FROM Employees;
```

Limiting Results with TOP

In SQL Server, you can use the TOP clause to limit the number of rows returned by a query.

Syntax:

```sql
SELECT TOP (n) column1, column2, ...
FROM table_name;
```

Examples:

1. Selecting the top 10 rows:

```sql
SELECT TOP (10) *
FROM Employees
ORDER BY Salary DESC;
```

2. Selecting the top 5 percent of rows:

```sql
SELECT TOP (5) PERCENT *
FROM Employees
ORDER BY HireDate DESC;
```

Handling NULL Values

NULL represents missing or unknown data in SQL. When working with NULL values, it's important to use the appropriate operators and functions.

- IS NULL: Checks if a value is NULL
- IS NOT NULL: Checks if a value is not NULL
- COALESCE(): Returns the first non-NULL value in a list

Examples:

1. Finding employees with no email address:

```
SELECT FirstName, LastName
FROM Employees
WHERE Email IS NULL;
```

2. Using COALESCE() to provide a default value:

```
SELECT FirstName, LastName, COALESCE(Email, 'No email provided')
AS Email
FROM Employees;
```

By mastering these basic SELECT statement techniques, you'll be able to retrieve and manipulate data effectively from your database tables. As you progress, you'll learn more advanced querying techniques that build upon these fundamental concepts.

Filtering Data with WHERE

The WHERE clause is a powerful feature in SQL that allows you to filter the rows returned by a SELECT statement based on specified conditions. It's an essential tool for retrieving specific data from your database tables.

Basic WHERE Clause Syntax

The basic syntax of a SELECT statement with a WHERE clause is as follows:

```
SELECT column1, column2, ...
FROM table_name
WHERE condition;
```

The WHERE clause comes after the FROM clause and before any other clauses like ORDER BY or GROUP BY.

Comparison Operators

SQL provides several comparison operators that you can use in WHERE clauses:

- Equal to: =
- Not equal to: <> or !=
- Greater than: >
- Less than: <
- Greater than or equal to: >=
- Less than or equal to: <=

Examples:

1. Employees with a salary greater than 50000:

```sql
SELECT FirstName, LastName, Salary
FROM Employees
WHERE Salary > 50000;
```

2. Employees hired before 2020:

```sql
SELECT FirstName, LastName, HireDate
FROM Employees
WHERE HireDate < '2020-01-01';
```

3. Employees in the Sales department:

```sql
SELECT FirstName, LastName, Department
FROM Employees
```

```
WHERE Department = 'Sales';
```

Logical Operators

Logical operators allow you to combine multiple conditions in a WHERE clause:

- AND: Both conditions must be true
- OR: At least one condition must be true
- NOT: Negates a condition

Examples:

1. Employees in Sales with a salary greater than 60000:

```
SELECT FirstName, LastName, Department, Salary
FROM Employees
WHERE Department = 'Sales' AND Salary > 60000;
```

2. Employees in either Sales or Marketing:

```
SELECT FirstName, LastName, Department
FROM Employees
WHERE Department = 'Sales' OR Department = 'Marketing';
```

3. Employees not in the IT department:

```
SELECT FirstName, LastName, Department
FROM Employees
WHERE NOT Department = 'IT';
```

BETWEEN Operator

The BETWEEN operator selects values within a given range (inclusive).

Syntax:

```
SELECT column1, column2, ...
FROM table_name
WHERE column_name BETWEEN value1 AND value2;
```

Example:

```
SELECT FirstName, LastName, Salary
FROM Employees
WHERE Salary BETWEEN 50000 AND 75000;
```

IN Operator

The IN operator allows you to specify multiple values in a WHERE clause.

Syntax:

```
SELECT column1, column2, ...
FROM table_name
WHERE column_name IN (value1, value2, ...);
```

Example:

```
SELECT FirstName, LastName, Department
FROM Employees
WHERE Department IN ('Sales', 'Marketing', 'HR');
```

LIKE Operator

The LIKE operator is used for pattern matching with wildcard characters:

- % : Represents zero, one, or multiple characters

- _ : Represents a single character

Syntax:

```
SELECT column1, column2, ...
FROM table_name
WHERE column_name LIKE pattern;
```

Examples:

1. Employees whose last name starts with 'S':

```
SELECT FirstName, LastName
FROM Employees
WHERE LastName LIKE 'S%';
```

2. Employees with a five-letter first name:

```
SELECT FirstName, LastName
FROM Employees
WHERE FirstName LIKE '_____';
```

NULL Values in WHERE Clauses

To check for NULL values, use IS NULL or IS NOT NULL:

Examples:

1. Employees with no manager:

```
SELECT FirstName, LastName
FROM Employees
WHERE ManagerID IS NULL;
```

2. Employees with a specified manager:

```sql
SELECT FirstName, LastName, ManagerID
FROM Employees
WHERE ManagerID IS NOT NULL;
```

Combining Multiple Conditions

You can combine multiple conditions using parentheses to control the order of evaluation:

Example:

```sql
SELECT FirstName, LastName, Department, Salary
FROM Employees
WHERE (Department = 'Sales' OR Department = 'Marketing')
  AND Salary > 60000;
```

This query retrieves employees in either Sales or Marketing departments with a salary greater than 60000.

Using Subqueries in WHERE Clauses

Subqueries can be used within WHERE clauses to create more complex conditions:

Example:

```sql
SELECT FirstName, LastName, Salary
FROM Employees
WHERE Salary > (SELECT AVG(Salary) FROM Employees);
```

This query retrieves employees with a salary higher than the average salary.

EXISTS Operator

The EXISTS operator is used to test for the existence of rows that satisfy a sub-query:

Example:

```
SELECT FirstName, LastName
FROM Employees e
WHERE EXISTS (
    SELECT 1
    FROM Orders o
    WHERE o.EmployeeID = e.EmployeeID
);
```

This query retrieves employees who have associated orders.

Using Functions in WHERE Clauses

You can use various SQL functions in WHERE clauses to perform calculations or transformations:

Example:

```
SELECT FirstName, LastName, HireDate
FROM Employees
WHERE YEAR(HireDate) = 2020;
```

This query retrieves employees hired in the year 2020.

By mastering the WHERE clause and its various operators and techniques, you'll be able to efficiently filter and retrieve specific data from your database tables. This skill is crucial for data analysis, reporting, and building efficient database queries.

Sorting Data with ORDER BY

The ORDER BY clause is used to sort the result set of a SELECT statement in ascending or descending order based on one or more columns. Sorting data is crucial for presenting information in a meaningful and organized manner.

Basic ORDER BY Syntax

The basic syntax of a SELECT statement with an ORDER BY clause is as follows:

```
SELECT column1, column2, ...
FROM table_name
ORDER BY column1 [ASC|DESC], column2 [ASC|DESC], ...;
```

The ORDER BY clause comes after the WHERE clause (if present) and before the TOP clause (if used).

Sorting in Ascending Order

By default, ORDER BY sorts data in ascending order (ASC). You can explicitly specify ASC, but it's not necessary.

Example:

```
SELECT FirstName, LastName, Salary
FROM Employees
ORDER BY Salary;
```

This query retrieves employee names and salaries, sorted by salary in ascending order.

Sorting in Descending Order

To sort data in descending order, use the DESC keyword after the column name.

Example:

```
SELECT FirstName, LastName, HireDate
FROM Employees
ORDER BY HireDate DESC;
```

This query retrieves employee names and hire dates, sorted by hire date in descending order (most recent first).

Sorting by Multiple Columns

You can sort by multiple columns by listing them in the ORDER BY clause, separated by commas. The sort order is applied in the order the columns are listed.

Example:

```
SELECT FirstName, LastName, Department, Salary
FROM Employees
ORDER BY Department ASC, Salary DESC;
```

This query sorts employees first by department in ascending order, then by salary in descending order within each department.

Sorting by Column Position

Instead of column names, you can use the position of the column in the SELECT list to specify the sort order.

Example:

```
SELECT FirstName, LastName, Salary
FROM Employees
```

```
ORDER BY 3 DESC;
```

This query sorts the result set by the third column (Salary) in descending order.

Sorting by Expressions

You can use expressions in the ORDER BY clause to sort based on calculated values.

Example:

```
SELECT FirstName, LastName, Salary, Salary * 0.1 AS Bonus
FROM Employees
ORDER BY Salary * 0.1 DESC;
```

This query calculates a bonus for each employee and sorts the result set based on the bonus amount in descending order.

Sorting with NULL Values

In SQL Server, NULL values are considered to be the lowest possible value when sorting in ascending order, and the highest possible value when sorting in descending order.

Example:

```
SELECT FirstName, LastName, ManagerID
FROM Employees
ORDER BY ManagerID;
```

In this query, employees with no manager (NULL ManagerID) will appear first in the result set.

Using CASE in ORDER BY

You can use a CASE expression in the ORDER BY clause to create custom sorting logic.

Example:

```
SELECT FirstName, LastName, Department
FROM Employees
ORDER BY
    CASE
        WHEN Department = 'Sales' THEN 1
        WHEN Department = 'Marketing' THEN 2
        WHEN Department = 'IT' THEN 3
        ELSE 4
    END;
```

This query sorts employees by department in a custom order: Sales first, then Marketing, then IT, and finally all other departments.

Sorting with TOP

When using the TOP clause to limit the number of rows returned, the ORDER BY clause determines which rows are included in the result set.

Example:

```
SELECT TOP 5 FirstName, LastName, Salary
FROM Employees
ORDER BY Salary DESC;
```

This query retrieves the top 5 highest-paid employees.

Sorting with OFFSET-FETCH

SQL Server 2012 introduced the OFFSET-FETCH clause, which can be used with ORDER BY to implement paging.

Example:

```
SELECT FirstName, LastName, Salary
FROM Employees
ORDER BY Salary DESC
OFFSET 10 ROWS
FETCH NEXT 10 ROWS ONLY;
```

This query skips the first 10 rows and retrieves the next 10 rows, effectively giving you the second page of results when sorted by salary in descending order.

Performance Considerations

While ORDER BY is a powerful tool for presenting data, it can have performance implications, especially on large datasets. Here are some tips to optimize ORDER BY operations:

1. Create indexes on columns frequently used in ORDER BY clauses.
2. Avoid sorting on computed columns or expressions if possible.
3. Be cautious when sorting on large text columns.
4. Consider using indexed views for frequently used complex queries with sorting.

Combining ORDER BY with Other Clauses

ORDER BY can be used in combination with other SQL clauses to create more complex queries:

Example:

```
SELECT Department, AVG(Salary) AS AvgSalary
FROM Employees
WHERE HireDate >= '2020-01-01'
GROUP BY Department
HAVING AVG(Salary) > 50000
ORDER BY AVG(Salary) DESC;
```

This query calculates the average salary for each department for employees hired since 2020, filters departments with an average salary above 50000, and sorts the results by average salary in descending order.

By mastering the ORDER BY clause, you can effectively control how your query results are presented, making it easier to analyze and interpret data. Whether you're creating reports, implementing pagination, or simply organizing data for better readability, ORDER BY is an essential tool in your SQL toolkit.

Conclusion

In this chapter, we've covered the fundamental concepts of SQL, focusing on the basic structure of SELECT statements, filtering data with WHERE clauses, and sorting results with ORDER BY. These foundational skills form the basis for more advanced SQL techniques and are essential for anyone working with relational databases.

We started by exploring the different categories of SQL commands: DDL for defining database structures, DML for manipulating data, and DCL for controlling access to data. Understanding these categories helps in organizing and managing database operations effectively.

Next, we delved into the structure of SELECT statements, learning how to retrieve specific columns, use aliases, remove duplicates with DISTINCT, and limit results with TOP. These techniques allow for precise data retrieval and presentation.

The WHERE clause was introduced as a powerful tool for filtering data based on specific conditions. We covered various comparison and logical operators, as well as special operators like BETWEEN, IN, and LIKE. These filtering capabilities are crucial for extracting relevant data from large datasets.

Finally, we explored the ORDER BY clause, which enables sorting of query results. We learned how to sort in ascending and descending order, sort by multiple columns, and even use expressions and CASE statements for custom sorting logic.

By mastering these basic SQL concepts, you've laid a strong foundation for more advanced database querying and manipulation techniques. As you continue to work with SQL, you'll find that these fundamental skills are used repeatedly in more complex queries and database operations.

Remember that practice is key to becoming proficient in SQL. Try writing various queries using different combinations of these clauses, and experiment with real-world datasets to gain practical experience. As you become more comfortable with these basics, you'll be well-prepared to tackle more advanced SQL topics in the following chapters.

Part 2: Core T-SQL Features

Chapter 4: Data Types and Variables

Overview of T-SQL Data Types

T-SQL (Transact-SQL) provides a wide range of data types to store and manipulate various kinds of information efficiently. Understanding these data types is crucial for designing effective database schemas and writing optimized queries. Let's explore the main categories of T-SQL data types:

1. Numeric Data Types

Numeric data types are used to store numerical values. T-SQL offers several options to accommodate different ranges and precision requirements:

a) Integer Types:

- `tinyint`: 0 to 255 (1 byte)
- `smallint`: -32,768 to 32,767 (2 bytes)
- `int`: -2,147,483,648 to 2,147,483,647 (4 bytes)
- `bigint`: -9,223,372,036,854,775,808 to 9,223,372,036,854,775,807 (8 bytes)

These types are suitable for whole numbers and are commonly used for primary keys, counters, and other integer-based data.

b) Decimal Types:

- `decimal(p,s)` or `numeric(p,s)`: Fixed-precision and scale numbers
- p: precision (total number of digits)
- s: scale (number of digits to the right of the decimal point)
- `money`: Currency values with 4 decimal places (8 bytes)
- `smallmoney`: Currency values with 4 decimal places (4 bytes)

Decimal types are ideal for financial calculations and other scenarios requiring exact decimal representation.

c) Floating-Point Types:

- `float(n)`: -1.79E+308 to 1.79E+308 (4 or 8 bytes)
- `real`: -3.40E+38 to 3.40E+38 (4 bytes)

Floating-point types are suitable for scientific calculations and scenarios where approximate representations are acceptable.

2. Character String Data Types

Character string data types are used to store textual information:

a) Fixed-Length Strings:

- `char(n)`: Fixed-length non-Unicode string (up to 8,000 characters)

b) Variable-Length Strings:

- `varchar(n)`: Variable-length non-Unicode string (up to 8,000 characters)
- `varchar(max)`: Variable-length non-Unicode string (up to 2^31-1 bytes)

c) Unicode Strings:

- `nchar(n)`: Fixed-length Unicode string (up to 4,000 characters)
- `nvarchar(n)`: Variable-length Unicode string (up to 4,000 characters)
- `nvarchar(max)`: Variable-length Unicode string (up to $2^{30}-1$ characters)

Unicode strings are essential for storing multilingual data or characters from various writing systems.

3. Date and Time Data Types

T-SQL provides several data types for handling date and time information:

- `date`: Date only (3 bytes)
- `time`: Time only (3-5 bytes)
- `datetime`: Date and time (8 bytes)
- `datetime2`: Date and time with higher precision (6-8 bytes)
- `datetimeoffset`: Date and time with time zone awareness (8-10 bytes)
- `smalldatetime`: Date and time with less precision (4 bytes)

These types allow for efficient storage and manipulation of temporal data, catering to various precision and time zone requirements.

4. Binary Data Types

Binary data types are used to store raw binary information:

- `binary(n)`: Fixed-length binary data (up to 8,000 bytes)
- `varbinary(n)`: Variable-length binary data (up to 8,000 bytes)

- `varbinary(max)`: Variable-length binary data (up to 2^31-1 bytes)
- `image`: Variable-length binary data (deprecated, use varbinary(max) instead)

These types are suitable for storing files, images, or any other binary data.

5. Other Data Types

T-SQL includes several other specialized data types:

- `bit`: Boolean values (0 or 1)
- `uniqueidentifier`: Globally unique identifier (GUID)
- `xml`: XML data
- `sql_variant`: Can store values of various data types
- `table`: Temporary storage of a set of rows
- `cursor`: Reference to a cursor object

These types serve specific purposes and are used in various scenarios depending on the application requirements.

Declaring and Using Variables

Variables in T-SQL are used to store temporary data within a batch or stored procedure. They provide a way to hold and manipulate values during query execution. Let's explore how to declare and use variables in T-SQL:

Variable Declaration

To declare a variable in T-SQL, you use the DECLARE statement followed by the variable name and its data type. The general syntax is:

```
DECLARE @variable_name data_type
```

For example:

```
DECLARE @employee_id INT
DECLARE @first_name NVARCHAR(50)
DECLARE @hire_date DATE
DECLARE @salary DECIMAL(10, 2)
```

You can also declare multiple variables in a single DECLARE statement:

```
DECLARE @employee_id INT, @first_name NVARCHAR(50), @hire_date DATE, @salary DECIMAL(10, 2)
```

Assigning Values to Variables

There are several ways to assign values to variables in T-SQL:

1. Using the SET statement:

```
DECLARE @employee_id INT
SET @employee_id = 1001
```

2. Using the SELECT statement:

```
DECLARE @employee_count INT
SELECT @employee_count = COUNT(*) FROM Employees
```

3. Assigning values during declaration:

```
DECLARE @tax_rate DECIMAL(5, 2) = 0.08
```

4. Using the UPDATE statement (less common):

```
DECLARE @total_sales DECIMAL(10, 2)
UPDATE @total_sales = SUM(SalesAmount) FROM Sales
```

Using Variables in Queries

Once declared and assigned, variables can be used in various parts of your T-SQL statements:

1. In WHERE clauses:

```
DECLARE @department_id INT = 5
SELECT * FROM Employees WHERE DepartmentID = @department_id
```

2. In INSERT statements:

```
DECLARE @new_employee_id INT = 1002
DECLARE @new_employee_name NVARCHAR(50) = 'John Doe'
INSERT INTO Employees (EmployeeID, EmployeeName) VALUES
(@new_employee_id, @new_employee_name)
```

3. In UPDATE statements:

```
DECLARE @salary_increase DECIMAL(5, 2) = 0.05
UPDATE Employees SET Salary = Salary * (1 + @salary_increase)
WHERE DepartmentID = 3
```

4. In stored procedure parameters:

```
CREATE PROCEDURE GetEmployeesByDepartment
    @dept_id INT
AS
BEGIN
    SELECT * FROM Employees WHERE DepartmentID = @dept_id
END
```

Variable Scope

Variables in T-SQL have a limited scope. They are only accessible within the batch or stored procedure where they are declared. Once the batch or stored procedure execution is complete, the variables are destroyed, and their values are lost.

If you need to use a variable across multiple batches or stored procedures, you can consider using temporary tables or table variables instead.

Best Practices for Using Variables

1. Use meaningful and descriptive variable names to improve code readability.
2. Initialize variables with default values when appropriate to avoid unexpected behavior.
3. Use the appropriate data type for your variables to ensure data integrity and optimize performance.
4. Be mindful of variable scope and avoid declaring variables with overly broad scopes.
5. Use variables to improve code maintainability and reduce redundancy in your queries.

Type Conversions and Casting

Type conversion, also known as type casting, is the process of changing a value from one data type to another. In T-SQL, type conversions can occur implicitly (automatically) or explicitly (manually). Understanding type conversions is crucial for writing correct and efficient queries.

Implicit Conversions

Implicit conversions occur automatically when T-SQL needs to convert a value from one data type to another without explicit instructions from the developer. These conversions follow predefined rules and are generally safe, but they can sometimes lead to unexpected results or performance issues.

Common scenarios for implicit conversions include:

1. Comparing values of different data types:

```
DECLARE @int_value INT = 10
DECLARE @varchar_value VARCHAR(20) = '10'

IF @int_value = @varchar_value
    PRINT 'Values are equal'
```

In this example, SQL Server implicitly converts the VARCHAR value to an INT for comparison.

2. Assigning values of one data type to a variable of another data type:

```
DECLARE @decimal_value DECIMAL(10, 2)
SET @decimal_value = 10 -- Implicit conversion from INT to
DECIMAL
```

3. Using functions that expect a specific data type:

```
DECLARE @date_string VARCHAR(10) = '2023-05-15'
SELECT DATEADD(day, 1, @date_string)
```

Here, SQL Server implicitly converts the VARCHAR value to a DATE for use with the DATEADD function.

While implicit conversions can be convenient, they can also lead to performance issues, especially when used in WHERE clauses or JOIN conditions on large tables. It's generally better to use explicit conversions when possible to ensure clarity and maintain control over the conversion process.

Explicit Conversions

Explicit conversions are performed using specific T-SQL functions or the CAST operator. These conversions give you more control over the conversion process and can help prevent unexpected results.

The two main methods for explicit conversions in T-SQL are:

1. CAST Function:

The CAST function converts a value to a specified data type. The syntax is:

```
CAST(expression AS data_type [(length)])
```

Examples:

```
-- Convert INT to VARCHAR
DECLARE @int_value INT = 42
DECLARE @string_value VARCHAR(10) = CAST(@int_value AS
VARCHAR(10))

-- Convert VARCHAR to DATE
DECLARE @date_string VARCHAR(10) = '2023-05-15'
```

```
DECLARE @date_value DATE = CAST(@date_string AS DATE)

-- Convert DECIMAL to INT (truncation occurs)
DECLARE @decimal_value DECIMAL(10, 2) = 123.45
DECLARE @int_result INT = CAST(@decimal_value AS INT)
```

2. CONVERT Function:

The CONVERT function is similar to CAST but provides additional options for formatting, especially for date and time conversions. The syntax is:

```
CONVERT(data_type [(length)], expression [, style])
```

Examples:

```
-- Convert DATE to VARCHAR with specific format
DECLARE @date_value DATE = '2023-05-15'
DECLARE @formatted_date VARCHAR(20) = CONVERT(VARCHAR(20),
@date_value, 107) -- May 15, 2023

-- Convert VARCHAR to DATETIME with specific format
DECLARE @datetime_string VARCHAR(20) = '15/05/2023 14:30'
DECLARE @datetime_value DATETIME = CONVERT(DATETIME,
@datetime_string, 103)

-- Convert DECIMAL to VARCHAR with specific format
DECLARE @amount DECIMAL(10, 2) = 1234.56
DECLARE @formatted_amount VARCHAR(20) = CONVERT(VARCHAR(20),
@amount, 1) -- 1,234.56
```

The style parameter in the CONVERT function allows you to specify different formatting options, especially useful for date and time conversions.

Best Practices for Type Conversions

1. Use explicit conversions when possible to make your code more readable and maintainable.
2. Be aware of potential data loss or truncation when converting between data types with different ranges or precisions.
3. Consider performance implications, especially when using conversions in WHERE clauses or JOIN conditions on large tables.
4. Use appropriate data types for your columns and variables to minimize the need for conversions.
5. Be cautious when converting between string and date/time data types, as format mismatches can lead to errors or incorrect results.
6. Use the TRY_CAST or TRY_CONVERT functions when dealing with potentially invalid data to handle conversion errors gracefully.

Common Conversion Scenarios and Challenges

1. String to Date Conversions:

Converting string representations of dates to actual DATE or DATETIME values can be tricky due to different date formats. Always use unambiguous date formats (e.g., ISO 8601) when possible, or specify the format explicitly using the CONVERT function.

```
-- Unambiguous ISO 8601 format
DECLARE @date_string VARCHAR(10) = '2023-05-15'
DECLARE @date_value DATE = CONVERT(DATE, @date_string, 120)

-- Ambiguous format, use style parameter
DECLARE @ambiguous_date VARCHAR(10) = '05/15/2023'
```

```
DECLARE @date_value2 DATE = CONVERT(DATE, @ambiguous_date, 101)
-- US format (mm/dd/yyyy)
```

2. Numeric Precision and Scale:

When converting between numeric types with different precisions or scales, be aware of potential data loss or rounding.

```
DECLARE @decimal_value DECIMAL(10, 2) = 123.45
DECLARE @int_value INT = CAST(@decimal_value AS INT) -- Result:
123 (truncation)
DECLARE @float_value FLOAT = CAST(@decimal_value AS FLOAT) --
Potential loss of precision
```

3. Unicode to Non-Unicode Conversions:

Converting from NVARCHAR (Unicode) to VARCHAR (non-Unicode) can result in data loss if the text contains characters outside the code page of the non-Unicode collation.

```
DECLARE @unicode_text NVARCHAR(50) = N'Hello, 世界'
DECLARE @non_unicode_text VARCHAR(50) = CONVERT(VARCHAR(50),
@unicode_text)
-- Potential data loss for non-ASCII characters
```

4. Handling NULL Values:

Be cautious when converting NULL values, as the result of the conversion will also be NULL.

```
DECLARE @null_value INT = NULL
DECLARE @converted_value VARCHAR(10) = CAST(@null_value AS
VARCHAR(10))
-- @converted_value will be NULL, not an empty string
```

5. Converting Large Objects:

When converting large object types (e.g., VARCHAR(MAX), VARBINARY(MAX)), be aware of potential memory usage and performance implications.

```
DECLARE @large_text VARCHAR(MAX) = 'Very long text...'
DECLARE @converted_ntext NTEXT = CAST(@large_text AS NTEXT)
-- This conversion can be memory-intensive for very large strings
```

6. Implicit Conversions in Queries:

Implicit conversions in WHERE clauses or JOIN conditions can lead to poor query performance, especially on large tables.

```
-- Potential performance issue due to implicit conversion
SELECT * FROM Orders WHERE OrderID = '1000' -- OrderID is an INT
column

-- Better performance with explicit conversion
SELECT * FROM Orders WHERE OrderID = CAST('1000' AS INT)
```

7. Handling Invalid Conversions:

Use TRY_CAST or TRY_CONVERT to handle potential conversion errors gracefully.

```
DECLARE @invalid_date VARCHAR(10) = 'not a date'
DECLARE @converted_date DATE = TRY_CONVERT(DATE, @invalid_date)
-- @converted_date will be NULL instead of raising an error
```

Advanced Type Conversion Techniques

1. Dynamic SQL and Type Conversions:

When working with dynamic SQL, be extra cautious with type conversions to prevent SQL injection vulnerabilities.

```
DECLARE @table_name NVARCHAR(128) = N'Employees'
DECLARE @column_name NVARCHAR(128) = N'Salary'
DECLARE @threshold DECIMAL(10, 2) = 50000.00

DECLARE @sql NVARCHAR(MAX) = N'
SELECT * FROM ' + QUOTENAME(@table_name) + N'
WHERE ' + QUOTENAME(@column_name) + N' > @threshold'

EXEC sp_executesql @sql, N'@threshold DECIMAL(10, 2)', @threshold
```

2. XML and JSON Conversions:

T-SQL provides functions for converting between XML/JSON and relational data.

```
-- Convert table data to XML
SELECT TOP 5 CustomerID, CompanyName, ContactName
FROM Customers
FOR XML PATH('Customer'), ROOT('Customers')

-- Convert XML to table
DECLARE @xml XML = '<Customers>
  <Customer>
    <CustomerID>ALFKI</CustomerID>
    <CompanyName>Alfreds Futterkiste</CompanyName>
  </Customer>
</Customers>'

SELECT
  Customer.value('(CustomerID)[1]', 'NCHAR(5)') AS CustomerID,
  Customer.value('(CompanyName)[1]', 'NVARCHAR(40)') AS
CompanyName
FROM @xml.nodes('/Customers/Customer') AS T(Customer)

-- Convert table data to JSON
SELECT TOP 5 CustomerID, CompanyName, ContactName
FROM Customers
FOR JSON PATH
```

```sql
-- Convert JSON to table
DECLARE @json NVARCHAR(MAX) = N'[
  {"CustomerID": "ALFKI", "CompanyName": "Alfreds Futterkiste"},
  {"CustomerID": "ANATR", "CompanyName": "Ana Trujillo
Emparedados y helados"}
]'

SELECT *
FROM OPENJSON(@json)
WITH (
  CustomerID NCHAR(5),
  CompanyName NVARCHAR(40)
)
```

3. Spatial Data Type Conversions:

SQL Server supports conversions between spatial data types and other formats.

```sql
-- Convert WKT (Well-Known Text) to geometry
DECLARE @wkt NVARCHAR(100) = 'POINT(30 10)'
DECLARE @geom GEOMETRY = GEOMETRY::STGeomFromText(@wkt, 4326)

-- Convert geometry to WKT
SELECT @geom.STAsText() AS WKT

-- Convert latitude and longitude to geography point
DECLARE @lat DECIMAL(9, 6) = 47.643417
DECLARE @lon DECIMAL(9, 6) = -122.130799
DECLARE @geo GEOGRAPHY = GEOGRAPHY::Point(@lat, @lon, 4326)

-- Convert geography to latitude and longitude
SELECT @geo.Lat AS Latitude, @geo.Long AS Longitude
```

4. CLR User-Defined Type Conversions:

If you're using CLR (Common Language Runtime) user-defined types, you can implement custom conversion methods.

```
-- Assuming a CLR type called 'Point'
DECLARE @point Point
SET @point = CONVERT(Point, '10,20')

DECLARE @text NVARCHAR(20) = CONVERT(NVARCHAR(20), @point)
```

5. Handling Time Zones:

When working with DATETIMEOFFSET, you may need to convert between different time zones.

```
DECLARE @utc_time DATETIMEOFFSET = '2023-05-15 14:30:00 +00:00'
DECLARE @pst_time DATETIMEOFFSET = SWITCHOFFSET(@utc_time,
'-08:00')

SELECT
    @utc_time AS UTCTime,
    @pst_time AS PSTTime,
    CONVERT(DATETIME2, @pst_time) AS LocalDateTime
```

Performance Considerations for Type Conversions

1. Implicit vs. Explicit Conversions:

Explicit conversions are generally preferred for clarity and control, but they may not always offer better performance. In some cases, the query optimizer can handle implicit conversions efficiently.

2. Index Usage:

Conversions in WHERE clauses or JOIN conditions can prevent the use of indexes, leading to table scans. Always try to match the data types of compared columns and parameters.

3. Computed Columns:

For frequently used conversions, consider using persisted computed columns with appropriate indexing.

```
ALTER TABLE Orders ADD
  OrderDateString AS CONVERT(VARCHAR(10), OrderDate, 120)
PERSISTED

CREATE INDEX IX_Orders_OrderDateString ON Orders(OrderDateString)
```

4. Collation Conflicts:

When joining tables with different collations, implicit conversions can occur, impacting performance. Use the COLLATE clause to explicitly specify the collation when necessary.

```
SELECT *
FROM TableA a
JOIN TableB b ON a.Column = b.Column COLLATE DATABASE_DEFAULT
```

5. Batch Conversions:

For large-scale data conversions, consider using batch processing techniques to improve performance and reduce resource consumption.

```
DECLARE @batch_size INT = 10000
DECLARE @max_id INT

SELECT @max_id = MAX(ID) FROM SourceTable

DECLARE @current_id INT = 0

WHILE @current_id < @max_id
BEGIN
  INSERT INTO TargetTable (ID, ConvertedValue)
    SELECT TOP (@batch_size) ID, CAST(OriginalValue AS NewDataType)
```

```
FROM SourceTable
WHERE ID > @current_id
ORDER BY ID

SET @current_id = SCOPE_IDENTITY()

CHECKPOINT -- For minimally logged operations
end
```

Conclusion

Understanding T-SQL data types, variables, and type conversions is fundamental to writing efficient and correct SQL Server code. By mastering these concepts, you can design better database schemas, write more maintainable queries, and optimize performance. Remember to choose appropriate data types for your columns and variables, use explicit conversions when necessary, and be aware of the potential pitfalls and performance implications of type conversions. With practice and attention to detail, you'll become proficient in handling various data scenarios in your T-SQL development.

Chapter 5: Functions in T-SQL

Functions are essential building blocks in T-SQL programming, allowing you to perform various operations on data, manipulate values, and create more complex and efficient queries. This chapter will dive deep into four main categories of functions in T-SQL: scalar functions, aggregate functions, string manipulation functions, and date and time functions.

Scalar Functions

Scalar functions in T-SQL are functions that operate on a single value and return a single value. These functions can be used in SELECT statements, WHERE clauses, and other parts of a T-SQL query to perform calculations or transformations on individual data points.

Mathematical Scalar Functions

T-SQL provides a wide range of mathematical scalar functions for performing various calculations:

1. ABS(numeric_expression)

   - Returns the absolute value of a given number.

- Example: `SELECT ABS(-15)` returns 15.

2. CEILING(numeric_expression)

- Returns the smallest integer greater than or equal to the given number.
- Example: `SELECT CEILING(15.2)` returns 16.

3. FLOOR(numeric_expression)

- Returns the largest integer less than or equal to the given number.
- Example: `SELECT FLOOR(15.8)` returns 15.

4. POWER(base, exponent)

- Returns the value of the base raised to the power of the exponent.
- Example: `SELECT POWER(2, 3)` returns 8.

5. ROUND(numeric_expression, length)

- Rounds a numeric expression to the specified number of decimal places.
- Example: `SELECT ROUND(15.678, 2)` returns 15.68.

6. SQRT(float_expression)

- Returns the square root of a given positive number.
- Example: `SELECT SQRT(16)` returns 4.

Logical Scalar Functions

Logical scalar functions in T-SQL help in evaluating conditions and returning appropriate results:

1. ISNULL(check_expression, replacement_value)

- Returns the replacement value if the check expression is NULL; otherwise, it returns the check expression.
- Example: `SELECT ISNULL(NULL, 'Default')` returns 'Default'.

2. COALESCE(expression1, expression2, ..., expressionN)

- Returns the first non-NULL expression in the list.
- Example: `SELECT COALESCE(NULL, NULL, 'Third', 'Fourth')` returns 'Third'.

3. NULLIF(expression1, expression2)

- Returns NULL if expression1 equals expression2; otherwise, it returns expression1.
- Example: `SELECT NULLIF(10, 10)` returns NULL, while `SELECT NULLIF(10, 20)` returns 10.

4. CHOOSE(index, val1, val2, ..., valN)

- Returns the item at the specified index from a list of values.

- Example: `SELECT CHOOSE(2, 'Apple', 'Banana', 'Cherry')` returns 'Banana'.

5. IIF(boolean_expression, true_value, false_value)

- Returns the true_value if the boolean expression is true; otherwise, it returns the false_value.
- Example: `SELECT IIF(10 > 5, 'Greater', 'Less')` returns 'Greater'.

System Scalar Functions

T-SQL also provides various system scalar functions that return information about the database environment:

1. @@VERSION

- Returns the version information of the SQL Server instance.
- Example: `SELECT @@VERSION`

2. @@SERVERNAME

- Returns the name of the SQL Server instance.
- Example: `SELECT @@SERVERNAME`

3. @@SPID

- Returns the session ID of the current user process.

- Example: `SELECT @@SPID`

4. CURRENT_USER

- Returns the name of the current user in the current database context.
- Example: `SELECT CURRENT_USER`

5. SYSTEM_USER

- Returns the login name of the current user.
- Example: `SELECT SYSTEM_USER`

Aggregate Functions

Aggregate functions in T-SQL perform calculations on a set of values and return a single result. These functions are commonly used with the GROUP BY clause to generate summary statistics for groups of rows.

Basic Aggregate Functions

1. COUNT(expression)

- Returns the number of items in a group.
- Example: `SELECT COUNT(*) FROM Employees`

2. SUM(expression)

- Calculates the sum of a set of values.
- Example: `SELECT SUM(Salary) FROM Employees`

3. AVG(expression)

- Calculates the average value of a set of values.
- Example: `SELECT AVG(Salary) FROM Employees`

4. MIN(expression)

- Returns the minimum value in a set of values.
- Example: `SELECT MIN(Salary) FROM Employees`

5. MAX(expression)

- Returns the maximum value in a set of values.
- Example: `SELECT MAX(Salary) FROM Employees`

Advanced Aggregate Functions

1. STDEV(expression)

- Calculates the statistical standard deviation of all values in the specified expression.
- Example: `SELECT STDEV(Salary) FROM Employees`

2. VAR(expression)

- Calculates the statistical variance of all values in the specified expression.
- Example: `SELECT VAR(Salary) FROM Employees`

3. GROUPING(column_name)

- Indicates whether a specified column in a GROUP BY list is aggregated or not.
- Returns 1 for aggregated or 0 for not aggregated in the result set.
- Example:

```
SELECT Department, GROUPING(Department) AS IsAggregated,
COUNT(*) AS EmployeeCount
FROM Employees
GROUP BY ROLLUP(Department)
```

4. STRING_AGG(expression, separator)

- Concatenates the values of string expressions and places separator values between them.
- Example:

```
SELECT Department, STRING_AGG(FirstName, ', ') AS
Employees
FROM Employees
GROUP BY Department
```

Using Aggregate Functions with GROUP BY

The GROUP BY clause is often used in conjunction with aggregate functions to group rows that have the same values in specified columns. This allows you to perform calculations on each group of rows.

Example:

```
SELECT Department, COUNT(*) AS EmployeeCount, AVG(Salary) AS
AverageSalary
FROM Employees
GROUP BY Department
```

This query groups employees by department and calculates the count of employees and average salary for each department.

Window Functions

Window functions perform calculations across a set of rows that are related to the current row. They operate on a window of data and return a value for each row in the result set.

1. ROW_NUMBER()

- Assigns a unique sequential integer to rows within a partition of a result set.
- Example:

```
SELECT
    FirstName,
    Salary,
    ROW_NUMBER() OVER (ORDER BY Salary DESC) AS
SalaryRank
FROM Employees
```

2. RANK()

- Assigns a rank to each row within a partition of a result set.
- Example:

```
SELECT
    FirstName,
    Salary,
    RANK() OVER (ORDER BY Salary DESC) AS SalaryRank
FROM Employees
```

3. DENSE_RANK()

- Similar to RANK(), but without gaps in the ranking values.
- Example:

```
SELECT
    FirstName,
    Salary,
    DENSE_RANK() OVER (ORDER BY Salary DESC) AS
SalaryRank
FROM Employees
```

4. NTILE(n)

- Distributes rows into a specified number of groups.
- Example:

```
SELECT
    FirstName,
    Salary,
    NTILE(4) OVER (ORDER BY Salary DESC) AS
SalaryQuartile
FROM Employees
```

5. LAG(column, offset, default) and LEAD(column, offset, default)

- LAG returns data from a previous row in the result set.
- LEAD returns data from a subsequent row in the result set.
- Example:

```
SELECT
    FirstName,
    Salary,
    LAG(Salary, 1, 0) OVER (ORDER BY Salary DESC) AS
PreviousSalary,
    LEAD(Salary, 1, 0) OVER (ORDER BY Salary DESC) AS
NextSalary
FROM Employees
```

String Manipulation Functions

String manipulation functions in T-SQL allow you to perform various operations on string data, such as concatenation, substring extraction, and case conversion.

Basic String Functions

1. LEN(string_expression)

- Returns the number of characters in the given string expression.
- Example: `SELECT LEN('Hello, World!')` returns 13.

2. LEFT(string_expression, number_of_characters)

- Returns the specified number of characters from the left side of the string.
- Example: `SELECT LEFT('Hello, World!', 5)` returns 'Hello'.

3. RIGHT(string_expression, number_of_characters)

- Returns the specified number of characters from the right side of the string.
- Example: `SELECT RIGHT('Hello, World!', 6)` returns 'World!'.

4. SUBSTRING(string_expression, start, length)

- Returns a substring starting at the specified position with the given length.
- Example: `SELECT SUBSTRING('Hello, World!', 8, 5)` returns 'World'.

5. LTRIM(string_expression) and RTRIM(string_expression)

- LTRIM removes leading spaces from the string.
- RTRIM removes trailing spaces from the string.
- Example: `SELECT LTRIM('    Hello')` returns 'Hello'.

6. TRIM(string_expression)

- Removes both leading and trailing spaces from the string.
- Example: `SELECT TRIM('    Hello    ')` returns 'Hello'.

String Concatenation

1. CONCAT(string1, string2, ..., stringN)

- Concatenates two or more strings together.
- Example: `SELECT CONCAT('Hello', ' ', 'World')` returns 'Hello World'.

2. CONCAT_WS(separator, string1, string2, ..., stringN)

- Concatenates two or more strings together with the specified separator.
- Example: `SELECT CONCAT_WS(', ', 'Apple', 'Banana', 'Cherry')` returns 'Apple, Banana, Cherry'.

    - operator

- Can be used to concatenate strings, but be cautious with NULL values.
- Example: `SELECT 'Hello' + ' ' + 'World'` returns 'Hello World'.

Case Conversion

1. UPPER(string_expression)

- Converts all characters in the string to uppercase.
- Example: `SELECT UPPER('Hello, World!')` returns 'HELLO, WORLD!'.

2. LOWER(string_expression)

- Converts all characters in the string to lowercase.
- Example: `SELECT LOWER('Hello, World!')` returns 'hello, world!'.

3. INITCAP(string_expression)

- Converts the first letter of each word to uppercase and the rest to lower-case.
- Example: `SELECT INITCAP('hello world')` returns 'Hello World'.

String Searching and Replacing

1. CHARINDEX(substring, string [, start_location])

- Returns the starting position of the specified substring within a string.
- Example: `SELECT CHARINDEX('World', 'Hello, World!')` returns 8.

2. PATINDEX(pattern, expression)

- Returns the starting position of the first occurrence of a pattern in a specified expression.
- Example: `SELECT PATINDEX('%World%', 'Hello, World!')` returns 8.

3. REPLACE(string_expression, string_pattern, string_replacement)

- Replaces all occurrences of a specified string value with another string value.
- Example: `SELECT REPLACE('Hello, World!', 'World', 'Universe')` returns 'Hello, Universe!'.

4. STUFF(string_expression, start, length, replacementString)

- Deletes a specified length of characters and inserts another set of characters at a specified starting point.
- Example: `SELECT STUFF('Hello, World!', 7, 5, 'Beautiful')` returns 'Hello, Beautiful!'.

Advanced String Functions

1. FORMAT(value, format [, culture])

- Formats a value with the specified format and optional culture.
- Example: `SELECT FORMAT(1234567.89, 'N2', 'en-US')` returns '1,234,567.89'.

2. STRING_SPLIT(string, separator)

- Splits a string into rows of substrings based on a specified separator.
- Example:

```
SELECT value
```

```
FROM STRING_SPLIT('Apple,Banana,Cherry', ',')
```

3. STRING_ESCAPE(string, type)

- Escapes special characters in a string and returns the result.
- Example: `SELECT STRING_ESCAPE('It''s a "quote"', 'json')`
  returns "It's a "quote"".

4. TRANSLATE(inputString, characters, translations)

- Replaces a set of characters with another set of characters in a string.
- Example: `SELECT  TRANSLATE('2*[3+4]/{7-2}', '[]{}', '()`
  `()')` returns '2*(3+4)/(7-2)'.

Date and Time Functions

Date and time functions in T-SQL are crucial for working with temporal data, allowing you to perform calculations, extract specific parts of dates, and format date and time values.

Current Date and Time

1. GETDATE()

- Returns the current system date and time as a datetime value.
- Example: `SELECT GETDATE()`

2. SYSDATETIME()

- Returns the current system date and time with higher precision (date-time2).
- Example: `SELECT SYSDATETIME()`

3. CURRENT_TIMESTAMP

- Returns the current system date and time (synonym for GETDATE()).
- Example: `SELECT CURRENT_TIMESTAMP`

4. GETUTCDATE()

- Returns the current UTC date and time.
- Example: `SELECT GETUTCDATE()`

Date and Time Parts

1. DATEPART(datepart, date)

- Returns an integer representing the specified datepart of the given date.
- Example: `SELECT DATEPART(YEAR, '2023-05-15')` returns 2023.

2. YEAR(date), MONTH(date), DAY(date)

- Extract the year, month, or day from a date.

- Example: `SELECT YEAR('2023-05-15')` returns 2023.

3. DATENAME(datepart, date)

- Returns a string representing the specified datepart of the given date.
- Example: `SELECT DATENAME(MONTH, '2023-05-15')` returns 'May'.

4. DATETRUNC(datepart, date)

- Returns a date truncated to the specified datepart.
- Example: `SELECT DATETRUNC(MONTH, '2023-05-15')` returns '2023-05-01'.

Date and Time Arithmetic

1. DATEADD(datepart, number, date)

- Adds a specified number of dateparts to a date and returns the new date.
- Example: `SELECT DATEADD(DAY, 7, '2023-05-15')` returns '2023-05-22'.

2. DATEDIFF(datepart, startdate, enddate)

- Returns the number of datepart boundaries crossed between two dates.

- Example: `SELECT DATEDIFF(DAY, '2023-05-01',` `'2023-05-15')` returns 14.

3. EOMONTH(start_date [, month_to_add])

- Returns the last day of the month for a specified date, with an optional offset.
- Example: `SELECT EOMONTH('2023-05-15')` returns '2023-05-31'.

Date and Time Formatting

1. CONVERT(data_type [(length)], expression [, style])

- Converts a date to a specified format using style codes.
- Example: `SELECT CONVERT(VARCHAR(20), GETDATE(), 107)` returns 'May 15, 2023'.

2. FORMAT(value, format [, culture])

- Formats a date value using specified format strings and culture.
- Example: `SELECT FORMAT(GETDATE(), 'dd-MM-yyyy')` returns '15-05-2023'.

Working with Time Zones

1. SWITCHOFFSET(datetimeoffset, time_zone)

- Changes the time zone offset of a datetimeoffset value.
- Example: `SELECT SWITCHOFFSET('2023-05-15 12:00:00 +01:00', '-08:00')`

2. TODATETIMEOFFSET(expression, time_zone)

- Converts a datetime2 value to a datetimeoffset value.
- Example: `SELECT TODATETIMEOFFSET('2023-05-15 12:00:00', '-08:00')`

3. AT TIME ZONE

- Converts an input date and time value to a target time zone.
- Example: `SELECT GETDATE() AT TIME ZONE 'Pacific Standard Time'`

Date and Time Validation

1. ISDATE(expression)

- Returns 1 if the expression is a valid date, time, or datetime value; otherwise, returns 0.

- Example: `SELECT ISDATE('2023-05-15')` returns 1.

2. TRY_CONVERT(data_type [(length)], expression [, style])

- Converts a value to the specified data type and returns NULL if the conversion fails.
- Example: `SELECT TRY_CONVERT(DATE, '2023-05-15')` returns '2023-05-15'.

3. TRY_CAST(expression AS data_type [(length)])

- Converts a value to the specified data type and returns NULL if the conversion fails.
- Example: `SELECT TRY_CAST('2023-05-15' AS DATE)` returns '2023-05-15'.

Conclusion

Functions in T-SQL are powerful tools that enable you to manipulate data, perform calculations, and transform results in various ways. By mastering scalar functions, aggregate functions, string manipulation functions, and date and time functions, you can write more efficient and expressive queries.

Remember to consider performance implications when using functions, especially in large datasets or frequently executed queries. In some cases, it may be more efficient to use built-in T-SQL constructs or to perform calculations in application code rather than relying heavily on functions within queries.

As you continue to work with T-SQL, practice using these functions in different scenarios to become more proficient in writing complex and efficient queries. Additionally, keep in mind that SQL Server is constantly evolving, and new functions may be introduced in future versions, so it's essential to stay updated with the latest features and best practices in T-SQL programming.

Chapter 6: Joins and Sub-queries

Introduction

In this chapter, we'll dive deep into the world of joins and subqueries in T-SQL. These powerful features allow you to combine data from multiple tables and create complex queries that can extract valuable insights from your database. We'll explore various types of joins, learn how to write efficient join operations, and master the art of subqueries and Common Table Expressions (CTEs). By the end of this chapter, you'll have a solid understanding of these advanced T-SQL concepts and be able to apply them to real-world scenarios.

Types of Joins

Joins are essential operations in relational databases that allow you to combine data from two or more tables based on a related column between them. T-SQL supports several types of joins, each with its own use case and behavior. Let's explore the main types of joins:

1. INNER JOIN

An INNER JOIN returns only the rows that have matching values in both tables being joined. It's the most common type of join and is used when you want to retrieve data that exists in both tables.

Syntax:

```
SELECT columns
FROM table1
INNER JOIN table2 ON table1.column = table2.column;
```

Example:

```
SELECT o.OrderID, c.CustomerName, o.OrderDate
FROM Orders o
INNER JOIN Customers c ON o.CustomerID = c.CustomerID;
```

In this example, we're joining the Orders and Customers tables based on the CustomerID column. The result will include only the orders that have a matching customer in the Customers table.

2. OUTER JOIN

OUTER JOINs allow you to retrieve data from both tables, even if there's no match in one of the tables. There are three types of OUTER JOINs:

a. LEFT OUTER JOIN (or simply LEFT JOIN)

A LEFT JOIN returns all rows from the left table and the matching rows from the right table. If there's no match, NULL values are returned for the right table's columns.

Syntax:

```
SELECT columns
FROM table1
```

```
LEFT JOIN table2 ON table1.column = table2.column;
```

Example:

```
SELECT c.CustomerName, o.OrderID, o.OrderDate
FROM Customers c
LEFT JOIN Orders o ON c.CustomerID = o.CustomerID;
```

This query will return all customers, even those who haven't placed any orders. For customers without orders, the OrderID and OrderDate columns will contain NULL values.

    b. RIGHT OUTER JOIN (or simply RIGHT JOIN)

    A RIGHT JOIN is similar to a LEFT JOIN, but it returns all rows from the right table and the matching rows from the left table. If there's no match, NULL values are returned for the left table's columns.

    Syntax:

```
SELECT columns
FROM table1
RIGHT JOIN table2 ON table1.column = table2.column;
```

Example:

```
SELECT o.OrderID, o.OrderDate, c.CustomerName
FROM Orders o
RIGHT JOIN Customers c ON o.CustomerID = c.CustomerID;
```

This query will return all customers and their orders, including customers who haven't placed any orders. For customers without orders, the OrderID and Order-Date columns will contain NULL values.

    c. FULL OUTER JOIN (or simply FULL JOIN)

    A FULL JOIN returns all rows from both tables, with NULL values in place of missing matches on either side.

    Syntax:

```
SELECT columns
FROM table1
FULL JOIN table2 ON table1.column = table2.column;
```

Example:

```
SELECT e.EmployeeID, e.EmployeeName, d.DepartmentName
FROM Employees e
FULL JOIN Departments d ON e.DepartmentID = d.DepartmentID;
```

This query will return all employees and all departments, even if there are employees without departments or departments without employees.

3. CROSS JOIN

A CROSS JOIN returns the Cartesian product of both tables, meaning it combines each row from the first table with every row from the second table. This type of join doesn't require a joining condition.

Syntax:

```
SELECT columns
FROM table1
CROSS JOIN table2;
```

Example:

```
SELECT p.ProductName, c.CategoryName
FROM Products p
CROSS JOIN Categories c;
```

This query will create all possible combinations of products and categories, regardless of whether a product belongs to a specific category.

Writing Efficient Joins

While joins are powerful, they can also be resource-intensive if not used properly. Here are some tips for writing efficient joins:

1. Use appropriate indexes:

Ensure that the columns used in the join conditions are properly indexed. This can significantly improve join performance, especially for large tables.

Example:

```
CREATE INDEX IX_CustomerID ON Orders (CustomerID);
CREATE INDEX IX_CustomerID ON Customers (CustomerID);
```

2. Join on equality whenever possible:

Equality joins (using the = operator) are generally more efficient than inequality joins or complex join conditions.

3. Avoid unnecessary joins:

Only join tables that are required for your query. Unnecessary joins can lead to performance degradation and potentially incorrect results.

4. Use appropriate join types:

Choose the right type of join based on your requirements. For example, use an INNER JOIN when you only need matching rows, and use OUTER JOINs when you need to include non-matching rows.

5. Optimize join order:

The order in which tables are joined can affect performance. Generally, start with the largest table and join smaller tables to it. However, the SQL Server query optimizer usually determines the best join order automatically.

6. Use table aliases:

Table aliases make your queries more readable and can slightly improve performance by reducing the amount of text the query engine needs to parse.

Example:

```
SELECT o.OrderID, c.CustomerName
FROM Orders o
INNER JOIN Customers c ON o.CustomerID = c.CustomerID;
```

7. Avoid joining on computed columns:

Joining on computed columns can prevent the use of indexes and lead to poor performance. If possible, join on non-computed columns.

8. Consider using indexed views:

For complex joins that are frequently used, consider creating an indexed view to materialize the join results and improve query performance.

Example:

```
CREATE VIEW vw_OrderCustomer WITH SCHEMABINDING AS
SELECT o.OrderID, o.OrderDate, c.CustomerName
FROM dbo.Orders o
INNER JOIN dbo.Customers c ON o.CustomerID = c.CustomerID;

CREATE UNIQUE CLUSTERED INDEX IX_vw_OrderCustomer ON
vw_OrderCustomer (OrderID);
```

9. Use HASH JOIN hints for large tables:

For very large tables, you can use the HASH JOIN hint to potentially improve performance. However, use this sparingly and only after testing, as the query optimizer usually chooses the best join method automatically.

Example:

```sql
SELECT o.OrderID, c.CustomerName
FROM Orders o
INNER HASH JOIN Customers c ON o.CustomerID = c.CustomerID;
```

10. Monitor and analyze join performance:

Use tools like SQL Server Profiler, Dynamic Management Views (DMVs), and execution plans to identify and optimize poorly performing joins.

Subqueries and Correlated Subqueries

Subqueries are queries nested within another query. They can be used in various parts of a SQL statement, such as the SELECT, FROM, WHERE, and HAVING clauses. Subqueries can return a single value, a single row, a single column, or a table result set.

Types of Subqueries

1. Scalar Subquery:

Returns a single value and can be used wherever a single value expression is allowed.

Example:

```sql
SELECT ProductName, UnitPrice
```

```
FROM Products
WHERE UnitPrice > (SELECT AVG(UnitPrice) FROM Products);
```

2. Row Subquery:

Returns a single row and can be compared using operators like =, <, >, etc.

Example:

```
SELECT *
FROM Employees
WHERE (Salary, DepartmentID) = (SELECT MAX(Salary), DepartmentID
FROM Employees WHERE DepartmentID = 10);
```

3. Column Subquery:

Returns a single column of one or more values and is often used with IN, ANY, or ALL operators.

Example:

```
SELECT ProductName
FROM Products
WHERE ProductID IN (SELECT ProductID FROM OrderDetails WHERE
Quantity > 100);
```

4. Table Subquery:

Returns a table result set and is often used in the FROM clause as a derived table.

Example:

```
SELECT d.DepartmentName, e.EmployeeCount
FROM Departments d
INNER JOIN (
    SELECT DepartmentID, COUNT(*) AS EmployeeCount
    FROM Employees
    GROUP BY DepartmentID
) e ON d.DepartmentID = e.DepartmentID;
```

Correlated Subqueries

A correlated subquery is a subquery that depends on the outer query for its values. It is executed once for each row processed by the outer query.

Example:

```sql
SELECT e.EmployeeName, e.Salary
FROM Employees e
WHERE e.Salary > (
    SELECT AVG(Salary)
    FROM Employees
    WHERE DepartmentID = e.DepartmentID
);
```

In this example, the subquery calculates the average salary for each department, and the outer query compares each employee's salary to their department's average.

Best Practices for Subqueries

1. Use subqueries judiciously:

While subqueries can be powerful, they can also impact performance. Consider using joins or other SQL constructs when appropriate.

2. Optimize correlated subqueries:

Correlated subqueries can be slow for large datasets. Consider rewriting them as joins or using derived tables when possible.

3. Use EXISTS for efficiency:

When checking for the existence of related rows, use EXISTS instead of IN, as it's generally more efficient.

Example:

```
SELECT CustomerName
FROM Customers c
WHERE EXISTS (
    SELECT 1
    FROM Orders o
    WHERE o.CustomerID = c.CustomerID
);
```

4. Avoid unnecessary subqueries:

If a subquery returns a constant value, consider replacing it with the actual value to improve performance.

5. Use table variables or temporary tables:

For complex subqueries that are reused multiple times in a query, consider storing the results in a table variable or temporary table.

Example:

```
DECLARE @HighValueOrders TABLE (OrderID INT);

INSERT INTO @HighValueOrders
SELECT OrderID
FROM Orders
WHERE TotalAmount > 10000;

SELECT c.CustomerName, o.OrderID, o.TotalAmount
FROM Customers c
INNER JOIN Orders o ON c.CustomerID = o.CustomerID
WHERE o.OrderID IN (SELECT OrderID FROM @HighValueOrders);
```

Common Table Expressions (CTEs)

Common Table Expressions (CTEs) provide a way to define named temporary result sets that exist only within the scope of a single SQL statement. CTEs can simplify complex queries, improve readability, and allow for recursive queries.

Basic CTE Syntax

```
WITH CTE_Name AS (
    -- CTE definition
    SELECT column1, column2
    FROM SomeTable
    WHERE SomeCondition
)
-- Main query using the CTE
SELECT *
FROM CTE_Name
WHERE AnotherCondition;
```

Benefits of CTEs

1. Improved readability:

CTEs make complex queries easier to understand by breaking them down into logical, named components.

2. Reusability within a query:

You can reference a CTE multiple times within the same query, reducing redundancy.

3. Recursive capabilities:

CTEs support recursive queries, which are useful for hierarchical or tree-structured data.

4. Modularization:

CTEs allow you to modularize your query logic, making it easier to maintain and modify.

Examples of CTEs

1. Basic CTE:

```
WITH TopCustomers AS (
    SELECT TOP 10 CustomerID, SUM(TotalAmount) AS TotalPurchases
    FROM Orders
    GROUP BY CustomerID
    ORDER BY TotalPurchases DESC
)
SELECT c.CustomerName, tc.TotalPurchases
FROM TopCustomers tc
INNER JOIN Customers c ON tc.CustomerID = c.CustomerID;
```

2. Multiple CTEs:

```
WITH
OrderStats AS (
    SELECT CustomerID, COUNT(*) AS OrderCount, SUM(TotalAmount)
AS TotalSpent
    FROM Orders
    GROUP BY CustomerID
),
CustomerCategories AS (
    SELECT CustomerID,
```

```
        CASE
            WHEN TotalSpent > 10000 THEN 'High Value'
            WHEN TotalSpent > 5000 THEN 'Medium Value'
            ELSE 'Low Value'
        END AS CustomerCategory
    FROM OrderStats
)
SELECT c.CustomerName, os.OrderCount, os.TotalSpent,
cc.CustomerCategory
FROM Customers c
LEFT JOIN OrderStats os ON c.CustomerID = os.CustomerID
LEFT JOIN CustomerCategories cc ON c.CustomerID = cc.CustomerID;
```

3. Recursive CTE:

```
WITH EmployeeHierarchy AS (
    -- Anchor member
    SELECT EmployeeID, EmployeeName, ManagerID, 0 AS Level
    FROM Employees
    WHERE ManagerID IS NULL

    UNION ALL

    -- Recursive member
    SELECT e.EmployeeID, e.EmployeeName, e.ManagerID, eh.Level +
1
    FROM Employees e
    INNER JOIN EmployeeHierarchy eh ON e.ManagerID =
eh.EmployeeID
)
SELECT EmployeeID, EmployeeName, Level
FROM EmployeeHierarchy
ORDER BY Level, EmployeeName;
```

Best Practices for CTEs

1. Use meaningful names:

Choose descriptive names for your CTEs to enhance readability and self-documentation.

2. Limit CTE complexity:

While CTEs can simplify complex queries, avoid creating overly complex CTEs that are difficult to understand.

3. Consider performance:

CTEs are optimized by the query engine, but in some cases, temporary tables or table variables might perform better for very large datasets.

4. Use CTEs for code organization:

Leverage CTEs to organize complex query logic into manageable, logical units.

5. Be cautious with recursive CTEs:

Ensure that recursive CTEs have a proper termination condition to avoid infinite loops.

6. Combine CTEs with other T-SQL features:

CTEs can be used in conjunction with other T-SQL features like window functions, PIVOT, and UNPIVOT for powerful data analysis.

Conclusion

In this chapter, we've explored the various types of joins in T-SQL, including INNER, OUTER, and CROSS joins. We've discussed best practices for writing efficient joins and provided tips for optimizing join performance. We've also delved into subqueries and correlated subqueries, examining their types, use cases, and best practices.

Finally, we've introduced Common Table Expressions (CTEs) as a powerful tool for simplifying complex queries, improving code readability, and enabling recursive queries. By mastering these concepts, you'll be well-equipped to write sophisticated T-SQL queries that can handle complex data relationships and analysis tasks.

Remember that while these features provide great flexibility and power, it's essential to use them judiciously and always consider query performance. Regular testing, monitoring, and optimization are key to ensuring that your T-SQL code remains efficient and maintainable as your database and application needs evolve.

Chapter 7: Advanced Query Techniques

Grouping and Aggregation

Grouping and aggregation are powerful features in T-SQL that allow you to summarize and analyze data in meaningful ways. These techniques are essential for generating reports, performing data analysis, and extracting valuable insights from large datasets.

GROUP BY Clause

The GROUP BY clause is used to group rows that have the same values in specified columns. It is often used in conjunction with aggregate functions to perform calculations on each group of rows.

Syntax:

```
SELECT column1, column2, ..., aggregate_function(column)
FROM table_name
GROUP BY column1, column2, ...
```

Example:

```
SELECT Department, COUNT(*) AS EmployeeCount
FROM Employees
GROUP BY Department
```

This query groups employees by department and counts the number of employees in each department.

Aggregate Functions

Aggregate functions perform calculations on a set of values and return a single result. Common aggregate functions include:

1. COUNT(): Counts the number of rows or non-null values
2. SUM(): Calculates the sum of a set of values
3. AVG(): Calculates the average of a set of values
4. MAX(): Returns the maximum value in a set
5. MIN(): Returns the minimum value in a set

Example using multiple aggregate functions:

```
SELECT
    Department,
    COUNT(*) AS EmployeeCount,
    AVG(Salary) AS AverageSalary,
    MAX(Salary) AS HighestSalary,
    MIN(Salary) AS LowestSalary
FROM Employees
GROUP BY Department
```

Grouping Sets

Grouping sets allow you to specify multiple grouping combinations in a single query. This is useful when you need to generate subtotals and grand totals in a single result set.

Syntax:

```
SELECT column1, column2, ..., aggregate_function(column)
FROM table_name
GROUP BY
GROUPING SETS (
    (column1, column2, ...),
    (column1),
    (column2),
    ()
)
```

Example:

```
SELECT
    COALESCE(Department, 'All Departments') AS Department,
    COALESCE(JobTitle, 'All Job Titles') AS JobTitle,
    COUNT(*) AS EmployeeCount
FROM Employees
GROUP BY
GROUPING SETS (
    (Department, JobTitle),
    (Department),
    (JobTitle),
    ()
)
```

This query generates a report with subtotals for each department, each job title, and a grand total for all employees.

ROLLUP and CUBE

ROLLUP and CUBE are extensions of the GROUP BY clause that generate additional summary rows.

- ROLLUP: Generates a hierarchy of subtotals and a grand total
- CUBE: Generates all possible combinations of groupings

Example using ROLLUP:

```
SELECT
    COALESCE(Department, 'All Departments') AS Department,
    COALESCE(JobTitle, 'All Job Titles') AS JobTitle,
    COUNT(*) AS EmployeeCount
FROM Employees
GROUP BY ROLLUP (Department, JobTitle)
```

Example using CUBE:

```
SELECT
    COALESCE(Department, 'All Departments') AS Department,
    COALESCE(JobTitle, 'All Job Titles') AS JobTitle,
    COUNT(*) AS EmployeeCount
FROM Employees
GROUP BY CUBE (Department, JobTitle)
```

HAVING vs WHERE Clauses

Both HAVING and WHERE clauses are used to filter data in SQL queries, but they serve different purposes and are applied at different stages of query execution.

WHERE Clause

The WHERE clause is used to filter rows before any grouping or aggregation occurs. It is applied to individual rows in the base table(s).

Key points about the WHERE clause:

- Filters rows before grouping
- Can use any column from the base table(s)
- Cannot use aggregate functions

Example:

```
SELECT Department, COUNT(*) AS EmployeeCount
FROM Employees
WHERE Salary > 50000
GROUP BY Department
```

In this query, the WHERE clause filters out employees with salaries of 50,000 or less before grouping and counting.

HAVING Clause

The HAVING clause is used to filter groups after grouping and aggregation have been performed. It is applied to the result set of a GROUP BY operation.

Key points about the HAVING clause:

- Filters groups after grouping
- Can only use columns or expressions in the SELECT list or GROUP BY clause
- Can use aggregate functions

Example:

```
SELECT Department, COUNT(*) AS EmployeeCount
FROM Employees
GROUP BY Department
HAVING COUNT(*) > 10
```

This query groups employees by department and then filters out departments with 10 or fewer employees.

Combining WHERE and HAVING

You can use both WHERE and HAVING clauses in the same query to apply filters at different stages of query execution.

Example:

```
SELECT Department, AVG(Salary) AS AverageSalary
FROM Employees
WHERE HireDate >= '2020-01-01'
GROUP BY Department
HAVING AVG(Salary) > 60000
```

This query:

1. Filters employees hired on or after January 1, 2020 (using WHERE)
2. Groups the remaining employees by department
3. Calculates the average salary for each department
4. Filters out departments with an average salary of 60,000 or less (using HAVING)

Window Functions

Window functions perform calculations across a set of rows that are related to the current row. They are powerful tools for performing complex analyses and calculations within a query.

Key features of window functions:

- Operate on a window (set of rows) defined by a PARTITION BY clause
- Can include an ORDER BY clause to determine the order of rows within each partition
- Do not reduce the number of rows returned by the query

Types of Window Functions

1. Ranking Functions

- ROW_NUMBER()
- RANK()
- DENSE_RANK()
- NTILE()

2. Offset Functions

- LAG()
- LEAD()
- FIRST_VALUE()
- LAST_VALUE()

3. Aggregate Functions

- SUM()
- AVG()
- COUNT()
- MIN()
- MAX()

Syntax

The general syntax for window functions is:

```
window_function(arguments)
OVER (
    [PARTITION BY partition_expression, ...]
    [ORDER BY sort_expression [ASC | DESC], ...]
    [ROWS | RANGE frame_extent]
)
```

ROW_NUMBER()

ROW_NUMBER() assigns a unique integer to each row within its partition.

Example:

```
SELECT
    EmployeeID,
    FirstName,
    LastName,
    Department,
    Salary,
    ROW_NUMBER() OVER (PARTITION BY Department ORDER BY Salary
DESC) AS SalaryRank
FROM Employees
```

This query assigns a rank to each employee within their department based on their salary.

RANK() and DENSE_RANK()

RANK() and DENSE_RANK() are similar to ROW_NUMBER(), but they handle ties differently:

- RANK() assigns the same rank to ties and skips the next rank(s)
- DENSE_RANK() assigns the same rank to ties but doesn't skip the next rank

Example:

```
SELECT
    EmployeeID,
    FirstName,
    LastName,
    Department,
    Salary,
    ROW_NUMBER() OVER (ORDER BY Salary DESC) AS RowNum,
    RANK() OVER (ORDER BY Salary DESC) AS SalaryRank,
    DENSE_RANK() OVER (ORDER BY Salary DESC) AS DenseRank
FROM Employees
```

LAG() and LEAD()

LAG() and LEAD() allow you to access data from other rows in relation to the current row.

- LAG(): Accesses data from a previous row in the result set
- LEAD(): Accesses data from a subsequent row in the result set

Example:

```
SELECT
    EmployeeID,
    FirstName,
    LastName,
    Salary,
    LAG(Salary) OVER (ORDER BY Salary) AS PreviousSalary,
    LEAD(Salary) OVER (ORDER BY Salary) AS NextSalary
FROM Employees
```

This query shows each employee's salary along with the salaries of the employees immediately below and above them in the salary range.

Running Totals and Moving Averages

Window functions are excellent for calculating running totals and moving averages.

Example of a running total:

```
SELECT
    OrderDate,
    OrderTotal,
    SUM(OrderTotal) OVER (ORDER BY OrderDate) AS RunningTotal
FROM Orders
```

Example of a 3-day moving average:

```
SELECT
    OrderDate,
    OrderTotal,
    AVG(OrderTotal) OVER (
        ORDER BY OrderDate
        ROWS BETWEEN 1 PRECEDING AND 1 FOLLOWING
    ) AS MovingAverage
FROM Orders
```

PIVOT and UNPIVOT

PIVOT and UNPIVOT are powerful operators in T-SQL that allow you to transform data from rows to columns (PIVOT) and vice versa (UNPIVOT). These operations are particularly useful for generating reports and restructuring data for analysis.

PIVOT

The PIVOT operator rotates a table-valued expression by turning the unique values from one column into multiple columns in the output, and performs aggregations on any remaining column values.

Syntax:

```
SELECT ...
FROM
    (<SELECT query that produces the base data>) AS SourceTable
PIVOT
(
    <aggregate function>(<column being aggregated>)
    FOR
    <column whose values will become column headers>
    IN ( [first pivoted column], [second pivoted column], ...
[last pivoted column] )
) AS PivotTable
```

Example:

Let's say we have a table of sales data:

```
CREATE TABLE Sales (
    SalesDate DATE,
    Category VARCHAR(50),
    Amount DECIMAL(10, 2)
)

INSERT INTO Sales VALUES
('2023-01-01', 'Electronics', 1000),
('2023-01-01', 'Clothing', 500),
('2023-01-02', 'Electronics', 1500),
('2023-01-02', 'Furniture', 2000),
('2023-01-03', 'Clothing', 750),
('2023-01-03', 'Furniture', 1800)
```

To pivot this data and show sales by category for each date:

```
SELECT *,
```

```
FROM
(
    SELECT SalesDate, Category, Amount
    FROM Sales
) AS SourceTable
PIVOT
(
    SUM(Amount)
    FOR Category IN ([Electronics], [Clothing], [Furniture])
) AS PivotTable
```

This query will produce a result set with columns: SalesDate, Electronics, Clothing, and Furniture.

Dynamic PIVOT

The previous example uses a static list of pivot columns. In many cases, you might not know the exact categories in advance. In such situations, you can use dynamic SQL to create a PIVOT query with a variable list of columns.

Example of dynamic PIVOT:

```
DECLARE @columns NVARCHAR(MAX) = '';
DECLARE @sql NVARCHAR(MAX) = '';

-- Generate the list of pivot columns dynamically
SELECT @columns += QUOTENAME(Category) + ','
FROM (SELECT DISTINCT Category FROM Sales) AS Categories
SET @columns = LEFT(@columns, LEN(@columns) - 1)

-- Construct the dynamic SQL
SET @sql =
N'SELECT *
FROM
(
    SELECT SalesDate, Category, Amount
    FROM Sales
) AS SourceTable
PIVOT
```

```
(
    SUM(Amount)
    FOR Category IN (' + @columns + ')
) AS PivotTable'

-- Execute the dynamic SQL
EXEC sp_executesql @sql
```

This approach allows the PIVOT operation to adapt to any categories present in the

Sales table.

UNPIVOT

The UNPIVOT operator performs the opposite operation of PIVOT. It rotates col-

umns of a table-valued expression into column values.

Syntax:

```
SELECT ...
FROM
    (<SELECT query that produces the base data>) AS SourceTable
UNPIVOT
(
    <column name for unpivoted values>
    FOR <column name for unpivoted column headers>
    IN ( [first column to unpivot], [second column to
unpivot], ... [last column to unpivot] )
) AS UnpivotTable
```

Example:

Let's assume we have a pivoted table of sales data:

```
CREATE TABLE PivotedSales (
    SalesDate DATE,
    Electronics DECIMAL(10, 2),
    Clothing DECIMAL(10, 2),
    Furniture DECIMAL(10, 2)
)
```

```
INSERT INTO PivotedSales VALUES
('2023-01-01', 1000, 500, NULL),
('2023-01-02', 1500, NULL, 2000),
('2023-01-03', NULL, 750, 1800)
```

To unpivot this data back into a format similar to our original Sales table:

```
SELECT SalesDate, Category, Amount
FROM PivotedSales
UNPIVOT
(
    Amount
    FOR Category IN (Electronics, Clothing, Furniture)
) AS UnpivotTable
WHERE Amount IS NOT NULL
```

This query transforms the data back into a format with columns: SalesDate, Category, and Amount. The `WHERE Amount IS NOT NULL` clause is added to remove rows with NULL values, which are typically not needed in the unpivoted result.

Dynamic UNPIVOT

Similar to dynamic PIVOT, you can create a dynamic UNPIVOT query when you don't know the exact columns to unpivot in advance.

Example of dynamic UNPIVOT:

```
DECLARE @columns NVARCHAR(MAX) = '';
DECLARE @sql NVARCHAR(MAX) = '';

-- Generate the list of columns to unpivot dynamically
SELECT @columns += QUOTENAME(COLUMN_NAME) + ','
FROM INFORMATION_SCHEMA.COLUMNS
WHERE TABLE_NAME = 'PivotedSales' AND COLUMN_NAME != 'SalesDate'
SET @columns = LEFT(@columns, LEN(@columns) - 1)

-- Construct the dynamic SQL
SET @sql =
N'SELECT SalesDate, Category, Amount
```

```
FROM PivotedSales
UNPIVOT
(
    Amount
    FOR Category IN (' + @columns + ')
) AS UnpivotTable
WHERE Amount IS NOT NULL'

-- Execute the dynamic SQL
EXEC sp_executesql @sql
```

This approach allows the UNPIVOT operation to adapt to any columns present in the PivotedSales table, excluding the SalesDate column.

Practical Applications and Best Practices

Use Cases for Advanced Query Techniques

1. Data Analysis and Reporting

- Use grouping and aggregation to summarize large datasets
- Apply window functions for ranking, running totals, and moving averages
- Utilize PIVOT for creating cross-tabulation reports

2. Data Transformation

- Use UNPIVOT to normalize data for further processing or analysis

- Apply window functions to calculate period-over-period changes

3. Performance Optimization

- Use window functions to avoid self-joins and subqueries
- Leverage PIVOT and UNPIVOT for efficient data reshaping

4. Complex Calculations

- Combine multiple window functions for sophisticated analyses
- Use GROUPING SETS, ROLLUP, or CUBE for multi-level aggregations

Best Practices

1. Choose the Right Technique

- Understand the differences between WHERE and HAVING clauses
- Select the appropriate window function for your specific need
- Consider readability and maintainability when choosing between different approaches

2. Optimize Performance

- Use appropriate indexes to support your queries
- Be cautious with large-scale PIVOT operations, as they can be resource-intensive

- Consider materializing intermediate results for complex queries

3. Ensure Data Integrity

- Be aware of how NULL values are handled in different operations
- Use COALESCE or ISNULL functions to handle missing values appropriately

4. Write Clear and Maintainable Code

- Use meaningful aliases for derived columns and subqueries
- Comment your code, especially for complex window functions or dynamic SQL
- Break down complex queries into manageable parts using CTEs or views

5. Test Thoroughly

- Verify results with smaller datasets before applying to large tables
- Test edge cases, especially with window functions and PIVOT/UNPIVOT operations

6. Consider Alternatives

- Evaluate whether client-side pivoting might be more appropriate for very dynamic scenarios

- Consider using APPLY operator as an alternative to certain window functions in some cases

By mastering these advanced query techniques, you'll be able to tackle complex data manipulation and analysis tasks efficiently in SQL Server. Remember that the key to becoming proficient with these techniques is practice and real-world application. As you use these methods in your projects, you'll develop a deeper understanding of when and how to apply each technique for optimal results.

Part 3: Advanced Programming with T-SQL

Chapter 8: Stored Procedures and User-Defined Functions

8.1 Introduction to Stored Procedures

Stored procedures are precompiled and stored collections of T-SQL statements that can be executed as a single unit. They are an essential component of SQL Server programming, offering numerous benefits such as improved performance, enhanced security, and code reusability.

Benefits of Stored Procedures

1. **Performance Optimization**: Stored procedures are compiled and cached in memory, resulting in faster execution compared to ad-hoc queries.
2. **Security Enhancement**: Stored procedures can be used to implement fine-grained access control, limiting direct access to underlying tables.
3. **Code Reusability**: Common database operations can be encapsulated in stored procedures, promoting code reuse across applications.

4. **Reduced Network Traffic**: By executing multiple statements on the server, stored procedures minimize the amount of data transferred between the client and server.

5. **Easier Maintenance**: Centralized business logic in stored procedures simplifies maintenance and updates.

8.2 Creating Stored Procedures

To create a stored procedure in SQL Server, you use the CREATE PROCEDURE statement. Here's the basic syntax:

```
CREATE PROCEDURE procedure_name
    [@parameter_name data_type [= default_value]]
AS
BEGIN
    -- SQL statements
END
```

Let's create a simple stored procedure that retrieves all customers from a hypothetical Customers table:

```
CREATE PROCEDURE GetAllCustomers
AS
BEGIN
    SELECT CustomerID, FirstName, LastName, Email
    FROM Customers
END
```

To execute this stored procedure, you would use the following command:

```
EXEC GetAllCustomers
```

Modifying Stored Procedures

To modify an existing stored procedure, you use the `ALTER PROCEDURE` statement:

```
ALTER PROCEDURE GetAllCustomers
AS
BEGIN
    SELECT CustomerID, FirstName, LastName, Email, PhoneNumber
    FROM Customers
    ORDER BY LastName, FirstName
END
```

Dropping Stored Procedures

To remove a stored procedure, use the `DROP PROCEDURE` statement:

```
DROP PROCEDURE GetAllCustomers
```

8.3 Parameterized Queries in Stored Procedures

Parameterized queries allow you to create more flexible and reusable stored procedures by accepting input parameters. These parameters can be used to filter results, provide values for insertions or updates, or control the behavior of the procedure.

Declaring Parameters

Parameters are declared in the procedure definition using the @ symbol, followed by the parameter name and data type:

```
CREATE PROCEDURE GetCustomersByCity
    @City NVARCHAR(50)
AS
BEGIN
    SELECT CustomerID, FirstName, LastName, Email
    FROM Customers
    WHERE City = @City
END
```

To execute this stored procedure with a parameter, you would use:

```
EXEC GetCustomersByCity @City = 'New York'
```

Optional Parameters and Default Values

You can make parameters optional by providing default values:

```
CREATE PROCEDURE GetCustomersByState
    @State NVARCHAR(2) = NULL
AS
BEGIN
    IF @State IS NULL
        SELECT CustomerID, FirstName, LastName, Email, State
        FROM Customers
    ELSE
        SELECT CustomerID, FirstName, LastName, Email, State
        FROM Customers
        WHERE State = @State
END
```

This procedure can be called with or without the @State parameter:

```
EXEC GetCustomersByState -- Returns all customers
```

```
EXEC GetCustomersByState @State = 'CA' -- Returns customers from
California
```

Output Parameters

Stored procedures can also return values through output parameters:

```
CREATE PROCEDURE GetCustomerCount
    @State NVARCHAR(2),
    @Count INT OUTPUT
AS
BEGIN
    SELECT @Count = COUNT(*)
    FROM Customers
    WHERE State = @State
END
```

To use this procedure and retrieve the output value:

```
DECLARE @CustomerCount INT
EXEC GetCustomerCount @State = 'NY', @Count = @CustomerCount
OUTPUT
PRINT 'Number of customers in NY: ' + CAST(@CustomerCount AS
NVARCHAR(10))
```

8.4 Advanced Stored Procedure Techniques

Error Handling in Stored Procedures

Proper error handling is crucial for robust stored procedures. SQL Server provides the `TRY...CATCH` construct for handling errors:

```sql
CREATE PROCEDURE InsertCustomer
    @FirstName NVARCHAR(50),
    @LastName NVARCHAR(50),
    @Email NVARCHAR(100)
AS
BEGIN
    BEGIN TRY
        INSERT INTO Customers (FirstName, LastName, Email)
        VALUES (@FirstName, @LastName, @Email)

        PRINT 'Customer inserted successfully.'
    END TRY
    BEGIN CATCH
        PRINT 'An error occurred: ' + ERROR_MESSAGE()
    END CATCH
END
```

Dynamic SQL in Stored Procedures

Dynamic SQL allows you to construct and execute SQL statements dynamically at runtime. This can be useful for creating flexible queries, but it should be used cautiously due to potential security risks:

```sql
CREATE PROCEDURE GetCustomersByColumn
    @ColumnName NVARCHAR(50),
    @SearchValue NVARCHAR(100)
AS
BEGIN
    DECLARE @SQL NVARCHAR(MAX)

    SET @SQL = 'SELECT CustomerID, FirstName, LastName, Email
FROM Customers WHERE ' +
                QUOTENAME(@ColumnName) + ' = @SearchValue'

    EXEC sp_executesql @SQL, N'@SearchValue NVARCHAR(100)',
@SearchValue
END
```

To execute this procedure:

```
EXEC GetCustomersByColumn @ColumnName = 'City', @SearchValue =
'Los Angeles'
```

8.5 Introduction to User-Defined Functions

User-Defined Functions (UDFs) are routines that accept parameters, perform actions, and return a result. Unlike stored procedures, UDFs can be used in SELECT statements and WHERE clauses. There are three types of UDFs in SQL Server:

1. Scalar Functions

2. Table-Valued Functions

3. Multi-Statement Table-Valued Functions

8.6 Scalar Functions

Scalar functions return a single value and can be used wherever an expression is allowed. They are created using the CREATE FUNCTION statement:

```
CREATE FUNCTION CalculateAge
(
    @BirthDate DATE
)
RETURNS INT
AS
BEGIN
    RETURN DATEDIFF(YEAR, @BirthDate, GETDATE()) -
        CASE
```

```
            WHEN (MONTH(@BirthDate) > MONTH(GETDATE())) OR
                 (MONTH(@BirthDate) = MONTH(GETDATE()) AND
DAY(@BirthDate) > DAY(GETDATE()))
                 THEN 1
                 ELSE 0
            END
END
```

To use this function:

```
SELECT CustomerID, FirstName, LastName,
dbo.CalculateAge(BirthDate) AS Age
FROM Customers
```

Modifying and Dropping Scalar Functions

To modify a scalar function, use the ALTER FUNCTION statement:

```
ALTER FUNCTION CalculateAge
(
    @BirthDate DATE
)
RETURNS INT
AS
BEGIN
    RETURN DATEDIFF(YEAR, @BirthDate, GETDATE())
END
```

To remove a function, use the DROP FUNCTION statement:

```
DROP FUNCTION CalculateAge
```

8.7 Table-Valued Functions

Table-Valued Functions (TVFs) return a table result set. There are two types of TVFs: Inline and Multi-Statement.

Inline Table-Valued Functions

Inline TVFs consist of a single SELECT statement and are defined using the RE-TURNS TABLE clause:

```
CREATE FUNCTION GetCustomersByState
(
    @State NVARCHAR(2)
)
RETURNS TABLE
AS
RETURN
(
    SELECT CustomerID, FirstName, LastName, Email
    FROM Customers
    WHERE State = @State
)
```

To use this function:

```
SELECT * FROM dbo.GetCustomersByState('CA')
```

Multi-Statement Table-Valued Functions

Multi-Statement TVFs can contain multiple statements and use a table variable to build the result set:

```
CREATE FUNCTION GetTopCustomersByState
(
    @State NVARCHAR(2),
```

```
    @TopN INT
)
RETURNS @Results TABLE
(
    CustomerID INT,
    FirstName NVARCHAR(50),
    LastName NVARCHAR(50),
    TotalPurchases DECIMAL(18,2)
)
AS
BEGIN
    INSERT INTO @Results
    SELECT TOP (@TopN) c.CustomerID, c.FirstName, c.LastName,
SUM(o.TotalAmount) AS TotalPurchases
    FROM Customers c
    JOIN Orders o ON c.CustomerID = o.CustomerID
    WHERE c.State = @State
    GROUP BY c.CustomerID, c.FirstName, c.LastName
    ORDER BY TotalPurchases DESC

    RETURN
END
```

To use this function:

```
SELECT * FROM dbo.GetTopCustomersByState('NY', 5)
```

8.8 Best Practices for Stored Procedures and User-Defined Functions

1. **Use Meaningful Names**: Choose clear, descriptive names for your procedures and functions.

2. **Comment Your Code**: Include comments to explain complex logic or the purpose of the routine.

3. **Handle Errors**: Implement proper error handling to make troubleshooting easier.

4. **Optimize Performance**: Use appropriate indexing and avoid unnecessary computations.

5. **Parameterize Queries**: Use parameters instead of concatenating strings to prevent SQL injection.

6. **Avoid Overuse of Dynamic SQL**: While powerful, dynamic SQL can be difficult to maintain and may introduce security risks.

7. **Test Thoroughly**: Create unit tests for your procedures and functions to ensure they work as expected.

8. **Use Schema Names**: Always prefix your objects with the schema name (e.g., `dbo.MyProcedure`) to avoid ambiguity.

9. **Limit the Scope**: Keep your procedures and functions focused on a single task or related set of tasks.

10. **Consider Set-Based Operations**: Favor set-based operations over cursors or loops for better performance.

8.9 Advanced Topics in Stored Procedures and Functions

Nesting Stored Procedures

Stored procedures can call other stored procedures, allowing for modular design:

```
CREATE PROCEDURE ProcessOrder
    @OrderID INT
AS
```

```
BEGIN
    EXEC ValidateOrder @OrderID
    EXEC UpdateInventory @OrderID
    EXEC GenerateInvoice @OrderID
END
```

Using Transactions in Stored Procedures

Transactions ensure that a series of operations are completed as a single unit of work:

```
CREATE PROCEDURE TransferFunds
    @FromAccount INT,
    @ToAccount INT,
    @Amount DECIMAL(18,2)
AS
BEGIN
    BEGIN TRY
        BEGIN TRANSACTION

        UPDATE Accounts SET Balance = Balance - @Amount WHERE
AccountID = @FromAccount
        UPDATE Accounts SET Balance = Balance + @Amount WHERE
AccountID = @ToAccount

        COMMIT TRANSACTION
        PRINT 'Funds transferred successfully.'
    END TRY
    BEGIN CATCH
        ROLLBACK TRANSACTION
        PRINT 'An error occurred: ' + ERROR_MESSAGE()
    END CATCH
END
```

Using CTEs in Functions

Common Table Expressions (CTEs) can be used in functions to create more readable and maintainable code:

```sql
CREATE FUNCTION GetCustomerHierarchy
(
    @CustomerID INT
)
RETURNS TABLE
AS
RETURN
(
    WITH CustomerCTE AS (
        SELECT CustomerID, ParentCustomerID, FirstName, LastName,
0 AS Level
        FROM Customers
        WHERE CustomerID = @CustomerID

        UNION ALL

        SELECT c.CustomerID, c.ParentCustomerID, c.FirstName,
c.LastName, cte.Level + 1
        FROM Customers c
        INNER JOIN CustomerCTE cte ON c.ParentCustomerID =
cte.CustomerID
    )
    SELECT CustomerID, ParentCustomerID, FirstName, LastName,
Level
    FROM CustomerCTE
)
```

Using Table-Valued Parameters

Table-Valued Parameters allow you to pass entire tables as parameters to stored procedures:

```sql
-- First, create a user-defined table type
```

```sql
CREATE TYPE OrderLineItemType AS TABLE
(
    ProductID INT,
    Quantity INT,
    UnitPrice DECIMAL(18,2)
)
GO

-- Now create a stored procedure that uses this type
CREATE PROCEDURE CreateOrder
    @CustomerID INT,
    @OrderDate DATE,
    @LineItems OrderLineItemType READONLY
AS
BEGIN
    DECLARE @OrderID INT

    -- Insert the order header
    INSERT INTO Orders (CustomerID, OrderDate)
    VALUES (@CustomerID, @OrderDate)

    SET @OrderID = SCOPE_IDENTITY()

    -- Insert the order details
    INSERT INTO OrderDetails (OrderID, ProductID, Quantity,
UnitPrice)
    SELECT @OrderID, ProductID, Quantity, UnitPrice
    FROM @LineItems
END
```

To use this procedure:

```sql
DECLARE @Items OrderLineItemType

INSERT INTO @Items (ProductID, Quantity, UnitPrice)
VALUES (1, 2, 10.99), (2, 1, 15.99), (3, 3, 5.99)

EXEC CreateOrder @CustomerID = 1, @OrderDate = '2023-05-01',
@LineItems = @Items
```

8.10 Performance Considerations

Execution Plan Caching

SQL Server caches execution plans for stored procedures, which can significantly improve performance for frequently executed procedures. However, this can sometimes lead to suboptimal plans if the data distribution changes significantly. In such cases, you may need to use the WITH RECOMPILE option or update statistics.

Avoiding Parameter Sniffing Issues

Parameter sniffing occurs when SQL Server creates an execution plan based on the first set of parameter values it encounters. This can lead to poor performance for subsequent executions with different parameter values. To mitigate this, you can use local variables:

```
CREATE PROCEDURE GetOrdersByDate
    @OrderDate DATE
AS
BEGIN
    DECLARE @LocalOrderDate DATE = @OrderDate

    SELECT OrderID, CustomerID, TotalAmount
    FROM Orders
    WHERE OrderDate = @LocalOrderDate
END
```

Optimizing Table-Valued Functions

Inline Table-Valued Functions generally perform better than Multi-Statement Table-Valued Functions because they can be optimized as part of the calling query. When possible, prefer inline TVFs:

```sql
-- Inline TVF (generally better performance)
CREATE FUNCTION GetActiveCustomers()
RETURNS TABLE
AS
RETURN
(
    SELECT CustomerID, FirstName, LastName, Email
    FROM Customers
    WHERE Status = 'Active'
)


-- Multi-Statement TVF
CREATE FUNCTION GetActiveCustomersMS()
RETURNS @Results TABLE
(
    CustomerID INT,
    FirstName NVARCHAR(50),
    LastName NVARCHAR(50),
    Email NVARCHAR(100)
)
AS
BEGIN
    INSERT INTO @Results
    SELECT CustomerID, FirstName, LastName, Email
    FROM Customers
    WHERE Status = 'Active'
    RETURN
END
```

8.11 Security Considerations

Ownership Chaining

Ownership chaining allows stored procedures to access objects that the user doesn't have direct permissions on, as long as the procedure and the objects have the same owner. This can simplify permission management but should be used carefully:

```
-- Create a table
CREATE TABLE SensitiveData (ID INT, Data NVARCHAR(100))

-- Create a procedure to access the table
CREATE PROCEDURE GetSensitiveData
AS
BEGIN
    SELECT * FROM SensitiveData
END

-- Grant execute permission to a user
GRANT EXECUTE ON GetSensitiveData TO SomeUser

-- SomeUser can now execute the procedure and see the data,
-- even without direct SELECT permission on SensitiveData table
```

Using EXECUTE AS

The EXECUTE AS clause allows you to specify the security context under which a stored procedure or function runs:

```
CREATE PROCEDURE UpdateCustomerStatus
WITH EXECUTE AS OWNER
AS
BEGIN
```

```
    UPDATE Customers SET Status = 'Inactive' WHERE LastOrderDate
< DATEADD(YEAR, -1, GETDATE())
END
```

This procedure will run with the permissions of the object owner, regardless of who executes it.

8.12 Debugging Stored Procedures and Functions

SQL Server Management Studio (SSMS) provides tools for debugging stored procedures and functions:

1. Set breakpoints in your code.
2. Use the "Debug" option when executing the procedure.
3. Step through the code line by line.
4. Inspect variable values and execution flow.

You can also use PRINT statements for basic debugging:

```
CREATE PROCEDURE DebugExample
    @Param1 INT,
    @Param2 INT
AS
BEGIN
    PRINT 'Param1: ' + CAST(@Param1 AS NVARCHAR(10))
    PRINT 'Param2: ' + CAST(@Param2 AS NVARCHAR(10))

    DECLARE @Result INT
    SET @Result = @Param1 + @Param2

    PRINT 'Result: ' + CAST(@Result AS NVARCHAR(10))

    -- Rest of the procedure...
```

8.13 Versioning and Source Control

Maintaining versions of your stored procedures and functions is crucial for tracking changes and rolling back if necessary. Some best practices include:

1. Use a source control system (e.g., Git) to store your SQL scripts.
2. Include version numbers or dates in your object names or comments.
3. Keep a change log for each object.
4. Use schema comparison tools to track differences between environments.

Example of versioning in comments:

```
/*
Procedure: GetCustomerOrders
Version: 1.2
Last Modified: 2023-05-01
Changes: Added OrderStatus column to result set
*/
CREATE PROCEDURE GetCustomerOrders
    @CustomerID INT
AS
BEGIN
    SELECT OrderID, OrderDate, TotalAmount, OrderStatus
    FROM Orders
    WHERE CustomerID = @CustomerID
END
```

Conclusion

Stored procedures and user-defined functions are powerful tools in SQL Server that can significantly enhance the performance, security, and maintainability of your database applications. By mastering these concepts and following best practices, you can create efficient, scalable, and robust database solutions. Remember to always consider performance implications, security aspects, and maintainability when designing and implementing stored procedures and functions in your SQL Server environment.

Chapter 9: Error Handling and Transactions

In this chapter, we'll dive deep into error handling and transaction management in SQL Server using T-SQL. These concepts are crucial for developing robust and reliable database applications. We'll explore the TRY...CATCH construct for error handling, as well as the intricacies of managing transactions, including nested transactions.

TRY...CATCH for Error Handling

Error handling is an essential aspect of database programming. It allows you to gracefully manage unexpected situations and provide meaningful feedback to users or calling applications. SQL Server introduced the TRY...CATCH construct in SQL Server 2005, providing a structured way to handle errors in T-SQL code.

Basic Syntax

The basic syntax of the TRY...CATCH construct is as follows:

```
BEGIN TRY
    -- Code that may cause an error
END TRY
BEGIN CATCH
    -- Error handling code
END CATCH
```

When an error occurs within the TRY block, execution immediately transfers to the CATCH block, where you can handle the error appropriately.

Error Functions

SQL Server provides several built-in functions that you can use within the CATCH block to retrieve information about the error:

1. ERROR_NUMBER(): Returns the number of the error.
2. ERROR_SEVERITY(): Returns the severity level of the error.
3. ERROR_STATE(): Returns the state number of the error.
4. ERROR_PROCEDURE(): Returns the name of the stored procedure or trigger where the error occurred.
5. ERROR_LINE(): Returns the line number at which the error occurred.
6. ERROR_MESSAGE(): Returns the complete text of the error message.

Here's an example of how to use these functions:

```
BEGIN TRY
    -- Some code that may cause an error
    SELECT 1/0; -- Division by zero error
END TRY
BEGIN CATCH
    SELECT
        ERROR_NUMBER() AS ErrorNumber,
        ERROR_SEVERITY() AS ErrorSeverity,
        ERROR_STATE() AS ErrorState,
        ERROR_PROCEDURE() AS ErrorProcedure,
        ERROR_LINE() AS ErrorLine,
        ERROR_MESSAGE() AS ErrorMessage;
END CATCH
```

Nesting TRY...CATCH Blocks

You can nest TRY...CATCH blocks to handle errors at different levels of your code. This allows for more granular error handling:

```
BEGIN TRY
    -- Outer TRY block
    BEGIN TRY
        -- Inner TRY block
        -- Some code that may cause an error
    END TRY
    BEGIN CATCH
        -- Handle specific errors in the inner block
        IF ERROR_NUMBER() = 1234
            -- Handle specific error
        ELSE
            -- Re-throw the error to the outer CATCH block
            THROW;
    END CATCH

    -- More code in the outer TRY block
END TRY
BEGIN CATCH
    -- Handle any errors not caught by the inner CATCH block
END CATCH
```

THROW Statement

The THROW statement, introduced in SQL Server 2012, allows you to raise an error or re-throw an existing error. It's often used in conjunction with TRY...CATCH blocks:

```
BEGIN TRY
    -- Some code that may cause an error
    IF (SomeCondition)
        THROW 50000, 'Custom error message', 1;
END TRY
```

```
BEGIN CATCH
    -- Handle the error or re-throw it
    THROW;
END CATCH
```

The THROW statement takes three parameters:

1. Error number (must be greater than or equal to 50000 for user-defined errors)
2. Error message
3. State (an integer from 0 to 255)

Best Practices for Error Handling

1. Always use TRY...CATCH blocks in stored procedures and important scripts.
2. Log errors for later analysis and troubleshooting.
3. Provide meaningful error messages to users or calling applications.
4. Use nested TRY...CATCH blocks for more granular error handling.
5. Consider using custom error numbers and messages for application-specific errors.

BEGIN TRANSACTION and COMMIT/ ROLLBACK

Transactions are a fundamental concept in database systems, ensuring data integrity and consistency. A transaction is a sequence of operations that are treated as a single unit of work. SQL Server provides commands to control transactions explicitly.

Basic Transaction Commands

1. BEGIN TRANSACTION: Marks the beginning of a transaction.
2. COMMIT: Saves all changes made in the transaction.
3. ROLLBACK: Undoes all changes made in the transaction.

Here's a basic example:

```
BEGIN TRANSACTION;

UPDATE Accounts SET Balance = Balance - 100 WHERE AccountID = 1;
UPDATE Accounts SET Balance = Balance + 100 WHERE AccountID = 2;

IF @@ERROR = 0
    COMMIT;
ELSE
    ROLLBACK;
```

Transaction Isolation Levels

SQL Server supports different transaction isolation levels, which determine how transactions interact with each other:

1. READ UNCOMMITTED: Allows dirty reads, non-repeatable reads, and phantom reads.
2. READ COMMITTED (default): Prevents dirty reads, but allows non-repeatable reads and phantom reads.

3. REPEATABLE READ: Prevents dirty reads and non-repeatable reads, but allows phantom reads.

4. SERIALIZABLE: Prevents dirty reads, non-repeatable reads, and phantom reads.

5. SNAPSHOT: Provides statement-level read consistency without using locks.

You can set the isolation level using the SET TRANSACTION ISOLATION LEVEL command:

```
SET TRANSACTION ISOLATION LEVEL READ COMMITTED;
```

Named Transactions

You can give a name to a transaction, which can be useful for managing nested transactions:

```
BEGIN TRANSACTION TransferFunds;
-- Transaction code
COMMIT TRANSACTION TransferFunds;
```

Savepoints

Savepoints allow you to create a point within a transaction to which you can later roll back:

```
BEGIN TRANSACTION;

INSERT INTO Orders (OrderID, CustomerID, OrderDate)
VALUES (1001, 'ALFKI', GETDATE());

SAVE TRANSACTION InsertOrder;
```

```
INSERT INTO OrderDetails (OrderID, ProductID, Quantity)
VALUES (1001, 1, 5);

IF @@ERROR <> 0
    ROLLBACK TRANSACTION InsertOrder;
ELSE
    COMMIT;
```

Managing Nested Transactions

Nested transactions occur when a transaction is started within another transaction. SQL Server supports nested transactions, but it's important to understand how they work to avoid unexpected behavior.

How Nested Transactions Work

1. SQL Server maintains a transaction count.
2. Each BEGIN TRANSACTION increments the count.
3. Each COMMIT decrements the count.
4. The outermost COMMIT (when the count reaches 0) actually commits the transaction.
5. Any ROLLBACK rolls back the entire transaction, regardless of nesting level.

Here's an example:

```
BEGIN TRANSACTION; -- Transaction count: 1
    -- Some operations
    BEGIN TRANSACTION; -- Transaction count: 2
        -- More operations
```

```
    IF @@ERROR <> 0
        ROLLBACK; -- Rolls back entire transaction
    ELSE
        COMMIT; -- Transaction count: 1
-- More operations
COMMIT; -- Actually commits the transaction
```

@@TRANCOUNT System Function

The @@TRANCOUNT function returns the current transaction count. It's useful for managing nested transactions:

```
BEGIN TRANSACTION;
PRINT @@TRANCOUNT; -- Output: 1

    BEGIN TRANSACTION;
    PRINT @@TRANCOUNT; -- Output: 2

        BEGIN TRANSACTION;
        PRINT @@TRANCOUNT; -- Output: 3

        COMMIT;
    COMMIT;
COMMIT;

PRINT @@TRANCOUNT; -- Output: 0
```

Best Practices for Nested Transactions

1. Be cautious when using nested transactions, as they can lead to complex and hard-to-maintain code.
2. Always ensure that the number of COMMIT statements matches the number of BEGIN TRANSACTION statements.

3. Use savepoints instead of nested transactions when possible.

4. Be aware that a ROLLBACK at any level will roll back the entire transaction.

Example: Handling Nested Transactions

Here's a more complex example demonstrating how to handle nested transactions:

```
CREATE PROCEDURE dbo.ProcessOrder
    @OrderID INT,
    @CustomerID NCHAR(5),
    @ProductID INT,
    @Quantity INT
AS
BEGIN
    SET NOCOUNT ON;

    DECLARE @TransactionCount INT = @@TRANCOUNT;

    BEGIN TRY
        IF @TransactionCount = 0
            BEGIN TRANSACTION;
        ELSE
            SAVE TRANSACTION ProcessOrder;

        -- Insert order
        INSERT INTO Orders (OrderID, CustomerID, OrderDate)
        VALUES (@OrderID, @CustomerID, GETDATE());

        -- Insert order details
        INSERT INTO OrderDetails (OrderID, ProductID, Quantity)
        VALUES (@OrderID, @ProductID, @Quantity);

        -- Update inventory
        UPDATE Products
        SET UnitsInStock = UnitsInStock - @Quantity
```

```
        WHERE ProductID = @ProductID;

        IF @TransactionCount = 0
            COMMIT;
    END TRY
    BEGIN CATCH
        IF @TransactionCount = 0
            ROLLBACK;
        ELSE IF XACT_STATE() <> -1
            ROLLBACK TRANSACTION ProcessOrder;

        THROW;
    END CATCH
END
```

This procedure can be called as part of a larger transaction or on its own. It uses savepoints and checks the initial transaction count to determine how to handle commits and rollbacks.

Combining Error Handling and Transactions

Error handling and transaction management often go hand in hand. Here's an example that demonstrates how to combine TRY...CATCH blocks with transaction management:

```
CREATE PROCEDURE dbo.TransferFunds
    @FromAccount INT,
    @ToAccount INT,
    @Amount DECIMAL(18,2)
AS
BEGIN
    SET NOCOUNT ON;

    DECLARE @TransactionCount INT = @@TRANCOUNT;
```

```sql
BEGIN TRY
    IF @TransactionCount = 0
        BEGIN TRANSACTION;
    ELSE
        SAVE TRANSACTION TransferFunds;

    -- Withdraw from the source account
    UPDATE Accounts
    SET Balance = Balance - @Amount
    WHERE AccountID = @FromAccount;

    IF @@ROWCOUNT = 0
        THROW 50001, 'Source account not found.', 1;

    -- Check for sufficient funds
    IF (SELECT Balance FROM Accounts WHERE AccountID =
@FromAccount) < 0
        THROW 50002, 'Insufficient funds.', 1;

    -- Deposit to the destination account
    UPDATE Accounts
    SET Balance = Balance + @Amount
    WHERE AccountID = @ToAccount;

    IF @@ROWCOUNT = 0
        THROW 50003, 'Destination account not found.', 1;

    IF @TransactionCount = 0
        COMMIT;

    SELECT 'Transfer successful' AS Result;
END TRY
BEGIN CATCH
    IF @TransactionCount = 0
        ROLLBACK;
    ELSE IF XACT_STATE() <> -1
        ROLLBACK TRANSACTION TransferFunds;

    DECLARE @ErrorMessage NVARCHAR(4000) = ERROR_MESSAGE();
    DECLARE @ErrorSeverity INT = ERROR_SEVERITY();
    DECLARE @ErrorState INT = ERROR_STATE();
```

```
      RAISERROR(@ErrorMessage, @ErrorSeverity, @ErrorState);
   END CATCH
END
```

This procedure demonstrates several important concepts:

1. It checks the initial transaction count to determine whether it's running within an existing transaction.
2. It uses savepoints to allow partial rollback if called as part of a larger transaction.
3. It uses custom THROW statements to raise specific errors.
4. The CATCH block handles rollbacks differently based on whether the procedure started its own transaction.
5. It re-raises the caught error using RAISERROR to propagate it to the caller.

Advanced Transaction Concepts

Distributed Transactions

Distributed transactions involve multiple resource managers, such as two different database servers or a database server and a message queue. SQL Server can participate in distributed transactions using the Microsoft Distributed Transaction Coordinator (MSDTC).

To start a distributed transaction, you can use the BEGIN DISTRIBUTED TRANSACTION statement:

```
BEGIN DISTRIBUTED TRANSACTION;
```

```
-- Operations on local SQL Server
INSERT INTO LocalTable (Column1, Column2) VALUES (1, 'Local');

-- Operations on linked server
INSERT INTO LinkedServer.Database.dbo.RemoteTable (Column1,
Column2)
VALUES (1, 'Remote');

COMMIT;
```

Transaction Marks

Transaction marks allow you to set named points within a transaction to which you can later roll back. They're similar to savepoints but work across multiple nesting levels:

```
BEGIN TRANSACTION;

INSERT INTO Orders (OrderID, CustomerID, OrderDate)
VALUES (1001, 'ALFKI', GETDATE());

SAVE TRANSACTION InsertOrder;

BEGIN TRANSACTION;

INSERT INTO OrderDetails (OrderID, ProductID, Quantity)
VALUES (1001, 1, 5);

SAVE TRANSACTION InsertOrderDetails;

-- If something goes wrong
ROLLBACK TRANSACTION InsertOrder;

COMMIT;
```

XACT_ABORT

The XACT_ABORT setting determines how SQL Server handles run-time errors. When SET XACT_ABORT is ON, any error that occurs during a transaction automatically rolls back the entire transaction and aborts the batch:

```sql
SET XACT_ABORT ON;

BEGIN TRY
    BEGIN TRANSACTION;

    -- Some operations that might cause an error

    COMMIT;
END TRY
BEGIN CATCH
    IF @@TRANCOUNT > 0
        ROLLBACK;

    THROW;
END CATCH
```

This can simplify error handling in some scenarios, as you don't need to check for errors after each statement.

Handling Deadlocks

Deadlocks occur when two or more transactions are waiting for each other to release locks. SQL Server automatically detects deadlocks and chooses one transaction as the deadlock victim, rolling it back to break the deadlock.

You can handle deadlocks in your code by checking for the specific deadlock error number (1205):

```sql
BEGIN TRY
    BEGIN TRANSACTION;
```

```
    -- Some operations that might cause a deadlock

    COMMIT;
END TRY
BEGIN CATCH
    IF ERROR_NUMBER() = 1205
    BEGIN
        -- Deadlock occurred, wait and retry
        WAITFOR DELAY '00:00:05'; -- Wait 5 seconds
        -- Retry the transaction
    END
    ELSE
    BEGIN
        IF @@TRANCOUNT > 0
            ROLLBACK;
        THROW;
    END
END CATCH
```

Best Practices for Error Handling and Transactions

1. Always use TRY...CATCH blocks in conjunction with transactions to ensure proper error handling and transaction management.

2. Be consistent in your use of BEGIN TRANSACTION and COMMIT/ROLLBACK. Ensure that every BEGIN TRANSACTION has a corresponding COMMIT or ROLLBACK.

3. Use nested transactions judiciously. They can add complexity to your code and may not always behave as expected.

4. Take advantage of savepoints for more granular control over transaction rollbacks.

5. When working with distributed transactions, be aware of the additional overhead and potential for increased lock times.

6. Use appropriate isolation levels to balance data consistency with concurrency requirements.

7. Consider using SET XACT_ABORT ON for simpler error handling in scenarios where you want any error to roll back the entire transaction.

8. Implement retry logic for deadlocks and other transient errors.

9. Log transaction errors for later analysis and troubleshooting.

10. Use meaningful custom error messages and error numbers for application-specific errors.

11. Be mindful of long-running transactions, as they can impact system performance and cause blocking.

12. Use the @@TRANCOUNT function to manage transaction nesting levels effectively.

13. Consider using table variables or temporary tables for complex operations within a transaction to reduce lock duration on production tables.

14. Use SET NOCOUNT ON in stored procedures to reduce network traffic and improve performance.

15. Implement proper error handling at the application level as well, not just within the database code.

Conclusion

Error handling and transaction management are critical aspects of developing robust and reliable database applications. By mastering the TRY...CATCH construct, understanding how transactions work (including nested transactions), and following best practices, you can create T-SQL code that gracefully handles errors and maintains data integrity.

Remember that while SQL Server provides powerful tools for error handling and transaction management, it's up to you as a developer to use them effectively. Always consider the specific requirements of your application and the potential impact on performance when implementing these techniques.

As you continue to work with SQL Server, you'll encounter more complex scenarios that require advanced error handling and transaction management. Keep practicing and exploring these concepts to become a more proficient T-SQL developer.

Chapter 10: Triggers and Events

What are Triggers?

Triggers are special types of stored procedures that automatically execute in response to specific events occurring in the database. They are powerful tools for enforcing business rules, maintaining data integrity, and automating complex processes. Triggers are often described as event-driven programming constructs within the database environment.

Key Characteristics of Triggers:

1. **Automatic Execution**: Triggers fire automatically when a predefined event occurs, without requiring explicit invocation.
2. **Event-Driven**: They are associated with specific database events, such as INSERT, UPDATE, or DELETE operations on tables.
3. **Implicit Transaction**: Triggers execute within the same transaction as the triggering event, ensuring atomicity.
4. **Invisible to Applications**: Triggers are transparent to client applications, operating behind the scenes.

5. **Multiple Triggers**: Multiple triggers can be defined for the same event on a table.

Types of Triggers:

1. **DML Triggers**: Respond to Data Manipulation Language (DML) operations (INSERT, UPDATE, DELETE).

- AFTER triggers
- INSTEAD OF triggers

2. **DDL Triggers**: Respond to Data Definition Language (DDL) operations (CREATE, ALTER, DROP).
3. **Logon Triggers**: Execute in response to LOGON events when a user session is established.

Common Use Cases for Triggers:

1. Enforcing complex business rules and data integrity constraints
2. Auditing and logging changes to sensitive data
3. Maintaining derived or calculated data
4. Implementing cascading actions across related tables
5. Preventing certain operations based on specific conditions
6. Automating notifications or alerts

Considerations When Using Triggers:

1. **Performance Impact**: Triggers can affect the performance of DML operations, especially if they perform complex operations.
2. **Debugging Challenges**: As triggers execute automatically, debugging can be more difficult compared to standard stored procedures.
3. **Nested Triggers**: Be cautious with nested triggers to avoid infinite loops or excessive cascading effects.
4. **Visibility**: Triggers operate behind the scenes, which can make troubleshooting application issues more challenging.
5. **Maintenance**: As business rules change, triggers need to be updated, which can be overlooked during system modifications.

DML Triggers: AFTER and INSTEAD OF

DML (Data Manipulation Language) triggers are the most commonly used type of triggers in SQL Server. They respond to INSERT, UPDATE, and DELETE operations on tables. There are two main categories of DML triggers: AFTER triggers and INSTEAD OF triggers.

AFTER Triggers

AFTER triggers, as the name suggests, execute after the triggering action has completed. They are used to perform additional actions or checks after the data modification has taken place.

Key Characteristics of AFTER Triggers:

1. **Execution Timing**: They run after the triggering action and any constraint checks have completed successfully.

2. **Multiple Triggers**: Multiple AFTER triggers can be defined for the same action on a table.

3. **Execution Order**: When multiple AFTER triggers exist, you can specify their execution order using sp_settriggerorder.

4. **Rollback Capability**: AFTER triggers can roll back the entire transaction if necessary.

5. **Table Types**: AFTER triggers can be created on regular tables but not on views.

Example of an AFTER Trigger:

```
CREATE TRIGGER trg_UpdateEmployeeAudit
ON Employees
AFTER UPDATE
AS
BEGIN
    INSERT INTO EmployeeAuditLog (EmployeeID, FieldChanged,
OldValue, NewValue, ChangeDate)
    SELECT
        i.EmployeeID,
        'Salary',
        d.Salary,
        i.Salary,
        GETDATE()
    FROM inserted i
    INNER JOIN deleted d ON i.EmployeeID = d.EmployeeID
    WHERE i.Salary <> d.Salary
END
```

This trigger logs changes to an employee's salary after an UPDATE operation on the Employees table.

INSTEAD OF Triggers

INSTEAD OF triggers replace the triggering action with the trigger's own logic. They are particularly useful for implementing complex business rules or for making views updatable.

Key Characteristics of INSTEAD OF Triggers:

1. **Execution Timing**: They execute in place of the triggering action, preventing the original operation from occurring directly.

2. **Custom Logic**: They allow complete control over how the data modification is handled.

3. **View Updates**: INSTEAD OF triggers are commonly used to make views updatable, especially for views that join multiple tables.

4. **Single Trigger**: Only one INSTEAD OF trigger can be defined per action (INSERT, UPDATE, DELETE) on a table or view.

5. **No Constraint Checks**: Since they replace the original action, constraint checks must be explicitly implemented within the trigger if required.

Example of an INSTEAD OF Trigger:

```
CREATE TRIGGER trg_InsertOrderDetails
ON OrderDetails
INSTEAD OF INSERT
AS
BEGIN
    -- Check if the product is in stock
    IF EXISTS (
        SELECT 1
        FROM inserted i
        INNER JOIN Products p ON i.ProductID = p.ProductID
        WHERE p.UnitsInStock < i.Quantity
    )
    BEGIN
```

```
        RAISERROR('Insufficient stock for one or more products.',
16, 1)
        RETURN
    END

    -- If stock is sufficient, proceed with the insert
    INSERT INTO OrderDetails (OrderID, ProductID, UnitPrice,
Quantity, Discount)
    SELECT OrderID, ProductID, UnitPrice, Quantity, Discount
    FROM inserted

    -- Update the stock levels
    UPDATE p
    SET UnitsInStock = p.UnitsInStock - i.Quantity
    FROM Products p
    INNER JOIN inserted i ON p.ProductID = i.ProductID
END
```

This trigger checks if there's sufficient stock before allowing an insert into the OrderDetails table, and updates the stock levels if the insert is successful.

Comparing AFTER and INSTEAD OF Triggers

Aspect	AFTER Triggers	INSTEAD OF Triggers
Execution Timing	After the triggering action	In place of the triggering action
Data Modification	Occurs before trigger execution	Controlled entirely by the trigger
Use on Views	Not applicable	Commonly used to make views updatable
Multiple Triggers	Multiple can be defined	Only one per action

Constraint Checks	Automatic	Must be implemented manually if needed
Typical Use Cases	Auditing, maintaining derived data	Complex business rules, view updates

Audit Logging with Triggers

Audit logging is one of the most common and valuable use cases for triggers in SQL Server. It allows you to automatically track changes to your data, providing a historical record of modifications, which is crucial for security, compliance, and data analysis purposes.

Benefits of Using Triggers for Audit Logging:

1. **Automatic and Transparent**: Changes are logged without requiring modifications to application code.
2. **Comprehensive**: Can capture details about the change, including old and new values, user information, and timestamps.
3. **Consistent**: Ensures that all changes are logged, regardless of how they were made (e.g., through an application, ad-hoc queries, or stored procedures).
4. **Transactional**: The audit log entry is created within the same transaction as the data change, ensuring consistency.

Key Considerations for Audit Logging:

1. **Performance Impact**: Audit triggers add overhead to DML operations, so they should be designed efficiently.
2. **Storage Requirements**: Audit logs can grow quickly, so consider data retention policies and archiving strategies.
3. **Sensitive Information**: Be mindful of storing sensitive data in audit logs and implement appropriate security measures.
4. **Scalability**: Design your audit logging solution to handle high-volume environments if necessary.

Implementing Audit Logging with Triggers

Here's a comprehensive example of implementing audit logging using triggers:

1. First, create an audit log table:

```sql
CREATE TABLE AuditLog (
    AuditLogID INT IDENTITY(1,1) PRIMARY KEY,
    TableName NVARCHAR(100) NOT NULL,
    PrimaryKeyColumn NVARCHAR(100) NOT NULL,
    PrimaryKeyValue NVARCHAR(1000) NOT NULL,
    ColumnName NVARCHAR(100) NOT NULL,
    OldValue NVARCHAR(MAX),
    NewValue NVARCHAR(MAX),
    UpdateDate DATETIME2 NOT NULL,
    UpdateBy NVARCHAR(128) NOT NULL
)
```

2. Create a trigger for each table you want to audit. Here's an example for a Customers table:

```sql
CREATE TRIGGER trg_AuditCustomers
ON Customers
AFTER INSERT, UPDATE, DELETE
AS
BEGIN
    SET NOCOUNT ON;

    DECLARE @TableName NVARCHAR(100) = 'Customers'
    DECLARE @PrimaryKeyColumn NVARCHAR(100) = 'CustomerID'
    DECLARE @UpdateDate DATETIME2 = SYSDATETIME()
    DECLARE @UpdateBy NVARCHAR(128) = SYSTEM_USER

    -- Handle INSERT
    IF EXISTS (SELECT 1 FROM inserted) AND NOT EXISTS (SELECT 1
FROM deleted)
    BEGIN
        INSERT INTO AuditLog (TableName, PrimaryKeyColumn,
PrimaryKeyValue, ColumnName, NewValue, UpdateDate, UpdateBy)
        SELECT
            @TableName,
            @PrimaryKeyColumn,
            i.CustomerID,
            c.name,
            CAST(i.[$(c.name)] AS NVARCHAR(MAX)),
            @UpdateDate,
            @UpdateBy
        FROM inserted i
        CROSS APPLY (
            SELECT name
            FROM sys.columns
            WHERE object_id = OBJECT_ID(@TableName)
              AND is_computed = 0
        ) c
    END

    -- Handle DELETE
    IF EXISTS (SELECT 1 FROM deleted) AND NOT EXISTS (SELECT 1
FROM inserted)
    BEGIN
        INSERT INTO AuditLog (TableName, PrimaryKeyColumn,
PrimaryKeyValue, ColumnName, OldValue, UpdateDate, UpdateBy)
        SELECT
```

```sql
                @TableName,
                @PrimaryKeyColumn,
                d.CustomerID,
                c.name,
                CAST(d.[$(c.name)] AS NVARCHAR(MAX)),
                @UpdateDate,
                @UpdateBy
        FROM deleted d
        CROSS APPLY (
            SELECT name
            FROM sys.columns
            WHERE object_id = OBJECT_ID(@TableName)
              AND is_computed = 0
        ) c
    END

    -- Handle UPDATE
    IF EXISTS (SELECT 1 FROM inserted) AND EXISTS (SELECT 1 FROM
deleted)
    BEGIN
        INSERT INTO AuditLog (TableName, PrimaryKeyColumn,
PrimaryKeyValue, ColumnName, OldValue, NewValue, UpdateDate,
UpdateBy)
        SELECT
            @TableName,
            @PrimaryKeyColumn,
            i.CustomerID,
            c.name,
            CAST(d.[$(c.name)] AS NVARCHAR(MAX)),
            CAST(i.[$(c.name)] AS NVARCHAR(MAX)),
            @UpdateDate,
            @UpdateBy
        FROM inserted i
        INNER JOIN deleted d ON i.CustomerID = d.CustomerID
        CROSS APPLY (
            SELECT name
            FROM sys.columns
            WHERE object_id = OBJECT_ID(@TableName)
              AND is_computed = 0
        ) c
        WHERE i.[$(c.name)] <> d.[$(c.name)]
```

```
         OR (i.[$(c.name)] IS NULL AND d.[$(c.name)] IS NOT
NULL)
         OR (i.[$(c.name)] IS NOT NULL AND d.[$(c.name)] IS
NULL)
    END
END
```

This trigger handles INSERT, UPDATE, and DELETE operations on the Customers table:

- For INSERTs, it logs all new values.
- For DELETEs, it logs all old values.
- For UPDATEs, it logs both old and new values, but only for columns that have changed.

The trigger uses dynamic SQL to iterate through all columns of the table, making it adaptable to schema changes without requiring modifications to the trigger itself.

Optimizing Audit Logging Performance

To minimize the performance impact of audit logging triggers, consider the following optimizations:

1. **Selective Logging**: Log only essential columns or changes, rather than every column for every change.
2. **Batch Inserts**: Instead of individual inserts into the audit log, consider using table variables or temporary tables to batch the inserts.
3. **Asynchronous Logging**: For very high-volume systems, consider using Service Broker or another asynchronous mechanism to offload the logging process.
4. **Partitioning**: Implement partitioning on the audit log table to improve query performance and facilitate easier archiving of old data.

5. **Indexed Views**: If you frequently query the audit log for specific types of changes, consider creating indexed views to optimize these queries.

Example of Optimized Audit Logging

Here's an example of how you might optimize the previous audit logging trigger:

```
CREATE TRIGGER trg_AuditCustomers_Optimized
ON Customers
AFTER INSERT, UPDATE, DELETE
AS
BEGIN
    SET NOCOUNT ON;

    DECLARE @TableName NVARCHAR(100) = 'Customers'
    DECLARE @PrimaryKeyColumn NVARCHAR(100) = 'CustomerID'
    DECLARE @UpdateDate DATETIME2 = SYSDATETIME()
    DECLARE @UpdateBy NVARCHAR(128) = SYSTEM_USER

    -- Table variable to batch inserts
    DECLARE @AuditEntries TABLE (
        TableName NVARCHAR(100),
        PrimaryKeyColumn NVARCHAR(100),
        PrimaryKeyValue NVARCHAR(1000),
        ColumnName NVARCHAR(100),
        OldValue NVARCHAR(MAX),
        NewValue NVARCHAR(MAX)
    )

    -- Handle INSERT
    IF EXISTS (SELECT 1 FROM inserted) AND NOT EXISTS (SELECT 1 FROM deleted)
    BEGIN
        INSERT INTO @AuditEntries (TableName, PrimaryKeyColumn, PrimaryKeyValue, ColumnName, NewValue)
        SELECT
            @TableName,
            @PrimaryKeyColumn,
```

```sql
            i.CustomerID,
            c.name,
            CAST(i.[$(c.name)] AS NVARCHAR(MAX))
        FROM inserted i
        CROSS APPLY (
            SELECT name
            FROM sys.columns
            WHERE object_id = OBJECT_ID(@TableName)
              AND is_computed = 0
              AND name IN ('CustomerName', 'Email',
'PhoneNumber') -- Only log specific columns
        ) c
    END

    -- Handle DELETE
    IF EXISTS (SELECT 1 FROM deleted) AND NOT EXISTS (SELECT 1
FROM inserted)
    BEGIN
        INSERT INTO @AuditEntries (TableName, PrimaryKeyColumn,
PrimaryKeyValue, ColumnName, OldValue)
        SELECT
            @TableName,
            @PrimaryKeyColumn,
            d.CustomerID,
            c.name,
            CAST(d.[$(c.name)] AS NVARCHAR(MAX))
        FROM deleted d
        CROSS APPLY (
            SELECT name
            FROM sys.columns
            WHERE object_id = OBJECT_ID(@TableName)
              AND is_computed = 0
              AND name IN ('CustomerName', 'Email',
'PhoneNumber') -- Only log specific columns
        ) c
    END

    -- Handle UPDATE
    IF EXISTS (SELECT 1 FROM inserted) AND EXISTS (SELECT 1 FROM
deleted)
    BEGIN
```

```sql
        INSERT INTO @AuditEntries (TableName, PrimaryKeyColumn,
PrimaryKeyValue, ColumnName, OldValue, NewValue)
        SELECT
            @TableName,
            @PrimaryKeyColumn,
            i.CustomerID,
            c.name,
            CAST(d.[$(c.name)] AS NVARCHAR(MAX)),
            CAST(i.[$(c.name)] AS NVARCHAR(MAX))
        FROM inserted i
        INNER JOIN deleted d ON i.CustomerID = d.CustomerID
        CROSS APPLY (
            SELECT name
            FROM sys.columns
            WHERE object_id = OBJECT_ID(@TableName)
              AND is_computed = 0
              AND name IN ('CustomerName', 'Email',
'PhoneNumber') -- Only log specific columns
        ) c
        WHERE i.[$(c.name)] <> d.[$(c.name)]
            OR (i.[$(c.name)] IS NULL AND d.[$(c.name)] IS NOT
NULL)
            OR (i.[$(c.name)] IS NOT NULL AND d.[$(c.name)] IS
NULL)
    END

    -- Batch insert into AuditLog table
    INSERT INTO AuditLog (TableName, PrimaryKeyColumn,
PrimaryKeyValue, ColumnName, OldValue, NewValue, UpdateDate,
UpdateBy)
    SELECT TableName, PrimaryKeyColumn, PrimaryKeyValue,
ColumnName, OldValue, NewValue, @UpdateDate, @UpdateBy
    FROM @AuditEntries
END
```

This optimized version includes the following improvements:

1. It uses a table variable to batch the inserts into the AuditLog table.

2. It only logs specific columns (CustomerName, Email, PhoneNumber) instead of all columns.

3. It performs a single INSERT operation into the AuditLog table at the end, reducing the number of individual inserts.

Advanced Audit Logging Techniques

1. **Compressed Storage**: If your audit logs contain a lot of repetitive data, consider using compressed storage to reduce space requirements.
2. **JSON or XML Storage**: For flexibility in storing varied data structures, consider using JSON or XML to store audit data, especially for complex objects.
3. **Temporal Tables**: SQL Server 2016 and later versions support temporal tables, which can be an alternative or complement to trigger-based auditing for maintaining historical data.
4. **Change Data Capture (CDC)**: For very large tables or databases where trigger overhead is a concern, consider using SQL Server's Change Data Capture feature instead of or in addition to triggers.
5. **Auditing Sensitive Operations**: For highly sensitive operations, consider additional logging such as capturing the client application name, host name, or even the full T-SQL statement that caused the change.

Here's an example of how you might implement some of these advanced techniques:

```
-- Create a compressed audit log table with JSON storage
CREATE TABLE AuditLogAdvanced (
    AuditLogID INT IDENTITY(1,1) PRIMARY KEY,
    TableName NVARCHAR(100) NOT NULL,
    PrimaryKeyValue NVARCHAR(1000) NOT NULL,
    ChangeData NVARCHAR(MAX),
    UpdateDate DATETIME2 NOT NULL,
```

```sql
    UpdateBy NVARCHAR(128) NOT NULL,
    ClientInfo NVARCHAR(1000),
    INDEX IX_AuditLogAdvanced_TableName_UpdateDate CLUSTERED
COLUMNSTORE
)

-- Create an advanced audit trigger
CREATE TRIGGER trg_AuditCustomers_Advanced
ON Customers
AFTER INSERT, UPDATE, DELETE
AS
BEGIN
    SET NOCOUNT ON;

    DECLARE @TableName NVARCHAR(100) = 'Customers'
    DECLARE @UpdateDate DATETIME2 = SYSDATETIME()
    DECLARE @UpdateBy NVARCHAR(128) = SYSTEM_USER
    DECLARE @ClientInfo NVARCHAR(1000) = (
        SELECT CONCAT(
            'App: ', ISNULL(APP_NAME(), 'Unknown'),
            ', Host: ', ISNULL(HOST_NAME(), 'Unknown'),
            ', SPID: ', @@SPID
        )
    )

    -- Handle INSERT
    IF EXISTS (SELECT 1 FROM inserted) AND NOT EXISTS (SELECT 1
FROM deleted)
    BEGIN
        INSERT INTO AuditLogAdvanced (TableName, PrimaryKeyValue,
ChangeData, UpdateDate, UpdateBy, ClientInfo)
        SELECT
            @TableName,
            i.CustomerID,
            (SELECT i.* FOR JSON PATH, WITHOUT_ARRAY_WRAPPER),
            @UpdateDate,
            @UpdateBy,
            @ClientInfo
        FROM inserted i
    END

    -- Handle DELETE
```

```sql
    IF EXISTS (SELECT 1 FROM deleted) AND NOT EXISTS (SELECT 1
FROM inserted)
    BEGIN
        INSERT INTO AuditLogAdvanced (TableName, PrimaryKeyValue,
ChangeData, UpdateDate, UpdateBy, ClientInfo)
        SELECT
            @TableName,
            d.CustomerID,
            (SELECT d.* FOR JSON PATH, WITHOUT_ARRAY_WRAPPER),
            @UpdateDate,
            @UpdateBy,
            @ClientInfo
        FROM deleted d
    END

    -- Handle UPDATE
    IF EXISTS (SELECT 1 FROM inserted) AND EXISTS (SELECT 1 FROM
deleted)
    BEGIN
        INSERT INTO AuditLogAdvanced (TableName, PrimaryKeyValue,
ChangeData, UpdateDate, UpdateBy, ClientInfo)
        SELECT
            @TableName,
            i.CustomerID,
            (SELECT
                i.CustomerID,
                (SELECT d.* FOR JSON PATH, WITHOUT_ARRAY_WRAPPER)
AS OldValues,
                (SELECT i.* FOR JSON PATH, WITHOUT_ARRAY_WRAPPER)
AS NewValues
            FOR JSON PATH, WITHOUT_ARRAY_WRAPPER),
            @UpdateDate,
            @UpdateBy,
            @ClientInfo
        FROM inserted i
        INNER JOIN deleted d ON i.CustomerID = d.CustomerID
    END
END
```

This advanced audit trigger:

1. Uses a columnstore index for improved compression and query performance.
2. Stores the entire row data as JSON, allowing for flexible querying and reduced storage for unchanged columns.
3. Captures additional client information, including the application name and host name.

Best Practices for Audit Logging with Triggers

1. **Separate Audit Database**: Consider storing audit logs in a separate database to isolate the performance impact and enhance security.
2. **Error Handling**: Implement robust error handling in your audit triggers to ensure that primary operations are not affected by audit logging failures.
3. **Monitoring and Maintenance**: Regularly monitor the size and performance of your audit logs, and implement a retention and archiving strategy.
4. **Security**: Ensure that access to audit logs is strictly controlled and that the logs themselves are protected from unauthorized modification.
5. **Testing**: Thoroughly test your audit triggers under various scenarios and load conditions to ensure they perform as expected without significantly impacting system performance.
6. **Documentation**: Maintain clear documentation of your auditing strategy, including which tables and columns are audited and how the audit data should be interpreted.

7. **Consistency**: Strive for a consistent approach to auditing across your database to simplify maintenance and data analysis.

By implementing these best practices and leveraging the power of SQL Server triggers, you can create a robust, efficient, and comprehensive audit logging system that meets your organization's compliance and data tracking needs while minimizing the impact on your database's performance.

Chapter 11: Working with XML and JSON

Introduction

In today's data-driven world, the ability to work with various data formats is crucial for database professionals. Two of the most common data interchange formats are XML (eXtensible Markup Language) and JSON (JavaScript Object Notation). SQL Server provides robust support for both XML and JSON, allowing developers and database administrators to seamlessly integrate these formats into their T-SQL code.

This chapter will explore the intricacies of working with XML and JSON in T-SQL, covering topics such as generating and parsing XML, querying JSON data, and practical use cases for both formats. By mastering these concepts, you'll be able to handle complex data structures and improve interoperability between different systems and applications.

Generating and Parsing XML in T-SQL

XML has been a part of SQL Server since version 2005, and it offers a powerful way to represent hierarchical data structures. SQL Server provides various methods for working with XML, including generating XML from relational data, parsing XML into relational format, and querying XML data.

Generating XML

SQL Server offers several ways to generate XML from relational data:

1. FOR XML clause
2. XML data type methods
3. SQLXML (SQL Server XML)

Let's explore each of these methods in detail.

FOR XML Clause

The FOR XML clause is the most common method for generating XML in T-SQL. It can be added to the end of a SELECT statement to produce XML output. There are four modes available:

- RAW
- AUTO
- EXPLICIT
- PATH

RAW Mode

The RAW mode generates a simple XML structure where each row in the result set becomes an element with the generic name "row".

```
SELECT CustomerID, CompanyName, ContactName
FROM Customers
WHERE Country = 'Germany'
FOR XML RAW;
```

This query will produce output similar to:

```
<row CustomerID="ALFKI" CompanyName="Alfreds Futterkiste"
ContactName="Maria Anders" />
<row CustomerID="BLAUS" CompanyName="Blauer See Delikatessen"
ContactName="Hanna Moos" />
```

AUTO Mode

The AUTO mode creates a nested XML structure based on the structure of the SELECT statement.

```sql
SELECT Customers.CustomerID, Customers.CompanyName,
       Orders.OrderID, Orders.OrderDate
FROM Customers
INNER JOIN Orders ON Customers.CustomerID = Orders.CustomerID
WHERE Customers.Country = 'Germany'
FOR XML AUTO, ELEMENTS;
```

This query will produce output similar to:

```xml
<Customers>
  <CustomerID>ALFKI</CustomerID>
  <CompanyName>Alfreds Futterkiste</CompanyName>
  <Orders>
    <OrderID>10643</OrderID>
    <OrderDate>1997-08-25T00:00:00</OrderDate>
  </Orders>
</Customers>
```

EXPLICIT Mode

The EXPLICIT mode provides the most control over the XML output structure but requires a specific query format.

```sql
SELECT 1 AS Tag,
       NULL AS Parent,
       CustomerID AS [Customer!1!CustomerID],
       CompanyName AS [Customer!1!CompanyName],
       NULL AS [Order!2!OrderID],
       NULL AS [Order!2!OrderDate]
```

```
FROM Customers
WHERE Country = 'Germany'
UNION ALL
SELECT 2 AS Tag,
       1 AS Parent,
       Customers.CustomerID,
       NULL,
       Orders.OrderID,
       Orders.OrderDate
FROM Customers
INNER JOIN Orders ON Customers.CustomerID = Orders.CustomerID
WHERE Customers.Country = 'Germany'
ORDER BY [Customer!1!CustomerID], [Order!2!OrderID]
FOR XML EXPLICIT;
```

This query will produce output similar to:

```
<Customer CustomerID="ALFKI" CompanyName="Alfreds Futterkiste">
  <Order OrderID="10643" OrderDate="1997-08-25T00:00:00" />
  <Order OrderID="10692" OrderDate="1997-10-03T00:00:00" />
</Customer>
```

PATH Mode

The PATH mode allows you to specify the XML structure using XPath-like expressions.

```
SELECT CustomerID AS [@CustomerID],
       CompanyName AS [CompanyInfo/Name],
       ContactName AS [CompanyInfo/Contact]
FROM Customers
WHERE Country = 'Germany'
FOR XML PATH('Customer'), ROOT('Customers');
```

This query will produce output similar to:

```
<Customers>
  <Customer CustomerID="ALFKI">
    <CompanyInfo>
      <Name>Alfreds Futterkiste</Name>
```

```
        <Contact>Maria Anders</Contact>
    </CompanyInfo>
  </Customer>
</Customers>
```

XML Data Type Methods

SQL Server provides an XML data type that comes with various methods for manipulating XML data. You can use these methods to generate XML programmatically.

```
DECLARE @xmlDoc XML;

SET @xmlDoc = (
    SELECT CustomerID AS [@ID],
           CompanyName AS [Name],
           ContactName AS [Contact]
    FROM Customers
    WHERE Country = 'Germany'
    FOR XML PATH('Customer'), ROOT('Customers')
);

SELECT @xmlDoc.query('/Customers/Customer[@ID="ALFKI"]');
```

This example demonstrates how to create an XML variable and then query it using
the query() method.

SQLXML

SQLXML is a technology that allows you to query SQL Server using XML and retrieve results as XML. While it's less commonly used now, it's still supported in SQL
Server and can be useful in certain scenarios.

```
-- This example uses SQLXML through a stored procedure
EXEC sp_xml_preparedocument @hdoc OUTPUT, '<root>
  <Customer CustomerID="ALFKI">
    <CompanyName>Alfreds Futterkiste</CompanyName>
    <ContactName>Maria Anders</ContactName>
```

```sql
    </Customer>
</root>';

SELECT *
FROM OPENXML(@hdoc, '/root/Customer')
WITH (
    CustomerID varchar(5),
    CompanyName nvarchar(40),
    ContactName nvarchar(30)
);

EXEC sp_xml_removedocument @hdoc;
```

Parsing XML

Parsing XML involves extracting data from XML documents and converting it into a relational format. SQL Server provides several methods for parsing XML:

1. XQuery functions

2. OPENXML

3. XML data type methods

XQuery Functions

SQL Server supports a subset of the XQuery language for querying XML data. Some commonly used XQuery functions include:

- `value()`: Extracts a single value from an XML fragment

- `query()`: Returns an XML fragment

- `nodes()`: Shreds XML into relational format

```sql
DECLARE @xmlDoc XML = '<Customers>
  <Customer CustomerID="ALFKI">
```

```
    <CompanyName>Alfreds Futterkiste</CompanyName>
    <ContactName>Maria Anders</ContactName>
  </Customer>
  <Customer CustomerID="ANATR">
    <CompanyName>Ana Trujillo Emparedados y helados</CompanyName>
    <ContactName>Ana Trujillo</ContactName>
  </Customer>
</Customers>';

-- Using value()
SELECT @xmlDoc.value('(/Customers/Customer/@CustomerID)[1]',
'varchar(5)') AS FirstCustomerID;

-- Using query()
SELECT @xmlDoc.query('/Customers/Customer[@CustomerID="ALFKI"]');

-- Using nodes()
SELECT
    Customer.value('@CustomerID', 'varchar(5)') AS CustomerID,
    Customer.value('(CompanyName)[1]', 'nvarchar(40)') AS
CompanyName,
    Customer.value('(ContactName)[1]', 'nvarchar(30)') AS
ContactName
FROM @xmlDoc.nodes('/Customers/Customer') AS T(Customer);
```

OPENXML

OPENXML is another method for parsing XML data, which can be useful when working with large XML documents.

```
DECLARE @xmlDoc XML = '<Customers>
  <Customer CustomerID="ALFKI">
    <CompanyName>Alfreds Futterkiste</CompanyName>
    <ContactName>Maria Anders</ContactName>
  </Customer>
  <Customer CustomerID="ANATR">
    <CompanyName>Ana Trujillo Emparedados y helados</CompanyName>
    <ContactName>Ana Trujillo</ContactName>
  </Customer>
</Customers>';
```

```
DECLARE @hdoc int;

EXEC sp_xml_preparedocument @hdoc OUTPUT, @xmlDoc;

SELECT *
FROM OPENXML(@hdoc, '/Customers/Customer', 2)
WITH (
    CustomerID varchar(5) '@CustomerID',
    CompanyName nvarchar(40) 'CompanyName',
    ContactName nvarchar(30) 'ContactName'
);

EXEC sp_xml_removedocument @hdoc;
```

XML Data Type Methods

The XML data type provides methods for parsing XML data, such as exist(), value(), and nodes().

```
DECLARE @xmlDoc XML = '<Customers>
  <Customer CustomerID="ALFKI">
    <CompanyName>Alfreds Futterkiste</CompanyName>
    <ContactName>Maria Anders</ContactName>
  </Customer>
  <Customer CustomerID="ANATR">
    <CompanyName>Ana Trujillo Emparedados y helados</CompanyName>
    <ContactName>Ana Trujillo</ContactName>
  </Customer>
</Customers>';

-- Check if a customer exists
SELECT @xmlDoc.exist('/Customers/Customer[@CustomerID="ALFKI"]')
AS CustomerExists;

-- Extract a single value
SELECT @xmlDoc.value('(/Customers/Customer[@CustomerID="ALFKI"]/
CompanyName)[1]', 'nvarchar(40)') AS CompanyName;

-- Shred XML into relational format
```

```
SELECT
    Customer.value('@CustomerID', 'varchar(5)') AS CustomerID,
    Customer.value('(CompanyName)[1]', 'nvarchar(40)') AS
CompanyName,
    Customer.value('(ContactName)[1]', 'nvarchar(30)') AS
ContactName
FROM @xmlDoc.nodes('/Customers/Customer') AS T(Customer);
```

Querying JSON Data in SQL Server

JSON support was introduced in SQL Server 2016, providing a set of functions and operators for working with JSON data. Unlike XML, JSON is not a native data type in SQL Server but is stored as NVARCHAR.

JSON Functions in SQL Server

SQL Server provides several functions for working with JSON data:

1. ISJSON
2. JSON_VALUE
3. JSON_QUERY
4. JSON_MODIFY
5. OPENJSON

Let's explore each of these functions in detail.

ISJSON

The ISJSON function checks if a string contains valid JSON.

```
DECLARE @json NVARCHAR(MAX) = N'{"name": "John", "age": 30}';
```

```
SELECT ISJSON(@json) AS IsValidJSON;
```

JSON_VALUE

JSON_VALUE extracts a scalar value from a JSON string.

```
DECLARE @json NVARCHAR(MAX) = N'{"name": "John", "age": 30}';
SELECT JSON_VALUE(@json, '$.name') AS Name,
       JSON_VALUE(@json, '$.age') AS Age;
```

JSON_QUERY

JSON_QUERY extracts an object or array from a JSON string.

```
DECLARE @json NVARCHAR(MAX) = N'{"name": "John", "address":
{"street": "123 Main St", "city": "New York"}}';
SELECT JSON_QUERY(@json, '$.address') AS Address;
```

JSON_MODIFY

JSON_MODIFY updates a value in a JSON string.

```
DECLARE @json NVARCHAR(MAX) = N'{"name": "John", "age": 30}';
SET @json = JSON_MODIFY(@json, '$.age', 31);
SELECT @json AS UpdatedJSON;
```

OPENJSON

OPENJSON parses JSON text and returns objects and properties as rows and columns.

```
DECLARE @json NVARCHAR(MAX) = N'[
   {"id": 1, "name": "John", "skills": ["C#", "SQL"]},
   {"id": 2, "name": "Jane", "skills": ["Python", "JavaScript"]}
]';
```

```
SELECT *
FROM OPENJSON(@json)
WITH (
    id INT '$.id',
    name NVARCHAR(50) '$.name',
    skills NVARCHAR(MAX) '$.skills' AS JSON
);
```

Querying JSON Data

Let's look at some more advanced examples of querying JSON data in SQL Server.

Filtering JSON Data

```
DECLARE @jsonTable TABLE (id INT, jsonData NVARCHAR(MAX));
INSERT INTO @jsonTable VALUES
(1, N'{"name": "John", "age": 30, "city": "New York"}'),
(2, N'{"name": "Jane", "age": 25, "city": "Los Angeles"}'),
(3, N'{"name": "Bob", "age": 35, "city": "Chicago"}');

SELECT id, JSON_VALUE(jsonData, '$.name') AS Name
FROM @jsonTable
WHERE CAST(JSON_VALUE(jsonData, '$.age') AS INT) > 28;
```

Aggregating JSON Data

```
DECLARE @jsonTable TABLE (id INT, jsonData NVARCHAR(MAX));
INSERT INTO @jsonTable VALUES
(1, N'{"name": "John", "sales": [100, 200, 300]}'),
(2, N'{"name": "Jane", "sales": [150, 250, 350]}'),
(3, N'{"name": "Bob", "sales": [120, 220, 320]}');

SELECT
    JSON_VALUE(jsonData, '$.name') AS Name,
    SUM(value) AS TotalSales
```

```sql
FROM @jsonTable
CROSS APPLY OPENJSON(JSON_QUERY(jsonData, '$.sales'))
GROUP BY JSON_VALUE(jsonData, '$.name');
```

Working with Nested JSON

```sql
DECLARE @json NVARCHAR(MAX) = N'{
  "employees": [
    {
      "name": "John",
      "department": "IT",
      "projects": [
        {"name": "Project A", "status": "In Progress"},
        {"name": "Project B", "status": "Completed"}
      ]
    },
    {
      "name": "Jane",
      "department": "HR",
      "projects": [
        {"name": "Project C", "status": "In Progress"}
      ]
    }
  ]
}';

SELECT
    e.name AS EmployeeName,
    e.department AS Department,
    p.name AS ProjectName,
    p.status AS ProjectStatus
FROM OPENJSON(@json, '$.employees')
WITH (
    name NVARCHAR(50) '$.name',
    department NVARCHAR(50) '$.department',
    projects NVARCHAR(MAX) '$.projects' AS JSON
) AS e
CROSS APPLY OPENJSON(e.projects)
WITH (
    name NVARCHAR(50) '$.name',
```

```
    status NVARCHAR(50) '$.status'
) AS p;
```

Practical Use Cases of XML and JSON in T-SQL

Both XML and JSON have numerous practical applications in database development and management. Let's explore some common use cases for each format.

XML Use Cases

1. **Data Exchange**: XML is widely used for exchanging data between different systems, especially in enterprise environments.

```
-- Exporting data as XML
SELECT CustomerID, CompanyName, ContactName, Country
FROM Customers
WHERE Country IN ('USA', 'UK', 'France')
FOR XML PATH('Customer'), ROOT('Customers');
```

2. **Configuration Storage**: XML is often used to store configuration data due to its hierarchical nature.

```
-- Storing and retrieving configuration data
CREATE TABLE AppConfig (
    ConfigID INT PRIMARY KEY,
    ConfigXML XML
);

INSERT INTO AppConfig (ConfigID, ConfigXML)
VALUES (1, '<Config>
```

```
  <Database>
    <ConnectionString>Server=myserver;Database=mydb;User
Id=myuser;Password=mypassword;</ConnectionString>
    <Timeout>30</Timeout>
  </Database>
  <Logging>
    <Level>Info</Level>
    <FilePath>C:\Logs\app.log</FilePath>
  </Logging>
</Config>');

-- Retrieving specific configuration values
SELECT
    ConfigXML.value('(/Config/Database/ConnectionString)[1]',
'nvarchar(max)') AS ConnectionString,
    ConfigXML.value('(/Config/Database/Timeout)[1]', 'int') AS
Timeout,
    ConfigXML.value('(/Config/Logging/Level)[1]', 'nvarchar(10)')
AS LogLevel
FROM AppConfig
WHERE ConfigID = 1;
```

3. **Storing Semi-Structured Data**: XML is useful for storing data that doesn't fit well into a traditional relational model.

```
-- Storing and querying product attributes
CREATE TABLE Products (
    ProductID INT PRIMARY KEY,
    ProductName NVARCHAR(50),
    Attributes XML
);

INSERT INTO Products (ProductID, ProductName, Attributes)
VALUES (1, 'Laptop', '<Attributes>
  <Processor>Intel Core i7</Processor>
  <RAM>16GB</RAM>
  <Storage>512GB SSD</Storage>
  <Display>
    <Size>15.6</Size>
    <Resolution>1920x1080</Resolution>
```

```
    </Display>
</Attributes>');

-- Querying specific attributes
SELECT
    ProductID,
    ProductName,
    Attributes.value('(/Attributes/Processor)[1]',
'nvarchar(50)') AS Processor,
    Attributes.value('(/Attributes/RAM)[1]', 'nvarchar(10)') AS
RAM,
    Attributes.value('(/Attributes/Display/Size)[1]',
'decimal(3,1)') AS DisplaySize
FROM Products;
```

4. **Generating Reports**: XML can be used to generate structured reports that can be easily transformed into other formats like HTML or PDF.

```
-- Generating a sales report as XML
SELECT
    YEAR(OrderDate) AS [@Year],
    MONTH(OrderDate) AS [@Month],
    SUM(TotalAmount) AS [@TotalSales],
    (
        SELECT TOP 3
            p.ProductName AS [@Name],
            SUM(od.Quantity) AS [@QuantitySold]
        FROM OrderDetails od
        JOIN Products p ON od.ProductID = p.ProductID
        WHERE YEAR(o.OrderDate) = YEAR(OrderDate) AND
MONTH(o.OrderDate) = MONTH(OrderDate)
        GROUP BY p.ProductName
        ORDER BY SUM(od.Quantity) DESC
        FOR XML PATH('TopProduct'), TYPE
    )
FROM Orders o
GROUP BY YEAR(OrderDate), MONTH(OrderDate)
ORDER BY YEAR(OrderDate), MONTH(OrderDate)
FOR XML PATH('Month'), ROOT('SalesReport');
```

JSON Use Cases

1. **API Integration**: JSON is the de facto standard for web APIs, making it essential for integrating with external services.

```sql
-- Storing API responses
CREATE TABLE APIResponses (
    ResponseID INT PRIMARY KEY,
    Endpoint NVARCHAR(100),
    ResponseData NVARCHAR(MAX)
);

INSERT INTO APIResponses (ResponseID, Endpoint, ResponseData)
VALUES (1, '/api/users', N'[
   {"id": 1, "name": "John Doe", "email": "john@example.com"},
   {"id": 2, "name": "Jane Smith", "email": "jane@example.com"}
]');

-- Querying API response data
SELECT
    u.id,
    u.name,
    u.email
FROM APIResponses ar
CROSS APPLY OPENJSON(ar.ResponseData)
WITH (
    id INT '$.id',
    name NVARCHAR(100) '$.name',
    email NVARCHAR(100) '$.email'
) AS u
WHERE ar.Endpoint = '/api/users';
```

2. **Flexible Schema**: JSON allows for storing data with varying structures in the same column.

```sql
-- Storing product data with flexible attributes
CREATE TABLE Products (
```

```sql
    ProductID INT PRIMARY KEY,
    ProductName NVARCHAR(50),
    Attributes NVARCHAR(MAX)
);

INSERT INTO Products (ProductID, ProductName, Attributes)
VALUES
(1, 'Laptop', N'{"processor": "Intel Core i7", "ram": "16GB",
"storage": "512GB SSD"}'),
(2, 'Smartphone', N'{"screen": "6.1 inch", "camera": "12MP",
"battery": "3000mAh"}');

-- Querying flexible attributes
SELECT
    ProductID,
    ProductName,
    JSON_VALUE(Attributes, '$.processor') AS Processor,
    JSON_VALUE(Attributes, '$.ram') AS RAM,
    JSON_VALUE(Attributes, '$.storage') AS Storage,
    JSON_VALUE(Attributes, '$.screen') AS Screen,
    JSON_VALUE(Attributes, '$.camera') AS Camera,
    JSON_VALUE(Attributes, '$.battery') AS Battery
FROM Products;
```

3. **Aggregating Data**: JSON can be used to aggregate related data into a single field.

```sql
-- Aggregating order details into JSON
SELECT
    o.OrderID,
    o.OrderDate,
    o.CustomerID,
    (
        SELECT od.ProductID, od.Quantity, od.UnitPrice
        FROM OrderDetails od
        WHERE od.OrderID = o.OrderID
        FOR JSON PATH
    ) AS OrderDetails
FROM Orders o;
```

4. **Storing Document-Oriented Data**: JSON is ideal for storing document-oriented data that doesn't fit well into a relational model.

```sql
-- Storing and querying document-oriented data
CREATE TABLE Documents (
    DocumentID INT PRIMARY KEY,
    DocumentData NVARCHAR(MAX)
);

INSERT INTO Documents (DocumentID, DocumentData)
VALUES (1, N'{
  "title": "Project Proposal",
  "author": "John Doe",
  "date": "2023-04-15",
  "sections": [
    {"name": "Introduction", "content": "This project aims
to..."},
    {"name": "Objectives", "content": "The main objectives
are..."},
    {"name": "Budget", "content": "The estimated budget is...",
     "details": {"amount": 50000, "currency": "USD"}}
  ],
  "tags": ["proposal", "project", "budget"]
}');

-- Querying document data
SELECT
    DocumentID,
    JSON_VALUE(DocumentData, '$.title') AS Title,
    JSON_VALUE(DocumentData, '$.author') AS Author,
    JSON_VALUE(DocumentData, '$.date') AS Date,
    JSON_QUERY(DocumentData, '$.tags') AS Tags,
    s.name AS SectionName,
    s.content AS SectionContent,
    JSON_VALUE(s.details, '$.amount') AS BudgetAmount,
    JSON_VALUE(s.details, '$.currency') AS BudgetCurrency
FROM Documents
CROSS APPLY OPENJSON(DocumentData, '$.sections')
WITH (
    name NVARCHAR(100) '$.name',
```

```
    content NVARCHAR(MAX) '$.content',
    details NVARCHAR(MAX) '$.details' AS JSON
) AS s;
```

Best Practices and Performance Considerations

When working with XML and JSON in T-SQL, keep the following best practices and performance considerations in mind:

1. **Indexing**: For frequently queried XML or JSON data, consider using selective XML indexes or computed columns with indexes.

```
-- Creating a computed column and index for JSON data
ALTER TABLE Products ADD
    ProcessorInfo AS JSON_VALUE(Attributes, '$.processor');

CREATE INDEX IX_Products_ProcessorInfo ON
Products(ProcessorInfo);
```

2. **Validation**: Use ISJSON or XML Schema validation to ensure data integrity.

```
-- Validating JSON data before insertion
CREATE TRIGGER tr_ValidateProductAttributes
ON Products
INSTEAD OF INSERT
AS
BEGIN
    IF EXISTS (SELECT 1 FROM inserted WHERE ISJSON(Attributes) =
0)
    BEGIN
        THROW 50000, 'Invalid JSON data in Attributes column', 1;
```

```
        RETURN;
    END

    INSERT INTO Products (ProductID, ProductName, Attributes)
    SELECT ProductID, ProductName, Attributes
    FROM inserted;
END;
```

3. **Avoid Overuse**: While XML and JSON are powerful, they shouldn't be used as a replacement for proper relational design when it's more appropriate.

4. **Optimize Queries**: When working with large XML or JSON datasets, optimize your queries to minimize parsing and improve performance.

```
-- Using CROSS APPLY for better performance
SELECT
    p.ProductID,
    p.ProductName,
    a.*
FROM Products p
CROSS APPLY OPENJSON(p.Attributes)
WITH (
    processor NVARCHAR(50) '$.processor',
    ram NVARCHAR(10) '$.ram',
    storage NVARCHAR(20) '$.storage'
) AS a;
```

5. **Use Appropriate Functions**: Choose the right function for the job. For example, use JSON_VALUE for scalar values and JSON_QUERY for objects or arrays.

6. **Consider Memory Usage**: Large XML or JSON operations can consume significant memory. Monitor and optimize memory usage in your queries.

7. **Versioning**: When storing configuration or schema-like data in XML or JSON, consider implementing a versioning system to manage changes over time.

```sql
-- Implementing basic versioning for configuration data
CREATE TABLE AppConfigVersioned (
    ConfigID INT,
    Version INT,
    ConfigData NVARCHAR(MAX),
    CreatedDate DATETIME2,
    PRIMARY KEY (ConfigID, Version)
);

--- Inserting a new version
INSERT INTO AppConfigVersioned (ConfigID, Version, ConfigData,
CreatedDate)
SELECT
    1,
    ISNULL(MAX(Version), 0) + 1,
    N'{"database": {"connectionString":
"Server=newserver;Database=newdb;User
Id=newuser;Password=newpassword;"}}',
    GETDATE()
FROM AppConfigVersioned
WHERE ConfigID = 1;

-- Retrieving the latest version
SELECT TOP 1
    ConfigID,
    Version,
    ConfigData,
    CreatedDate
FROM AppConfigVersioned
WHERE ConfigID = 1
ORDER BY Version DESC;
```

Conclusion

XML and JSON support in SQL Server provides powerful tools for working with semi-structured data within a relational database environment. By mastering these technologies, you can enhance your ability to integrate diverse data sources, implement flexible schemas, and create more versatile database solutions.

Remember that while XML and JSON offer great flexibility, they should be used judiciously. Always consider the trade-offs between the flexibility of semi-structured data and the performance and consistency benefits of traditional relational structures.

As you continue to work with XML and JSON in T-SQL, experiment with different techniques and use cases to find the best approaches for your specific requirements. Keep an eye on SQL Server updates, as Microsoft continues to improve and expand support for these data formats in each new version.

Part 4: Optimization and Best Practices

Chapter 12: Indexing and Performance Tuning

Introduction

In this chapter, we'll dive deep into the world of indexing and performance tuning in SQL Server. Understanding how to effectively use indexes and optimize query performance is crucial for any database professional. We'll explore various types of indexes, learn how to analyze query execution plans, and discover techniques for identifying and resolving slow queries.

Types of Indexes: Clustered and Non-Clustered

Indexes are essential database objects that improve query performance by allowing faster data retrieval. SQL Server supports two main types of indexes: clustered and non-clustered. Let's explore each type in detail.

Clustered Indexes

A clustered index determines the physical order of data in a table. It sorts and stores the data rows in the table based on the key values. Each table can have only one clustered index because the data rows themselves can be stored in only one order.

Key characteristics of clustered indexes:

1. **Physical order**: The data pages are arranged in order according to the clustered index key.

2. **Unique identifier**: If no clustered index is specified, SQL Server creates a hidden column called RID (Row Identifier) to uniquely identify each row.

3. **Leaf level**: The leaf level of a clustered index contains the actual data pages of the table.

4. **Performance impact**: Clustered indexes can significantly improve the performance of queries that retrieve a range of data or need to sort the result set based on the clustered index key.

Example of creating a clustered index:

```
CREATE CLUSTERED INDEX IX_Customers_CustomerID
ON Customers (CustomerID);
```

Non-Clustered Indexes

Non-clustered indexes have a structure separate from the data rows. They contain the index key values and row pointers to the actual data rows. A table can have multiple non-clustered indexes.

Key characteristics of non-clustered indexes:

1. **Separate structure**: Non-clustered indexes are stored separately from the table data.

2. **Multiple indexes**: A table can have up to 999 non-clustered indexes in SQL Server.

3. **Leaf level**: The leaf level of a non-clustered index contains the index key values and row locators pointing to the actual data rows.

4. **Performance impact**: Non-clustered indexes can improve the performance of queries that search for specific values or small ranges of data.

Example of creating a non-clustered index:

```
CREATE NONCLUSTERED INDEX IX_Customers_LastName
ON Customers (LastName);
```

Comparing Clustered and Non-Clustered Indexes

To better understand the differences between clustered and non-clustered indexes, let's compare their key aspects:

1. **Storage structure**:

- Clustered: Determines the physical order of data in the table.
- Non-clustered: Stored separately from the table data.

2. **Number of indexes per table**:

- Clustered: Only one per table.
- Non-clustered: Up to 999 per table.

3. **Leaf level content**:

- Clustered: Contains the actual data pages.
- Non-clustered: Contains index key values and row locators.

4. **Performance benefits**:

- Clustered: Best for range queries and sorting.
- Non-clustered: Best for searching specific values or small ranges.

5. **Impact on data modification**:

- Clustered: Can cause page splits and fragmentation when inserting new rows.
- Non-clustered: Less impact on data modification operations.

Choosing Between Clustered and Non-Clustered Indexes

When deciding which type of index to use, consider the following factors:

1. **Query patterns**: Analyze the most common queries and their access patterns.
2. **Data distribution**: Consider the uniqueness and distribution of values in the columns.
3. **Update frequency**: Evaluate how often the data is modified.
4. **Table size**: Consider the size of the table and the expected growth rate.

Generally, it's recommended to:

- Use a clustered index on the primary key column if it's used frequently in queries and joins.
- Create non-clustered indexes on columns frequently used in WHERE clauses, JOIN conditions, and ORDER BY clauses.
- Avoid over-indexing, as it can negatively impact insert, update, and delete performance.

Query Execution Plans

Query execution plans are a crucial tool for understanding how SQL Server processes queries and identifying performance bottlenecks. An execution plan shows the series of steps SQL Server takes to execute a query, including the indexes used, join methods, and data access strategies.

Types of Execution Plans

SQL Server provides three types of execution plans:

1. **Estimated Execution Plan**: Shows the plan SQL Server expects to use without actually running the query.
2. **Actual Execution Plan**: Displays the plan SQL Server actually used to execute the query, including runtime statistics.
3. **Cached Execution Plan**: Represents the plan stored in SQL Server's plan cache for previously executed queries.

Analyzing Execution Plans

To analyze an execution plan effectively, follow these steps:

1. **Generate the execution plan**:

   - For estimated plan: Right-click in the query window and select "Display Estimated Execution Plan" or use CTRL + L.
   - For actual plan: Enable "Include Actual Execution Plan" in SSMS or use SET STATISTICS XML ON.

2. **Identify the query cost**:

   - Look at the relative cost of each operation in the plan.
   - Focus on operations with high costs or unexpected behavior.

3. **Examine operators**:

   - Analyze the types of operators used (e.g., Table Scan, Index Seek, Nested Loops Join).
   - Check for inefficient operators like Table Scans on large tables.

4. **Review index usage**:

   - Look for missing index suggestions.
   - Identify unused or inefficient indexes.

5. **Analyze data flow**:

- Follow the data flow from right to left in the plan.
- Look for areas where large amounts of data are being processed.

6. **Check for warnings**:

- Look for yellow exclamation marks indicating potential issues.
- Review warnings such as implicit conversions or unmatched statistics.

Common Execution Plan Operators

Understanding the most common operators in execution plans is essential for effective analysis:

1. **Table Scan**: Reads all rows in a table. Can be inefficient for large tables.
2. **Clustered Index Scan**: Scans all pages in a clustered index.
3. **Index Seek**: Efficiently locates specific rows using an index.
4. **Nested Loops Join**: Joins two sets of rows by scanning one set and looking up matching rows in the other.
5. **Hash Match**: Builds a hash table from one input and probes it with the other input to find matches.
6. **Merge Join**: Joins two pre-sorted inputs by scanning them in parallel.
7. **Sort**: Sorts the input data based on specified columns.

Execution Plan Properties

Each operator in an execution plan has associated properties that provide valuable information:

- **Estimated Row Count**: The number of rows SQL Server expects the operator to process.
- **Actual Row Count**: The actual number of rows processed (available in actual execution plans).
- **Estimated I/O Cost**: The expected I/O cost of the operation.
- **Estimated CPU Cost**: The expected CPU cost of the operation.
- **Predicate**: Filters applied to the data.
- **Output List**: Columns output by the operator.

Using Execution Plans for Performance Tuning

Execution plans are invaluable for identifying performance issues and optimizing queries. Here are some ways to use execution plans for performance tuning:

1. **Identify missing indexes**:

- Look for "Missing Index" warnings in the plan.
- Evaluate the suggested indexes and create them if appropriate.

2. **Optimize join operations**:

- Analyze join types and look for opportunities to improve them.
- Consider adding indexes to support more efficient join methods.

3. **Reduce I/O operations**:

- Look for table scans on large tables and consider adding appropriate indexes.

- Identify opportunities to reduce the amount of data processed.

4. **Improve data access methods**:

- Replace table scans with index seeks where possible.
- Consider covering indexes for frequently executed queries.

5. **Address parameter sniffing issues**:

- Look for discrepancies between estimated and actual row counts.
- Consider using query hints or rewriting queries to mitigate parameter sniffing problems.

6. **Optimize sort operations**:

- Identify expensive sort operations and consider adding indexes to avoid sorting.
- Evaluate the need for sorting in queries and remove unnecessary ORDER BY clauses.

Identifying and Resolving Slow Queries

Identifying and resolving slow queries is a critical aspect of database performance tuning. This section will cover various techniques and tools to help you pinpoint problematic queries and optimize their performance.

Monitoring Tools and Techniques

1. **Dynamic Management Views (DMVs)**:

SQL Server provides various DMVs that offer insights into query performance:

- `sys.dm_exec_query_stats`: Shows aggregated performance statistics for cached query plans.
- `sys.dm_exec_requests`: Provides information about currently executing requests.
- `sys.dm_io_virtual_file_stats`: Offers I/O statistics for database files.

Example query to find top resource-consuming queries:

```
SELECT TOP 10
    qs.total_elapsed_time / qs.execution_count AS
avg_elapsed_time,
    qs.total_logical_reads / qs.execution_count AS
avg_logical_reads,
    qs.execution_count,
    SUBSTRING(st.text, (qs.statement_start_offset/2)+1,
        ((CASE qs.statement_end_offset
            WHEN -1 THEN DATALENGTH(st.text)
            ELSE qs.statement_end_offset
          END - qs.statement_start_offset)/2) + 1) AS query_text
FROM sys.dm_exec_query_stats qs
CROSS APPLY sys.dm_exec_sql_text(qs.sql_handle) st
ORDER BY avg_elapsed_time DESC;
```

2. **Extended Events**:

Extended Events provide a lightweight, flexible event-handling system for monitoring SQL Server performance:

- Create sessions to capture specific events related to query execution.
- Analyze captured data to identify patterns and problematic queries.

Example of creating an Extended Events session to capture slow queries:

```
CREATE EVENT SESSION [CaptureSlowQueries] ON SERVER
ADD EVENT sqlserver.sql_statement_completed
    (ACTION (sqlserver.sql_text, sqlserver.plan_handle)
    WHERE ([duration] > 1000000)) -- Capture queries taking more
than 1 second
ADD TARGET package0.event_file
    (SET filename=N'C:\Temp\CaptureSlowQueries.xel')
WITH (MAX_MEMORY=4096 KB,
EVENT_RETENTION_MODE=ALLOW_SINGLE_EVENT_LOSS,
    MAX_DISPATCH_LATENCY=30 SECONDS, MAX_EVENT_SIZE=0 KB,
    MEMORY_PARTITION_MODE=NONE, TRACK_CAUSALITY=OFF,
STARTUP_STATE=OFF);

-- Start the session
ALTER EVENT SESSION [CaptureSlowQueries] ON SERVER STATE = START;
```

3. **SQL Server Profiler**:

While deprecated in favor of Extended Events, SQL Server Profiler is still a useful tool for capturing and analyzing query performance:

- Create traces to capture specific events and filter based on duration, CPU usage, or other criteria.
- Analyze captured traces to identify slow queries and performance patterns.

4. **Query Store**:

Introduced in SQL Server 2016, Query Store provides a history of query execution statistics and plans:

- Automatically captures query execution statistics and plans over time.
- Offers built-in reports for identifying regressed queries and analyzing performance trends.

Example of querying Query Store data:

```
SELECT TOP 10
    q.query_id,
    qt.query_sql_text,
    p.plan_id,
    rs.avg_duration,
    rs.avg_logical_io_reads,
    rs.count_executions
FROM sys.query_store_query q
JOIN sys.query_store_query_text qt ON q.query_text_id =
qt.query_text_id
JOIN sys.query_store_plan p ON q.query_id = p.query_id
JOIN sys.query_store_runtime_stats rs ON p.plan_id = rs.plan_id
ORDER BY rs.avg_duration DESC;
```

Common Causes of Slow Queries

Understanding the common causes of slow queries can help you quickly identify and resolve performance issues:

1. **Missing or inefficient indexes**:

- Lack of appropriate indexes can lead to full table scans and poor query performance.
- Over-indexing can negatively impact insert, update, and delete performance.

2. **Suboptimal query design**:

- Inefficient join conditions or excessive use of subqueries can slow down query execution.
- Improper use of wildcards in LIKE predicates can prevent index usage.

3. **Outdated statistics**:

- Stale statistics can lead to poor query plan choices by the optimizer.
- Ensure statistics are up-to-date, especially for frequently changing tables.

4. **Parameter sniffing issues**:

- The query plan generated for one set of parameter values may not be optimal for other values.
- Can lead to inconsistent query performance.

5. **Blocking and locking**:

- Excessive blocking can cause queries to wait for resources, leading to slow performance.
- Identify and resolve deadlocks and long-running transactions.

6. **Resource contention**:

- CPU, memory, or I/O bottlenecks can impact overall query performance.
- Monitor system resources and address any contention issues.

7. **Large result sets**:

- Returning excessive amounts of data can slow down query execution and network transfer.
- Implement proper filtering and pagination techniques.

Techniques for Resolving Slow Queries

Once you've identified slow queries, use these techniques to optimize their performance:

1. **Index optimization**:

- Create appropriate indexes based on query patterns and execution plans.
- Consider covering indexes for frequently executed queries.
- Remove unused or redundant indexes.

Example of creating a covering index:

```
CREATE NONCLUSTERED INDEX IX_Orders_CustomerID_OrderDate_IncTotal
ON Orders (CustomerID, OrderDate)
INCLUDE (TotalAmount);
```

2. **Query rewriting**:

- Simplify complex queries by breaking them into smaller, more manageable parts.
- Use CTEs or derived tables instead of deeply nested subqueries.

- Optimize JOIN conditions and ensure proper filtering.

Example of simplifying a query using a CTE:

```
WITH CustomerOrders AS (
    SELECT CustomerID, COUNT(*) AS OrderCount
    FROM Orders
    GROUP BY CustomerID
)
SELECT c.CustomerName, co.OrderCount
FROM Customers c
LEFT JOIN CustomerOrders co ON c.CustomerID = co.CustomerID
WHERE co.OrderCount > 10;
```

3. **Statistics management**:

- Regularly update statistics, especially for frequently changing tables.
- Consider using auto-update statistics or manually updating statistics for critical queries.

Example of updating statistics:

```
UPDATE STATISTICS Orders WITH FULLSCAN;
```

4. **Query hints**:

- Use query hints judiciously to guide the optimizer when necessary.
- Be cautious, as hints can prevent the optimizer from adapting to changing data distributions.

Example of using a query hint:

```
SELECT *
FROM Orders WITH (INDEX(IX_Orders_OrderDate))
```

```
WHERE OrderDate > '2023-01-01';
```

5. **Parameterization**:

- Use parameterized queries to improve plan reuse and reduce compilation overhead.
- Consider using the OPTIMIZE FOR hint to address parameter sniffing issues.

Example of using OPTIMIZE FOR hint:

```
SELECT *
FROM Orders
WHERE CustomerID = @CustomerID
OPTION (OPTIMIZE FOR (@CustomerID = 1000));
```

6. **Partitioning**:

- Implement table partitioning for very large tables to improve query performance and manageability.
- Use partition elimination to reduce the amount of data scanned.

Example of creating a partitioned table:

```
CREATE PARTITION FUNCTION PF_OrderDate (datetime)
AS RANGE RIGHT FOR VALUES ('2022-01-01', '2023-01-01',
'2024-01-01');

CREATE PARTITION SCHEME PS_OrderDate
AS PARTITION PF_OrderDate ALL TO ([PRIMARY]);

CREATE TABLE Orders (
    OrderID int IDENTITY(1,1) PRIMARY KEY,
    CustomerID int,
    OrderDate datetime,
```

```
    TotalAmount decimal(18,2)
) ON PS_OrderDate(OrderDate);
```

7. **Temporary tables and table variables**:

- Use temporary tables for complex intermediate results in multi-step queries.
- Consider table variables for small datasets or when you need to pass table-valued parameters.

Example of using a temporary table:

```
CREATE TABLE #TempResults (
    CustomerID int,
    TotalOrders int,
    TotalAmount decimal(18,2)
);

INSERT INTO #TempResults (CustomerID, TotalOrders, TotalAmount)
SELECT CustomerID, COUNT(*), SUM(TotalAmount)
FROM Orders
GROUP BY CustomerID;

-- Use #TempResults in subsequent queries
```

8. **Materialized views**:

- Use indexed views (materialized views) to pre-compute and store complex aggregations or joins.
- Particularly useful for data warehouse scenarios with complex, frequently executed queries.

Example of creating an indexed view:

```
CREATE VIEW vw_CustomerOrderSummary
```

```
WITH SCHEMABINDING
AS
SELECT CustomerID, COUNT_BIG(*) AS TotalOrders, SUM(TotalAmount)
AS TotalAmount
FROM dbo.Orders
GROUP BY CustomerID;

CREATE UNIQUE CLUSTERED INDEX IX_vw_CustomerOrderSummary
ON vw_CustomerOrderSummary (CustomerID);
```

9. **Query plan guides**:

- Use plan guides to force specific execution plans for problematic queries.
- Useful when you can't modify the original query or when query hints are not sufficient.

Example of creating a plan guide:

```
EXEC sp_create_plan_guide
    @name = N'PG_GetCustomerOrders',
    @stmt = N'SELECT * FROM Orders WHERE CustomerID =
@CustomerID',
    @type = N'SQL',
    @module_or_batch = NULL,
    @params = N'@CustomerID int',
    @hints = N'OPTION (OPTIMIZE FOR (@CustomerID = 1000))';
```

10. **In-Memory OLTP**:

- For extreme performance requirements, consider using In-Memory OLTP (memory-optimized tables) for appropriate tables and workloads.
- Particularly effective for high-concurrency, low-latency scenarios.
  Example of creating a memory-optimized table:

```
CREATE TABLE dbo.OrderDetails
(
    OrderID int NOT NULL,
    ProductID int NOT NULL,
    Quantity int NOT NULL,
    UnitPrice decimal(18,2) NOT NULL,
    INDEX IX_OrderDetails_OrderID NONCLUSTERED (OrderID)
)
WITH (MEMORY_OPTIMIZED = ON, DURABILITY =
SCHEMA_AND_DATA);
```

Performance Tuning Best Practices

To maintain optimal database performance, follow these best practices:

1. **Regular monitoring**:

- Implement a proactive monitoring strategy to identify performance issues early.
- Use tools like SQL Server Management Studio reports, Performance Monitor, and custom scripts.

2. **Periodic index maintenance**:

- Regularly rebuild or reorganize indexes to reduce fragmentation.
- Consider using Ola Hallengren's IndexOptimize script for automated index maintenance.

3. **Query performance baseline**:

- Establish performance baselines for critical queries and monitor for deviations.
- Use Query Store to track query performance over time.

4. **Code reviews**:

- Implement a code review process that includes performance considerations.
- Use tools like SQL Server Data Tools (SSDT) to analyze query performance during development.

5. **Testing and staging environments**:

- Test performance optimizations in a non-production environment before applying them to production.
- Use realistic data volumes and concurrency levels in your testing.

6. **Documentation**:

- Maintain documentation of performance tuning efforts, including the rationale for optimizations and their impacts.
- Keep track of index strategies and query optimization techniques used in your database.

7. **Continuous education**:

- Stay up-to-date with new SQL Server features and performance tuning techniques.

- Attend conferences, webinars, and training sessions to enhance your skills.

Conclusion

Indexing and performance tuning are critical skills for any database professional working with SQL Server. By understanding the different types of indexes, mastering the art of analyzing query execution plans, and applying various techniques to identify and resolve slow queries, you can significantly improve the performance and efficiency of your database systems.

Remember that performance tuning is an ongoing process. As your data grows and query patterns change, you'll need to continually monitor and optimize your database performance. By following the best practices and techniques outlined in this chapter, you'll be well-equipped to tackle even the most challenging performance issues in your SQL Server environments.

Chapter 13: Security and Permissions

Granting and Revoking Permissions

In SQL Server, managing permissions is crucial for maintaining the security and integrity of your database. Permissions control what actions users can perform on various database objects. Let's explore the process of granting and revoking permissions in detail.

Understanding Permission Types

SQL Server offers several types of permissions:

1. **Object-level permissions**: These apply to specific database objects like tables, views, stored procedures, and functions.
2. **Schema-level permissions**: These apply to all objects within a schema.
3. **Database-level permissions**: These apply to the entire database.
4. **Server-level permissions**: These apply to the entire SQL Server instance.

GRANT Statement

The GRANT statement is used to give permissions to users or roles. The basic syntax is:

```
GRANT <permission> ON <object> TO <principal>
```

Where:

- <permission> is the type of permission (e.g., SELECT, INSERT, UP-DATE, DELETE, EXECUTE)
- <object> is the database object (e.g., table, view, stored procedure)
- <principal> is the user or role receiving the permission

Examples:

```
-- Grant SELECT permission on a table
GRANT SELECT ON dbo.Customers TO User1;

-- Grant EXECUTE permission on a stored procedure
GRANT EXECUTE ON dbo.GetCustomerOrders TO User2;

-- Grant multiple permissions at once
GRANT SELECT, INSERT, UPDATE ON dbo.Orders TO User3;
```

REVOKE Statement

The REVOKE statement is used to remove permissions from users or roles. The basic syntax is similar to GRANT:

```
REVOKE <permission> ON <object> FROM <principal>
```

Examples:

```
-- Revoke SELECT permission on a table
REVOKE SELECT ON dbo.Customers FROM User1;
```

```
-- Revoke EXECUTE permission on a stored procedure
REVOKE EXECUTE ON dbo.GetCustomerOrders FROM User2;

-- Revoke multiple permissions at once
REVOKE SELECT, INSERT, UPDATE ON dbo.Orders FROM User3;
```

WITH GRANT OPTION

When granting permissions, you can use the WITH GRANT OPTION clause to allow the recipient to grant the same permission to others:

```
GRANT SELECT ON dbo.Customers TO User1 WITH GRANT OPTION;
```

To revoke this cascading grant ability, use the CASCADE option:

```
REVOKE SELECT ON dbo.Customers FROM User1 CASCADE;
```

Checking Permissions

To view the permissions granted to a user or role, you can use the sys.database_permissions system view:

```
SELECT
    dp.state_desc,
    dp.permission_name,
    OBJECT_NAME(dp.major_id) AS object_name,
    dp.class_desc,
    SCHEMA_NAME(obj.schema_id) AS schema_name
FROM sys.database_permissions dp
LEFT JOIN sys.objects obj ON dp.major_id = obj.object_id
WHERE dp.grantee_principal_id = USER_ID('User1');
```

Best Practices for Managing Permissions

1. **Least Privilege Principle**: Grant only the minimum necessary permissions for each user or role.
2. **Use Roles**: Group users with similar access needs into roles for easier management.
3. **Regular Audits**: Periodically review and update permissions to ensure they remain appropriate.
4. **Document Changes**: Keep a record of permission changes for auditing and troubleshooting.
5. **Use Schema-Level Permissions**: When possible, grant permissions at the schema level rather than individual objects for easier management.

Securing Sensitive Data

Protecting sensitive data is a critical aspect of database security. SQL Server provides various mechanisms to ensure that confidential information remains secure.

Data Encryption

SQL Server offers two main types of encryption:

1. **Transparent Data Encryption (TDE)**: Encrypts the entire database at rest.
2. **Column-level encryption**: Encrypts specific columns containing sensitive data.

Transparent Data Encryption (TDE)

TDE encrypts the entire database file, including backups. To implement TDE:

1. Create a master key in the master database:

```
USE master;
GO
CREATE MASTER KEY ENCRYPTION BY PASSWORD = 'StrongPassword123!';
```

2. Create a certificate protected by the master key:

```
CREATE CERTIFICATE TDECert
WITH SUBJECT = 'TDE Certificate';
```

3. Create a database encryption key and enable TDE:

```
USE YourDatabase;
GO
CREATE DATABASE ENCRYPTION KEY
WITH ALGORITHM = AES_256
ENCRYPTION BY SERVER CERTIFICATE TDECert;
GO
ALTER DATABASE YourDatabase
SET ENCRYPTION ON;
```

Column-level Encryption

For more granular control, you can encrypt specific columns:

1. Create a master key in the database:

```
CREATE MASTER KEY ENCRYPTION BY PASSWORD = 'StrongPassword123!';
```

2. Create a certificate:

```
CREATE CERTIFICATE MyCertificate
WITH SUBJECT = 'Column Encryption Certificate';
```

3. Create a symmetric key:

```
CREATE SYMMETRIC KEY MySymmetricKey
WITH ALGORITHM = AES_256
ENCRYPTION BY CERTIFICATE MyCertificate;
```

4. Use the symmetric key to encrypt data:

```
-- Open the symmetric key
OPEN SYMMETRIC KEY MySymmetricKey
DECRYPTION BY CERTIFICATE MyCertificate;

-- Insert encrypted data
INSERT INTO Customers (CustomerName, CreditCardNumber)
VALUES ('John Doe', EncryptByKey(Key_GUID('MySymmetricKey'),
'1234-5678-9012-3456'));

-- Close the symmetric key
CLOSE SYMMETRIC KEY MySymmetricKey;
```

Data Masking

Dynamic Data Masking (DDM) is a feature that limits sensitive data exposure by masking it to non-privileged users. To implement DDM:

```
ALTER TABLE Customers
ALTER COLUMN CreditCardNumber ADD MASKED WITH (FUNCTION =
'partial(0,"XXXX-XXXX-XXXX-",4)');
```

This masks the credit card number, showing only the last four digits.

Always Encrypted

Always Encrypted is a feature that keeps sensitive data encrypted in the database, during transit, and even in memory. To use Always Encrypted:

1. Generate encryption keys using SQL Server Management Studio (SSMS).
2. Configure the column for encryption in SSMS.
3. Update your connection string to enable Always Encrypted:

```
"Column Encryption Setting=Enabled;"
```

Auditing

SQL Server Audit allows you to track and log events in the database. To set up auditing:

1. Create a server audit:

```
CREATE SERVER AUDIT MyAudit
TO FILE (FILEPATH = 'C:\SQLAudit\')
```

2. Create a database audit specification:

```
USE YourDatabase;
GO
CREATE DATABASE AUDIT SPECIFICATION MyDatabaseAuditSpec
FOR SERVER AUDIT MyAudit
ADD (SELECT, INSERT, UPDATE, DELETE ON dbo.Customers BY public)
```

```
WITH (STATE = ON);
```

Best Practices for Securing Sensitive Data

1. **Classify Data**: Identify and categorize sensitive data in your database.
2. **Use Strong Encryption**: Implement appropriate encryption methods for sensitive data.
3. **Key Management**: Securely manage and rotate encryption keys.
4. **Access Control**: Limit access to sensitive data using roles and permissions.
5. **Regular Audits**: Conduct periodic security audits and review audit logs.
6. **Data Minimization**: Only collect and retain necessary sensitive data.
7. **Secure Backups**: Ensure that backups of sensitive data are also encrypted.

Using Roles and Users for Access Control

Effective access control is crucial for maintaining database security. SQL Server provides a robust system of roles and users to manage access to database resources.

Understanding Principals

In SQL Server, principals are entities that can request SQL Server resources. The main types of principals are:

1. **Windows-level principals**: Windows users and groups
2. **SQL Server-level principals**: SQL Server logins
3. **Database-level principals**: Database users, roles, and application roles

Creating and Managing Logins

Logins are server-level principals used for authentication. There are two types:

1. **Windows Authentication logins**: Based on Windows accounts or groups
2. **SQL Server Authentication logins**: Username and password stored in SQL Server

To create a SQL Server Authentication login:

```
CREATE LOGIN JohnDoe
WITH PASSWORD = 'StrongPassword123!';
```

To create a Windows Authentication login:

```
CREATE LOGIN [DOMAIN\JohnDoe] FROM WINDOWS;
```

Creating and Managing Database Users

Database users are mapped to logins and provide access to a specific database. To create a database user:

```
USE YourDatabase;
GO
CREATE USER JohnDoe FOR LOGIN JohnDoe;
```

For a Windows login:

```
USE YourDatabase;
GO
CREATE USER [DOMAIN\JohnDoe] FOR LOGIN [DOMAIN\JohnDoe];
```

Fixed Server Roles

SQL Server provides built-in fixed server roles with predefined sets of permissions:

- sysadmin

- serveradmin

- securityadmin

- processadmin

- setupadmin

- bulkadmin

- diskadmin

- dbcreator

- public

To add a login to a fixed server role:

```
ALTER SERVER ROLE dbcreator ADD MEMBER JohnDoe;
```

Fixed Database Roles

Similar to server roles, there are fixed database roles:

- db_owner

- db_securityadmin

- db_accessadmin

- db_backupoperator

- db_ddladmin

- db_datawriter

- db_datareader

- db_denydatawriter

- db_denydatareader

To add a user to a fixed database role:

```
ALTER ROLE db_datareader ADD MEMBER JohnDoe;
```

Custom Roles

You can create custom roles to group permissions for specific business needs:

```
CREATE ROLE SalesTeam;
```

Grant permissions to the role:

```
GRANT SELECT, INSERT, UPDATE ON dbo.Sales TO SalesTeam;
```

Add users to the role:

```
ALTER ROLE SalesTeam ADD MEMBER JohnDoe;
```

Application Roles

Application roles are used to grant permissions to applications rather than users:

```
CREATE APPLICATION ROLE SalesApp
WITH PASSWORD = 'AppPassword123!';

GRANT SELECT, INSERT, UPDATE ON dbo.Sales TO SalesApp;
```

To use an application role, the application must execute:

```
EXEC sp_setapprole 'SalesApp', 'AppPassword123!';
```

Role Hierarchy

Roles can be nested to create a hierarchy:

```
CREATE ROLE JuniorSales;
CREATE ROLE SeniorSales;

ALTER ROLE SeniorSales ADD MEMBER JuniorSales;
```

Permissions granted to SeniorSales will also apply to JuniorSales.

Best Practices for Using Roles and Users

1. **Principle of Least Privilege**: Grant only the minimum necessary permissions.
2. **Use Roles**: Group users with similar access needs into roles for easier management.
3. **Avoid Using dbo**: Create and use custom roles instead of relying on the dbo user.
4. **Regular Audits**: Periodically review user and role memberships and permissions.
5. **Standardize Naming**: Use consistent naming conventions for roles and users.

6. **Document**: Maintain documentation of your role and user structure.

7. **Use Windows Authentication**: When possible, use Windows Authentication for better security.

8. **Limit sysadmin Members**: Minimize the number of logins with sysadmin privileges.

Monitoring and Auditing Access Control

Regularly monitor and audit your access control setup:

1. Use system views to review permissions:

```
SELECT
    dp.state_desc,
    dp.permission_name,
    OBJECT_NAME(dp.major_id) AS object_name,
    pr.name AS principal_name,
    pr.type_desc AS principal_type
FROM sys.database_permissions dp
JOIN sys.database_principals pr ON dp.grantee_principal_id =
pr.principal_id;
```

2. Review role memberships:

```
SELECT
    r.name AS role_name,
    m.name AS member_name
FROM sys.database_role_members rm
JOIN sys.database_principals r ON rm.role_principal_id =
r.principal_id
JOIN sys.database_principals m ON rm.member_principal_id =
m.principal_id;
```

3. Use SQL Server Audit to track permission changes and access attempts.
4. Implement a process for regular access reviews and permission cleanup.

Implementing Least Privilege

The principle of least privilege is fundamental to secure access control. Here are steps to implement it:

1. **Analyze Requirements**: Determine the minimum permissions each user or application needs.
2. **Create Granular Roles**: Design roles that align with specific job functions or access needs.
3. **Use Schema-Level Permissions**: When possible, grant permissions at the schema level rather than on individual objects.
4. **Implement Just-In-Time Access**: Use temporary role assignments for tasks that require elevated privileges.
5. **Regular Reviews**: Periodically review and adjust permissions to ensure they remain appropriate.

Handling Permission Conflicts

When a user is a member of multiple roles with conflicting permissions, SQL Server follows these rules:

1. DENY takes precedence over GRANT.
2. Permissions are cumulative (unless overridden by DENY).

To resolve conflicts:

1. Review role memberships and permissions.
2. Consider creating more specific roles to avoid overlaps.
3. Use DENY judiciously, as it can create complex permission scenarios.

Transferring Ownership

Object ownership can impact permissions. To transfer ownership:

```
ALTER AUTHORIZATION ON dbo.Customers TO JohnDoe;
```

Be cautious when transferring ownership, as it can affect existing permissions and the ability to access the object.

Using Contained Databases

Contained databases allow for database-level user authentication without server-level logins:

```
CREATE DATABASE ContainedDB CONTAINMENT = PARTIAL;

USE ContainedDB;
GO

CREATE USER JaneDoe WITH PASSWORD = 'StrongPassword456!';
```

This approach can simplify user management and improve portability between servers.

Implementing Row-Level Security (RLS)

Row-Level Security allows you to control access to rows in a table based on user characteristics:

1. Create a security predicate function:

```
CREATE FUNCTION dbo.fn_SecurityPredicate(@SalesRegion AS
nvarchar(50))
RETURNS TABLE
WITH SCHEMABINDING
AS
RETURN SELECT 1 AS fn_SecurityPredicate_Result
WHERE @SalesRegion = USER_NAME() OR USER_NAME() = 'SalesManager'
```

2. Create a security policy:

```
CREATE SECURITY POLICY SalesFilter
ADD FILTER PREDICATE dbo.fn_SecurityPredicate(SalesRegion)
ON dbo.Sales
WITH (STATE = ON);
```

This policy ensures users can only see sales data for their region, while the Sales-Manager can see all data.

Implementing Column-Level Security

While SQL Server doesn't have built-in column-level security, you can achieve it using views and permissions:

1. Create a view with restricted columns:

```
CREATE VIEW dbo.EmployeePublic AS
SELECT EmployeeID, FirstName, LastName, Department
```

```
FROM dbo.Employees;
```

2. Grant permissions on the view instead of the base table:

```
GRANT SELECT ON dbo.EmployeePublic TO HR_Assistant;
DENY SELECT ON dbo.Employees TO HR_Assistant;
```

Using Schema-Based Security

Organizing objects into schemas can simplify permission management:

1. Create a schema:

```
CREATE SCHEMA Sales;
```

2. Move objects into the schema:

```
ALTER SCHEMA Sales TRANSFER dbo.SalesOrders;
```

3. Grant permissions at the schema level:

```
GRANT SELECT ON SCHEMA::Sales TO SalesTeam;
```

This approach allows for more manageable and scalable permission structures.

Implementing Data-Driven Security

For complex security requirements, you can implement data-driven security using functions and views:

1. Create a security table:

```
CREATE TABLE dbo.UserRegions (
    UserName nvarchar(50),
    Region nvarchar(50)
);
```

2. Create a function to check access:

```
CREATE FUNCTION dbo.fn_UserHasAccess(@Region nvarchar(50))
RETURNS bit
AS
BEGIN
    RETURN CASE WHEN EXISTS (
        SELECT 1 FROM dbo.UserRegions
        WHERE UserName = USER_NAME() AND Region = @Region
    ) THEN 1 ELSE 0 END
END
```

3. Use the function in a view:

```
CREATE VIEW dbo.SalesData AS
SELECT * FROM dbo.Sales
WHERE dbo.fn_UserHasAccess(Region) = 1;
```

This approach allows for flexible, data-driven access control that can be easily updated by modifying the UserRegions table.

Handling Cross-Database Permissions

When dealing with cross-database access, consider these options:

1. **Use database roles and add users to roles in each database.**

2. **Create certificate-based users for cross-database ownership chaining.**

3. **Use EXECUTE AS to impersonate users with necessary permissions.**

Example of certificate-based user:

```sql
-- In master database
CREATE MASTER KEY ENCRYPTION BY PASSWORD = 'StrongMasterKey123!';

CREATE CERTIFICATE CrossDBCert
WITH SUBJECT = 'Certificate for cross-database access';

-- In Database1
CREATE USER CrossDBUser FROM CERTIFICATE CrossDBCert;
GRANT SELECT ON Schema1.Table1 TO CrossDBUser;

-- In Database2
CREATE USER CrossDBUser FROM CERTIFICATE CrossDBCert;
GRANT EXECUTE ON Schema2.StoredProc1 TO CrossDBUser;
```

Implementing Attribute-Based Access Control (ABAC)

ABAC allows for fine-grained access control based on attributes of the user, resource, and environment:

1. Create an attributes table:

```sql
CREATE TABLE dbo.UserAttributes (
    UserName nvarchar(50),
    AttributeName nvarchar(50),
    AttributeValue nvarchar(100)
);
```

2. Create a function to check attributes:

```
CREATE FUNCTION dbo.fn_CheckUserAttribute(
    @AttributeName nvarchar(50),
    @AttributeValue nvarchar(100)
)
RETURNS bit
AS
BEGIN
    RETURN CASE WHEN EXISTS (
        SELECT 1 FROM dbo.UserAttributes
        WHERE UserName = USER_NAME()
        AND AttributeName = @AttributeName
        AND AttributeValue = @AttributeValue
    ) THEN 1 ELSE 0 END
END
```

3. Use the function in views or stored procedures:

```
CREATE VIEW dbo.SensitiveData AS
SELECT * FROM dbo.AllData
WHERE dbo.fn_CheckUserAttribute('ClearanceLevel', 'Top Secret') =
1;
```

This approach allows for complex, attribute-based access control policies.

Implementing Just-In-Time Access

For scenarios where users need temporary elevated access:

1. Create a stored procedure to grant temporary access:

```
CREATE PROCEDURE dbo.GrantTemporaryAccess
    @UserName nvarchar(50),
    @Role nvarchar(50),
    @DurationMinutes int
```

```
AS
BEGIN
    -- Add user to role
    EXEC sp_addrolemember @rolename = @Role, @membername =
@UserName;

    -- Schedule removal
    DECLARE @SQL nvarchar(max) =
        N'EXEC sp_droprolemember @rolename = ''' + @Role +
        ''', @membername = ''' + @UserName + '''';

    EXEC sp_executesql N'WAITFOR DELAY @delay; EXEC (@SQL)',
        N'@delay char(8), @SQL nvarchar(max)',
        @delay = RIGHT('00' + CAST(@DurationMinutes/60 AS
varchar(2)), 2) + ':' +
                 RIGHT('00' + CAST(@DurationMinutes%60 AS
varchar(2)), 2) + ':00',
        @SQL = @SQL;
END
```

2. Use the procedure to grant temporary access:

```
EXEC dbo.GrantTemporaryAccess 'JohnDoe', 'db_owner', 60;
```

This grants JohnDoe db_owner privileges for 60 minutes.

Implementing Break-Glass Access

For emergency situations where immediate elevated access is required:

1. Create a break-glass role with necessary permissions:

```
CREATE ROLE EmergencyAccess;
GRANT CONTROL ON DATABASE::YourDatabase TO EmergencyAccess;
```

2. Create a stored procedure to grant and log emergency access:

```
CREATE PROCEDURE dbo.GrantEmergencyAccess
    @UserName nvarchar(50),
    @Reason nvarchar(max)
AS
BEGIN
    -- Grant access
    EXEC sp_addrolemember 'EmergencyAccess', @UserName;

    -- Log the access
    INSERT INTO dbo.EmergencyAccessLog (UserName, GrantTime,
Reason)
    VALUES (@UserName, GETDATE(), @Reason);

    -- Notify administrators (implement as needed)
    -- EXEC msdb.dbo.sp_send_dbmail ...
END
```

3. Use the procedure in emergencies:

```
EXEC dbo.GrantEmergencyAccess 'JaneDoe', 'Critical system
failure';
```

Ensure to have a process to review emergency access logs and revoke access once the emergency is resolved.

Conclusion

Effective security and permissions management in SQL Server requires a comprehensive approach that combines technical implementations with sound policies and procedures. By leveraging the various tools and techniques discussed in this chapter, you can create a robust security framework that protects your data while allowing appropriate access for users and applications.

Remember that security is an ongoing process. Regularly review and update your security measures, stay informed about new security features and best practices, and always prioritize the principle of least privilege in your database design and access control strategies.

Chapter 14: Best Practices for T-SQL Development

Writing Readable and Maintainable Code

Writing readable and maintainable T-SQL code is crucial for the long-term success of any database project. Well-structured and organized code not only makes it easier for you to understand and modify your own work but also facilitates collaboration with other developers. Here are some best practices to follow when writing T-SQL code:

1. Use Consistent Formatting

Consistent formatting makes your code easier to read and understand. Consider the following guidelines:

- Use indentation to show the logical structure of your code.
- Align related items vertically for better readability.
- Use uppercase for SQL keywords and lowercase for user-defined names.
- Place each major clause (SELECT, FROM, WHERE, etc.) on a separate line.

Example of well-formatted code:

```sql
SELECT
    c.CustomerID,
    c.FirstName,
    c.LastName,
    o.OrderDate,
    o.TotalAmount
FROM
    Customers c
    INNER JOIN Orders o ON c.CustomerID = o.CustomerID
WHERE
    o.OrderDate >= '2023-01-01'
    AND o.TotalAmount > 1000
ORDER BY
    o.OrderDate DESC,
    c.LastName ASC;
```

2. Use Meaningful Names

Choose descriptive and meaningful names for your database objects, variables, and aliases. This practice makes your code self-explanatory and reduces the need for extensive comments.

- Use clear and descriptive names for tables, views, and columns.
- Avoid abbreviations unless they are widely understood.
- Use prefixes or suffixes to indicate the object type (e.g., tbl_ for tables, vw_ for views).
- Use singular nouns for table names (e.g., Customer instead of Customers).

Example:

```sql
-- Good naming
CREATE TABLE tbl_Customer (
    CustomerID INT PRIMARY KEY,
    FirstName NVARCHAR(50),
```

```
    LastName NVARCHAR(50),
    DateOfBirth DATE
);

-- Poor naming
CREATE TABLE tbl_Cust (
    CustID INT PRIMARY KEY,
    FName NVARCHAR(50),
    LName NVARCHAR(50),
    DOB DATE
);
```

3. Comment Your Code

While well-written code should be mostly self-explanatory, comments are still valuable for providing context, explaining complex logic, or documenting assumptions. Use comments judiciously:

- Add header comments to stored procedures and functions to explain their purpose and parameters.
- Use inline comments to clarify complex calculations or business rules.
- Avoid redundant comments that simply restate the obvious.

Example:

```
-- Calculate the total sales for each product category in the
given year
CREATE PROCEDURE usp_GetCategorySales
    @Year INT
AS
BEGIN
    SELECT
        c.CategoryName,
        SUM(od.Quantity * od.UnitPrice) AS TotalSales
    FROM
        Categories c
```

```
        INNER JOIN Products p ON c.CategoryID = p.CategoryID
        INNER JOIN [Order Details] od ON p.ProductID =
od.ProductID
        INNER JOIN Orders o ON od.OrderID = o.OrderID
    WHERE
        YEAR(o.OrderDate) = @Year
    GROUP BY
        c.CategoryName
    ORDER BY
        TotalSales DESC;
END;
```

4. Use Common Table Expressions (CTEs) for Complex Queries

CTEs can make complex queries more readable by breaking them down into logical, named components. They are particularly useful for recursive queries or when you need to reference the same subquery multiple times.

Example:

```
WITH CustomerOrders AS (
    SELECT
        CustomerID,
        COUNT(*) AS OrderCount,
        SUM(TotalAmount) AS TotalSpent
    FROM
        Orders
    GROUP BY
        CustomerID
),
HighValueCustomers AS (
    SELECT
        CustomerID
    FROM
        CustomerOrders
    WHERE
        TotalSpent > 10000
```

```
)
SELECT
    c.CustomerID,
    c.FirstName,
    c.LastName,
    co.OrderCount,
    co.TotalSpent
FROM
    Customers c
    INNER JOIN CustomerOrders co ON c.CustomerID = co.CustomerID
    INNER JOIN HighValueCustomers hvc ON c.CustomerID =
hvc.CustomerID;
```

5. Use Stored Procedures and Functions

Encapsulate complex logic and frequently used queries in stored procedures and functions. This approach promotes code reuse, improves maintainability, and can enhance security by controlling access to underlying tables.

Example:

```
CREATE FUNCTION fn_GetCustomerTotalSpent
(
    @CustomerID INT
)
RETURNS DECIMAL(18,2)
AS
BEGIN
    DECLARE @TotalSpent DECIMAL(18,2);

    SELECT @TotalSpent = SUM(TotalAmount)
    FROM Orders
    WHERE CustomerID = @CustomerID;

    RETURN ISNULL(@TotalSpent, 0);
END;

GO
```

```
CREATE PROCEDURE usp_GetTopCustomers
    @TopN INT
AS
BEGIN
    SELECT TOP (@TopN)
        c.CustomerID,
        c.FirstName,
        c.LastName,
        dbo.fn_GetCustomerTotalSpent(c.CustomerID) AS TotalSpent
    FROM
        Customers c
    ORDER BY
        TotalSpent DESC;
END;
```

6. Use Schema Names

Always use schema names when referencing database objects. This practice improves code clarity and helps avoid naming conflicts.

Example:

```
SELECT
    o.OrderID,
    c.FirstName,
    c.LastName
FROM
    dbo.Orders o
    INNER JOIN dbo.Customers c ON o.CustomerID = c.CustomerID;
```

7. Use Table Aliases Consistently

When using table aliases, choose meaningful abbreviations and use them consistently throughout your query. This practice improves readability, especially in complex joins.

Example:

```
SELECT
    c.CustomerID,
    c.FirstName,
    c.LastName,
    o.OrderID,
    o.OrderDate,
    p.ProductName,
    od.Quantity
FROM
    dbo.Customers c
    INNER JOIN dbo.Orders o ON c.CustomerID = o.CustomerID
    INNER JOIN dbo.OrderDetails od ON o.OrderID = od.OrderID
    INNER JOIN dbo.Products p ON od.ProductID = p.ProductID;
```

8. Use SET-based Operations

Prefer SET-based operations over cursor-based or row-by-row processing whenever possible. SET-based operations are generally more efficient and scalable in SQL Server.

Example (using SET-based operation):

```
UPDATE o
SET o.TotalAmount = (
    SELECT SUM(od.Quantity * od.UnitPrice)
    FROM OrderDetails od
    WHERE od.OrderID = o.OrderID
)
FROM Orders o;
```

Instead of (using cursor):

```
DECLARE @OrderID INT;
DECLARE @TotalAmount DECIMAL(18,2);

DECLARE order_cursor CURSOR FOR
```

```sql
SELECT OrderID FROM Orders;

OPEN order_cursor;
FETCH NEXT FROM order_cursor INTO @OrderID;

WHILE @@FETCH_STATUS = 0
BEGIN
    SELECT @TotalAmount = SUM(Quantity * UnitPrice)
    FROM OrderDetails
    WHERE OrderID = @OrderID;

    UPDATE Orders
    SET TotalAmount = @TotalAmount
    WHERE OrderID = @OrderID;

    FETCH NEXT FROM order_cursor INTO @OrderID;
END

CLOSE order_cursor;
DEALLOCATE order_cursor;
```

9. Use Appropriate Data Types

Choose the most appropriate data types for your columns and variables. Using the correct data type improves performance, reduces storage requirements, and ensures data integrity.

Example:

```sql
-- Good practice
CREATE TABLE Employees (
    EmployeeID INT PRIMARY KEY,
    FirstName NVARCHAR(50),
    LastName NVARCHAR(50),
    BirthDate DATE,
    HireDate DATE,
    Salary DECIMAL(10,2)
);
```

```
-- Poor practice
CREATE TABLE Employees (
    EmployeeID BIGINT PRIMARY KEY,
    FirstName NVARCHAR(MAX),
    LastName NVARCHAR(MAX),
    BirthDate DATETIME,
    HireDate DATETIME,
    Salary FLOAT
);
```

10. Use Transactions for Data Integrity

Wrap related operations in transactions to ensure data consistency and integrity. This practice is especially important when modifying data across multiple tables.

Example:

```
BEGIN TRY
    BEGIN TRANSACTION;

    INSERT INTO Orders (CustomerID, OrderDate, TotalAmount)
    VALUES (@CustomerID, GETDATE(), @TotalAmount);

    DECLARE @OrderID INT = SCOPE_IDENTITY();

    INSERT INTO OrderDetails (OrderID, ProductID, Quantity,
UnitPrice)
    VALUES (@OrderID, @ProductID, @Quantity, @UnitPrice);

    UPDATE Inventory
    SET StockQuantity = StockQuantity - @Quantity
    WHERE ProductID = @ProductID;

    COMMIT TRANSACTION;
END TRY
BEGIN CATCH
    IF @@TRANCOUNT > 0
        ROLLBACK TRANSACTION;
```

```
    -- Handle the error (e.g., log it, rethrow it)
    THROW;
END CATCH;
```

Avoiding Common Pitfalls

When developing T-SQL code, it's important to be aware of common pitfalls that can lead to performance issues, logical errors, or maintainability problems. Here are some common pitfalls to avoid:

1. Overusing Cursors

Cursors are often used to process data row by row, but they can be slow and re-source-intensive, especially for large datasets. In most cases, set-based operations are more efficient.

Instead of using a cursor to update data, consider using a set-based UPDATE statement:

```
-- Avoid this:
DECLARE @CustomerID INT;
DECLARE @NewCreditLimit DECIMAL(10,2);

DECLARE customer_cursor CURSOR FOR
SELECT CustomerID FROM Customers WHERE CustomerType = 'Premium';

OPEN customer_cursor;
FETCH NEXT FROM customer_cursor INTO @CustomerID;

WHILE @@FETCH_STATUS = 0
BEGIN
    SET @NewCreditLimit = 10000;

    UPDATE Customers
```

```
      SET CreditLimit = @NewCreditLimit
      WHERE CustomerID = @CustomerID;

      FETCH NEXT FROM customer_cursor INTO @CustomerID;
END

CLOSE customer_cursor;
DEALLOCATE customer_cursor;

-- Use this instead:
UPDATE Customers
SET CreditLimit = 10000
WHERE CustomerType = 'Premium';
```

2. Ignoring Index Usage

Failing to consider index usage can lead to poor query performance. Always analyze your queries using execution plans and ensure appropriate indexes are in place.

Example of creating an index to improve query performance:

```
-- Slow query without proper indexing
SELECT OrderID, OrderDate, TotalAmount
FROM Orders
WHERE CustomerID = 1234 AND OrderDate >= '2023-01-01';

-- Create an index to improve performance
CREATE NONCLUSTERED INDEX IX_Orders_CustomerID_OrderDate
ON Orders (CustomerID, OrderDate)
INCLUDE (TotalAmount);
```

3. Using SELECT *

Using SELECT * can lead to unnecessary I/O and network traffic, especially when you only need a subset of columns. Always specify the exact columns you need.

```
-- Avoid this:
SELECT * FROM Customers;

-- Use this instead:
SELECT CustomerID, FirstName, LastName, Email
FROM Customers;
```

4. Ignoring Parameter Sniffing

Parameter sniffing can lead to suboptimal query plans in some scenarios. Be aware of this issue and use techniques like local variables or the OPTIMIZE FOR hint when necessary.

Example of using a local variable to mitigate parameter sniffing:

```
CREATE PROCEDURE usp_GetCustomerOrders
    @CustomerID INT
AS
BEGIN
    DECLARE @LocalCustomerID INT = @CustomerID;

    SELECT OrderID, OrderDate, TotalAmount
    FROM Orders
    WHERE CustomerID = @LocalCustomerID;
END;
```

5. Not Handling NULLs Properly

Improper handling of NULL values can lead to unexpected results. Always consider how NULL values will affect your queries and use appropriate NULL handling techniques.

Example of proper NULL handling:

```
-- Avoid this:
SELECT CustomerID, FirstName, LastName, City
```

```
FROM Customers
WHERE City = @City;

-- Use this instead:
SELECT CustomerID, FirstName, LastName, City
FROM Customers
WHERE City = @City OR (City IS NULL AND @City IS NULL);
```

6. Ignoring Concurrency Issues

Failing to handle concurrency can lead to data inconsistencies or deadlocks. Use appropriate isolation levels and consider implementing optimistic concurrency control when necessary.

Example of using optimistic concurrency control:

```
CREATE PROCEDURE usp_UpdateCustomer
    @CustomerID INT,
    @FirstName NVARCHAR(50),
    @LastName NVARCHAR(50),
    @LastModified DATETIME
AS
BEGIN
    UPDATE Customers
    SET
        FirstName = @FirstName,
        LastName = @LastName,
        LastModified = GETDATE()
    WHERE
        CustomerID = @CustomerID
        AND LastModified = @LastModified;

    IF @@ROWCOUNT = 0
        THROW 50000, 'Customer data has been modified by another
user.', 1;
END;
```

7. Not Using Parameterized Queries

Using string concatenation to build dynamic SQL can lead to SQL injection vulnerabilities. Always use parameterized queries or sp_executesql for dynamic SQL.

Example of using parameterized dynamic SQL:

```sql
DECLARE @SQL NVARCHAR(MAX);
DECLARE @Params NVARCHAR(MAX);

SET @SQL = N'SELECT CustomerID, FirstName, LastName FROM
Customers WHERE City = @City';
SET @Params = N'@City NVARCHAR(50)';

EXEC sp_executesql @SQL, @Params, @City = 'London';
```

8. Overusing Subqueries

While subqueries can be useful, overusing them can lead to performance issues. Consider using JOINs or CTEs as alternatives when appropriate.

Example of replacing a subquery with a JOIN:

```sql
-- Avoid this:
SELECT
    ProductID,
    ProductName,
    (SELECT AVG(UnitPrice) FROM OrderDetails WHERE ProductID =
p.ProductID) AS AvgPrice
FROM
    Products p;

-- Use this instead:
SELECT
    p.ProductID,
    p.ProductName,
    AVG(od.UnitPrice) AS AvgPrice
FROM
    Products p
```

```
    LEFT JOIN OrderDetails od ON p.ProductID = od.ProductID
GROUP BY
    p.ProductID, p.ProductName;
```

9. Not Using Schema Names

Failing to use schema names can lead to ambiguity and potential errors, especially when multiple schemas are involved.

Example of using schema names:

```
-- Avoid this:
SELECT * FROM Customers;

-- Use this instead:
SELECT * FROM dbo.Customers;
```

10. Ignoring Code Reusability

Not leveraging code reusability through stored procedures, functions, and views can lead to duplicated code and maintenance difficulties.

Example of improving code reusability:

```
-- Create a reusable function
CREATE FUNCTION dbo.fn_GetCustomerTotalOrders
(
    @CustomerID INT
)
RETURNS INT
AS
BEGIN
    DECLARE @TotalOrders INT;

    SELECT @TotalOrders = COUNT(*)
    FROM Orders
    WHERE CustomerID = @CustomerID;
```

```
    RETURN @TotalOrders;
END;

-- Use the function in multiple places
SELECT
    CustomerID,
    FirstName,
    LastName,
    dbo.fn_GetCustomerTotalOrders(CustomerID) AS TotalOrders
FROM
    Customers;
```

Tips for Debugging T-SQL Scripts

Debugging T-SQL scripts is an essential skill for any database developer. Here are some tips and techniques to help you effectively debug your T-SQL code:

1. Use PRINT Statements

Insert PRINT statements at key points in your code to output variable values or status messages. This can help you track the flow of your script and identify where issues might be occurring.

Example:

```
DECLARE @CustomerID INT = 1234;
DECLARE @OrderCount INT;

PRINT 'Starting process for CustomerID: ' + CAST(@CustomerID AS
NVARCHAR(10));

SELECT @OrderCount = COUNT(*)
FROM Orders
WHERE CustomerID = @CustomerID;
```

```
PRINT 'Order count: ' + CAST(@OrderCount AS NVARCHAR(10));

-- Rest of the script...
```

2. Use SET NOCOUNT ON

When debugging stored procedures or scripts that involve multiple statements, use SET NOCOUNT ON to suppress the rowcount messages. This can make your debug output cleaner and easier to read.

Example:

```
CREATE PROCEDURE usp_ProcessOrders
AS
BEGIN
    SET NOCOUNT ON;

    -- Your code here...

    PRINT 'Processing complete';
END;
```

3. Use Error Handling

Implement proper error handling in your scripts using TRY...CATCH blocks. This allows you to catch and handle errors gracefully, making it easier to identify and diagnose issues.

Example:

```
BEGIN TRY
    -- Your code here...
    SELECT 1/0; -- This will cause an error
END TRY
BEGIN CATCH
```

```
    PRINT 'Error occurred:';
    PRINT 'Error number: ' + CAST(ERROR_NUMBER() AS
NVARCHAR(10));
    PRINT 'Error message: ' + ERROR_MESSAGE();
    PRINT 'Error line: ' + CAST(ERROR_LINE() AS NVARCHAR(10));
END CATCH;
```

4. Use @@ROWCOUNT

After INSERT, UPDATE, or DELETE statements, check @@ROWCOUNT to verify that the expected number of rows were affected. This can help you identify issues where your statements aren't modifying the data as expected.

Example:

```
UPDATE Customers
SET CreditLimit = CreditLimit * 1.1
WHERE CustomerType = 'Premium';

IF @@ROWCOUNT = 0
    PRINT 'Warning: No customers were updated';
ELSE
    PRINT 'Updated ' + CAST(@@ROWCOUNT AS NVARCHAR(10)) + '
customers';
```

5. Use Table Variables or Temporary Tables

For complex queries or procedures, consider using table variables or temporary tables to store intermediate results. You can then query these tables to inspect the data at various stages of your script.

Example:

```
DECLARE @Results TABLE (
    CustomerID INT,
    TotalOrders INT,
```

```
    TotalAmount DECIMAL(18,2)
);

INSERT INTO @Results (CustomerID, TotalOrders, TotalAmount)
SELECT
    CustomerID,
    COUNT(*) AS TotalOrders,
    SUM(TotalAmount) AS TotalAmount
FROM
    Orders
GROUP BY
    CustomerID;

-- Inspect the results
SELECT * FROM @Results WHERE TotalOrders > 10;

-- Continue with the rest of your script...
```

6. Use SET STATISTICS IO and TIME ON

Enable these options to get detailed information about the I/O operations and execution time of your queries. This can be particularly useful for identifying performance bottlenecks.

Example:

```
SET STATISTICS IO ON;
SET STATISTICS TIME ON;

-- Your query here
SELECT * FROM Customers WHERE City = 'London';

SET STATISTICS IO OFF;
SET STATISTICS TIME OFF;
```

7. Use the SQL Server Profiler

For more complex debugging scenarios, use the SQL Server Profiler to capture and analyze the exact queries being executed, along with their execution plans and resource usage.

8. Use RAISERROR for Custom Error Messages

Use RAISERROR to generate custom error messages with specific error numbers and severity levels. This can help you distinguish between different types of errors in your scripts.

Example:

```
IF NOT EXISTS (SELECT 1 FROM Customers WHERE CustomerID =
@CustomerID)
    RAISERROR('Customer with ID %d not found', 16, 1,
@CustomerID);
```

9. Use Database Mail for Long-Running Scripts

For scripts that run for extended periods, consider using Database Mail to send progress updates or completion notifications. This can be especially useful for scheduled jobs or batch processes.

Example:

```
EXEC msdb.dbo.sp_send_dbmail
    @profile_name = 'YourMailProfile',
    @recipients = 'you@example.com',
    @subject = 'Long-running script completed',
    @body = 'The data processing script has finished
successfully.';
```

10. Use SET XACT_ABORT ON

Enable XACT_ABORT to ensure that any error will automatically roll back the entire transaction. This can help maintain data consistency and make it easier to identify where errors are occurring.

Example:

```sql
SET XACT_ABORT ON;

BEGIN TRY
    BEGIN TRANSACTION;

    -- Your code here...

    COMMIT TRANSACTION;
END TRY
BEGIN CATCH
    IF @@TRANCOUNT > 0
        ROLLBACK TRANSACTION;

    -- Handle or re-throw the error
    THROW;
END CATCH;
```

11. Use DBCC Commands

DBCC commands can be useful for diagnosing and fixing various database issues. For example, DBCC CHECKDB can help identify database corruption, while DBCC FREEPROCCACHE can clear the procedure cache if you suspect caching issues.

Example:

```sql
-- Check database integrity
DBCC CHECKDB ('YourDatabase');

-- Clear procedure cache
```

```
DBCC FREEPROCCACHE;
```

12. Use Dynamic Management Views (DMVs)

DMVs provide a wealth of information about the current state of your SQL Server instance. They can be extremely helpful for debugging performance issues or understanding query behavior.

Example:

```
-- Find currently executing queries
SELECT
    r.session_id,
    r.status,
    r.command,
    t.text,
    r.cpu_time,
    r.total_elapsed_time
FROM
    sys.dm_exec_requests r
    CROSS APPLY sys.dm_exec_sql_text(r.sql_handle) t
WHERE
    r.session_id > 50; -- Exclude system sessions
```

13. Use the OUTPUT Clause

The OUTPUT clause can be very useful for debugging INSERT, UPDATE, and DELETE operations by allowing you to capture the affected rows.

Example:

```
DECLARE @DeletedOrders TABLE (
    OrderID INT,
    CustomerID INT,
    OrderDate DATE
);
```

```
DELETE FROM Orders
OUTPUT DELETED.OrderID, DELETED.CustomerID, DELETED.OrderDate
INTO @DeletedOrders
WHERE OrderDate < '2020-01-01';

-- Inspect the deleted orders
SELECT * FROM @DeletedOrders;
```

14. Use SET PARSEONLY ON

When you're writing complex dynamic SQL, you can use SET PARSEONLY ON to check for syntax errors without actually executing the query.

Example:

```
DECLARE @SQL NVARCHAR(MAX) = N'
SELECT CustomerID, FirstName, LastName
FROM Customers
WHERE City = @City';

SET PARSEONLY ON;
EXEC sp_executesql @SQL, N'@City NVARCHAR(50)', @City = 'London';
SET PARSEONLY OFF;
```

15. Use Database Snapshots

For debugging scenarios where you need to compare data before and after a set of operations, consider using database snapshots. This allows you to create a read-only, point-in-time copy of your database.

Example:

```
-- Create a snapshot
CREATE DATABASE YourDatabaseSnapshot ON
```

```
( NAME = YourDatabase_Data, FILENAME = 'C:
\YourDatabaseSnapshot.ss' )
AS SNAPSHOT OF YourDatabase;

-- Perform your operations on YourDatabase

-- Compare data
SELECT *
FROM YourDatabase.dbo.Customers
EXCEPT
SELECT *
FROM YourDatabaseSnapshot.dbo.Customers;

-- Clean up
DROP DATABASE YourDatabaseSnapshot;
```

By following these best practices, avoiding common pitfalls, and utilizing these de-bugging techniques, you can significantly improve the quality, maintainability, and performance of your T-SQL code. Remember that writing good T-SQL is not just about getting the correct results; it's also about creating code that is efficient, read-able, and easy to maintain over time.

Part 5: Advanced Topics and Case Studies

Chapter 15: Dynamic SQL

Dynamic SQL is a powerful feature in SQL Server that allows you to construct and execute SQL statements at runtime. This chapter explores the concept of dynamic SQL, its applications, benefits, and potential risks. We'll also discuss best practices and provide practical examples to help you leverage dynamic SQL effectively in your database programming.

Understanding Dynamic SQL

Dynamic SQL refers to the practice of generating SQL statements as strings and executing them programmatically. Unlike static SQL, where the structure of the query is known at compile-time, dynamic SQL allows you to create and modify SQL statements on-the-fly based on various conditions or user inputs.

Key Characteristics of Dynamic SQL:

1. **Flexibility**: Dynamic SQL enables you to create queries that adapt to changing requirements or user inputs.
2. **Runtime Generation**: SQL statements are constructed and executed at runtime rather than being predefined.
3. **String Manipulation**: Dynamic SQL involves manipulating strings to build SQL statements.

4. **Execution Methods**: Dynamic SQL can be executed using methods like `EXEC()` or `sp_executesql`.

When to Use Dynamic SQL

While static SQL is generally preferred for its simplicity and better performance, there are scenarios where dynamic SQL becomes necessary or advantageous:

1. **Unknown Object Names**: When table or column names are not known until runtime, dynamic SQL allows you to construct queries using these names dynamically.

2. **Varying Search Conditions**: For complex search interfaces where the number and type of search conditions can vary, dynamic SQL enables you to build WHERE clauses based on user input.

3. **Dynamic Sorting**: When the sort column or direction is determined at runtime, dynamic SQL can construct the appropriate ORDER BY clause.

4. **Conditional JOINs**: In cases where the tables to be joined are not known in advance, dynamic SQL allows you to build JOIN clauses dynamically.

5. **Schema Changes**: For applications that need to work with different database schemas, dynamic SQL provides the flexibility to adapt queries to the current schema.

6. **Dynamic Pivot Operations**: When the number of pivot columns is not known in advance, dynamic SQL can generate pivot queries based on the data.

7. **Administrative Tasks**: For database administration tasks that involve working with multiple databases or objects, dynamic SQL can automate operations across different objects.

How to Use Dynamic SQL

There are two primary methods for executing dynamic SQL in SQL Server:

1. **EXEC() or EXECUTE()**
2. **sp_executesql**

Using EXEC()

The EXEC() function is the simplest way to execute dynamic SQL. It takes a string containing the SQL statement as an argument.

```
DECLARE @sql NVARCHAR(MAX);
SET @sql = 'SELECT * FROM Customers WHERE Country = ''USA''';
EXEC(@sql);
```

Using sp_executesql

The sp_executesql stored procedure offers more advanced features, including support for parameterized queries, which can help prevent SQL injection.

```
DECLARE @sql NVARCHAR(MAX);
DECLARE @country NVARCHAR(50) = 'USA';

SET @sql = N'SELECT * FROM Customers WHERE Country = @CountryParam';
```

```
EXEC sp_executesql @sql, N'@CountryParam NVARCHAR(50)',
@CountryParam = @country;
```

Risks and Mitigations

While dynamic SQL offers flexibility, it also comes with potential risks, the most significant being SQL injection vulnerabilities.

SQL Injection

SQL injection is a security vulnerability that occurs when untrusted data is used to construct SQL statements. An attacker can manipulate the input to alter the intended behavior of the query, potentially gaining unauthorized access to sensitive data or performing malicious operations.

Consider the following vulnerable dynamic SQL:

```
DECLARE @sql NVARCHAR(MAX);
DECLARE @userInput NVARCHAR(50) = 'USA'; -- This could be user
input

SET @sql = 'SELECT * FROM Customers WHERE Country = ''' +
@userInput + '''';
EXEC(@sql);
```

If an attacker provides the input 'USA' OR 1=1--, the resulting query would be:

```
SELECT * FROM Customers WHERE Country = 'USA' OR 1=1--'
```

This query would return all customers, regardless of their country, due to the injected OR 1=1 condition.

Mitigations

To mitigate the risk of SQL injection and other security vulnerabilities associated with dynamic SQL, consider the following best practices:

1. **Use Parameterized Queries**: Whenever possible, use parameterized queries with `sp_executesql` instead of concatenating strings.

```
DECLARE @sql NVARCHAR(MAX);
DECLARE @country NVARCHAR(50) = 'USA';

SET @sql = N'SELECT * FROM Customers WHERE Country =
@CountryParam';

EXEC sp_executesql @sql, N'@CountryParam NVARCHAR(50)',
@CountryParam = @country;
```

2. **Input Validation**: Always validate and sanitize user inputs before using them in dynamic SQL.

3. **Least Privilege**: Execute dynamic SQL under accounts with minimal necessary permissions.

4. **Use QUOTENAME() for Object Names**: When dynamically including object names (e.g., table names), use the `QUOTENAME()` function to properly escape them.

```
DECLARE @tableName NVARCHAR(128) = 'Customers';
DECLARE @sql NVARCHAR(MAX);

SET @sql = 'SELECT * FROM ' + QUOTENAME(@tableName);
EXEC(@sql);
```

5. **Avoid Direct User Input**: Whenever possible, use predefined lists or mappings instead of direct user input for constructing SQL statements.

6. **Use sp_executesql for Better Performance**: `sp_executesql` allows for query plan reuse, which can improve performance for frequently executed dynamic SQL.
7. **Implement Error Handling**: Proper error handling can prevent exposing sensitive information in error messages.

Practical Examples of Dynamic SQL

Let's explore some practical examples of dynamic SQL to illustrate its power and flexibility.

Example 1: Dynamic Sorting

Suppose you have a table of products, and you want to allow users to sort the results by different columns dynamically.

```
CREATE PROCEDURE dbo.GetSortedProducts
    @SortColumn NVARCHAR(50),
    @SortDirection NVARCHAR(4)
AS
BEGIN
    DECLARE @sql NVARCHAR(MAX);

    SET @sql = N'SELECT ProductID, ProductName, UnitPrice,
UnitsInStock
                FROM Products
                ORDER BY ' + QUOTENAME(@SortColumn) +
                CASE WHEN @SortDirection = 'DESC' THEN ' DESC'
ELSE ' ASC' END;

    EXEC sp_executesql @sql;
END;
```

You can then call this procedure with different sort options:

```
EXEC dbo.GetSortedProducts @SortColumn = 'UnitPrice',
@SortDirection = 'DESC';
```

Example 2: Dynamic Search Conditions

This example demonstrates how to build a dynamic search query based on multiple optional search criteria.

```
CREATE PROCEDURE dbo.SearchCustomers
    @CompanyName NVARCHAR(40) = NULL,
    @Country NVARCHAR(15) = NULL,
    @City NVARCHAR(15) = NULL
AS
BEGIN
    DECLARE @sql NVARCHAR(MAX);
    DECLARE @params NVARCHAR(MAX);

    SET @sql = N'SELECT CustomerID, CompanyName, Country, City
                FROM Customers
                WHERE 1 = 1';

    IF @CompanyName IS NOT NULL
        SET @sql = @sql + N' AND CompanyName LIKE @CompanyName +
''%''';

    IF @Country IS NOT NULL
        SET @sql = @sql + N' AND Country = @Country';

    IF @City IS NOT NULL
        SET @sql = @sql + N' AND City = @City';

    SET @params = N'@CompanyName NVARCHAR(40), @Country
NVARCHAR(15), @City NVARCHAR(15)';

    EXEC sp_executesql @sql, @params, @CompanyName, @Country,
@City;
```

```
END;
```

You can then call this procedure with different search criteria:

```
EXEC dbo.SearchCustomers @CompanyName = 'A', @Country = 'USA';
```

Example 3: Dynamic Pivot

This example shows how to create a dynamic pivot query to summarize sales by product and year.

```
CREATE PROCEDURE dbo.GetYearlySalesPivot
AS
BEGIN
    DECLARE @columns NVARCHAR(MAX) = '';
    DECLARE @sql NVARCHAR(MAX);

    -- Generate the column names dynamically
    SELECT @columns += ', [' + CAST(Year AS NVARCHAR(4)) + ']'
    FROM (SELECT DISTINCT YEAR(OrderDate) AS Year FROM Orders) AS
Years
    ORDER BY Year;

    SET @columns = STUFF(@columns, 1, 2, '');

    SET @sql = N'
    SELECT ProductName, ' + @columns + '
    FROM
    (
        SELECT p.ProductName,
                YEAR(o.OrderDate) AS Year,
                SUM(od.Quantity * od.UnitPrice) AS Sales
        FROM Products p
        JOIN [Order Details] od ON p.ProductID = od.ProductID
        JOIN Orders o ON od.OrderID = o.OrderID
        GROUP BY p.ProductName, YEAR(o.OrderDate)
    ) AS SourceData
    PIVOT
    (
```

```
        SUM(Sales)
        FOR Year IN (' + @columns + ')
    ) AS PivotTable
    ORDER BY ProductName;';

    EXEC sp_executesql @sql;
END;
```

This procedure will generate a pivot table showing sales for each product across different years, with the years as columns.

Example 4: Dynamic Schema Changes

This example demonstrates how to use dynamic SQL to add a new column to multiple tables with a similar naming convention.

```
CREATE PROCEDURE dbo.AddAuditColumnToTables
    @ColumnName NVARCHAR(128),
    @ColumnDefinition NVARCHAR(MAX)
AS
BEGIN
    DECLARE @sql NVARCHAR(MAX);
    DECLARE @tableName NVARCHAR(128);

    DECLARE table_cursor CURSOR FOR
    SELECT name
    FROM sys.tables
    WHERE name LIKE 'Audit_%';

    OPEN table_cursor;
    FETCH NEXT FROM table_cursor INTO @tableName;

    WHILE @@FETCH_STATUS = 0
    BEGIN
        SET @sql = N'ALTER TABLE ' + QUOTENAME(@tableName) +
                   N' ADD ' + QUOTENAME(@ColumnName) + N' ' +
@ColumnDefinition;

        EXEC sp_executesql @sql;
```

```
        FETCH NEXT FROM table_cursor INTO @tableName;
    END;

    CLOSE table_cursor;
    DEALLOCATE table_cursor;
END;
```

You can then call this procedure to add an audit column to all tables prefixed with "Audit_":

```
EXEC dbo.AddAuditColumnToTables @ColumnName = 'LastModifiedDate',
@ColumnDefinition = 'DATETIME DEFAULT GETDATE()';
```

Best Practices for Dynamic SQL

To ensure optimal performance, security, and maintainability when using dynamic SQL, consider the following best practices:

1. **Use Parameters**: Always use parameterized queries with `sp_executesql` when dealing with user inputs or variable data.
2. **Avoid String Concatenation**: Minimize string concatenation when building SQL statements to reduce the risk of SQL injection.
3. **Validate Inputs**: Implement thorough input validation, especially for values used in dynamic object names or SQL keywords.
4. **Use QUOTENAME() for Identifiers**: Always use `QUOTENAME()` when incorporating variable object names (tables, columns, etc.) into your dynamic SQL.
5. **Implement Error Handling**: Use proper error handling techniques to catch and manage any errors that may occur during the execution of dynamic SQL.

6. **Document Thoroughly**: Provide clear comments and documentation for dynamic SQL code, explaining the purpose and any potential risks.

7. **Test Extensively**: Thoroughly test dynamic SQL with various inputs and edge cases to ensure it behaves as expected.

8. **Monitor Performance**: Keep an eye on the performance of dynamic SQL queries, as they may not benefit from the same query plan optimizations as static SQL.

9. **Use sp_executesql for Frequent Execution**: For frequently executed dynamic SQL, use `sp_executesql` to take advantage of query plan caching.

10. **Limit Permissions**: Execute dynamic SQL under accounts with the minimum necessary permissions to reduce the potential impact of SQL injection attacks.

Conclusion

Dynamic SQL is a powerful tool in the SQL Server developer's toolkit, offering flexibility and adaptability in database programming. While it comes with inherent risks, particularly around security, these can be mitigated through careful implementation and adherence to best practices.

By understanding when and how to use dynamic SQL, along with the associated risks and mitigation strategies, you can leverage its power to create more flexible and dynamic database applications. The practical examples provided in this chapter serve as a starting point for exploring the capabilities of dynamic SQL in various scenarios.

Remember that while dynamic SQL offers solutions to complex problems, it should be used judiciously. Always consider whether a static SQL approach might be sufficient before resorting to dynamic SQL, and when you do use it, prioritize security and performance in your implementation.

Chapter 16: Working with Large Datasets

Bulk Operations with BULK INSERT

When dealing with large datasets, efficient data loading becomes crucial. SQL Server provides the BULK INSERT statement, which allows for rapid insertion of data from external files into database tables. This method is significantly faster than traditional INSERT statements, especially when handling millions of rows.

Syntax and Basic Usage

The basic syntax for BULK INSERT is as follows:

```
BULK INSERT target_table
FROM 'data_file_path'
WITH (
    FIELDTERMINATOR = ',',
    ROWTERMINATOR = '\n',
    FIRSTROW = 2
);
```

- `target_table`: The table where data will be inserted.
- `data_file_path`: The full path to the source file.
- `FIELDTERMINATOR`: Specifies the character that separates columns in the file.

- ROWTERMINATOR: Indicates the end of each row in the file.
- FIRSTROW: Specifies which row to start reading from (useful for skipping headers).

Advanced Options

BULK INSERT offers numerous options to customize the import process:

1. **DATAFILETYPE**: Specifies the file format (e.g., 'char' for text files, 'native' for native SQL Server format).
2. **MAXERRORS**: Sets the maximum number of errors allowed before the operation is aborted.
3. **BATCHSIZE**: Defines the number of rows in each batch of the bulk insert operation.
4. **CHECK_CONSTRAINTS**: Determines whether constraints are checked during the bulk insert.
5. **TABLOCK**: Specifies whether to acquire a table-level lock for the duration of the bulk insert.

Example with advanced options:

```
BULK INSERT Customers
FROM 'C:\Data\customers.csv'
WITH (
    DATAFILETYPE = 'char',
    FIELDTERMINATOR = ',',
    ROWTERMINATOR = '\n',
    MAXERRORS = 10,
    BATCHSIZE = 1000,
    CHECK_CONSTRAINTS = ON,
    TABLOCK
);
```

Performance Considerations

To maximize BULK INSERT performance:

1. Use a clustered index on the target table if possible.
2. Disable or drop non-clustered indexes before the operation and re-build them afterward.
3. Set the recovery model to BULK_LOGGED or SIMPLE during the operation.
4. Use TABLOCK for exclusive access to the table during the insert.

Error Handling and Logging

BULK INSERT provides options for handling and logging errors:

```
BULK INSERT Customers
FROM 'C:\Data\customers.csv'
WITH (
    FIELDTERMINATOR = ',',
    ROWTERMINATOR = '\n',
    MAXERRORS = 100,
    ERRORFILE = 'C:\Logs\bulk_insert_errors.log'
);
```

This configuration allows up to 100 errors before aborting and logs errors to the specified file.

Partitioning Tables and Queries

Table partitioning is a powerful feature in SQL Server that allows you to divide large tables into smaller, more manageable pieces called partitions. This can significantly improve query performance, data manageability, and maintenance operations.

Partition Function

The partition function defines how the table will be divided. It specifies the boundaries for the partitions based on a column value.

Example of creating a partition function:

```
CREATE PARTITION FUNCTION MyDateRangeFunction (datetime)
AS RANGE RIGHT FOR VALUES (
    '2021-01-01', '2022-01-01', '2023-01-01'
);
```

This creates a partition function that will divide data into four partitions based on date ranges.

Partition Scheme

The partition scheme maps the partitions defined by the partition function to filegroups.

Example of creating a partition scheme:

```
CREATE PARTITION SCHEME MyDateRangeScheme
AS PARTITION MyDateRangeFunction
TO (FG1, FG2, FG3, FG4);
```

This scheme maps each partition to a separate filegroup.

Creating a Partitioned Table

To create a partitioned table, you use the partition scheme in the CREATE TABLE statement:

```
CREATE TABLE Sales (
    SaleID int IDENTITY(1,1),
    SaleDate datetime,
    Amount decimal(10,2)
) ON MyDateRangeScheme(SaleDate);
```

This creates a Sales table partitioned by SaleDate using the previously defined scheme.

Querying Partitioned Tables

When querying partitioned tables, SQL Server can use partition elimination to improve performance by only scanning relevant partitions.

Example query benefiting from partition elimination:

```
SELECT * FROM Sales
WHERE SaleDate BETWEEN '2022-06-01' AND '2022-12-31';
```

SQL Server will only scan the partition(s) containing data for the second half of 2022.

Partition Switching

Partition switching is a powerful feature that allows you to move data in and out of a partitioned table almost instantaneously. This is particularly useful for loading new data or archiving old data.

Example of switching out a partition:

```
-- Create a staging table with the same schema as the Sales table
CREATE TABLE SalesStaging (
    SaleID int IDENTITY(1,1),
    SaleDate datetime,
    Amount decimal(10,2)
) ON FG5;

-- Switch out the oldest partition to the staging table
ALTER TABLE Sales SWITCH PARTITION 1 TO SalesStaging;
```

This moves all data from the oldest partition of the Sales table to the SalesStaging table.

Sliding Window Scenario

A common use case for partitioning is the sliding window scenario, where you maintain a rolling window of data in your table.

Example of implementing a sliding window:

```
-- Step 1: Prepare a new empty partition
ALTER PARTITION SCHEME MyDateRangeScheme
NEXT USED FG5;

ALTER PARTITION FUNCTION MyDateRangeFunction()
SPLIT RANGE ('2024-01-01');

-- Step 2: Switch out the oldest partition
ALTER TABLE Sales SWITCH PARTITION 1 TO SalesArchive;

-- Step 3: Merge the now-empty partition
ALTER PARTITION FUNCTION MyDateRangeFunction()
MERGE RANGE ('2021-01-01');
```

This process adds a new partition for future data, archives the oldest data, and removes the empty partition.

Considerations and Best Practices

1. Choose the partitioning column carefully - it should align with common query patterns.
2. Balance the number of partitions - too many can lead to management overhead.
3. Regularly maintain statistics on partitioned tables.
4. Be aware of the impact on indexes, especially non-aligned indexes.
5. Test thoroughly to ensure partitioning benefits your specific workload.

Working with Temp Tables and Table Variables

Temporary tables and table variables are powerful tools in T-SQL for storing intermediate results or for breaking down complex queries into more manageable parts.

Temporary Tables

Temporary tables are created in the tempdb database and are automatically dropped when they go out of scope.

Local Temporary Tables

Local temporary tables are prefixed with a single hash (#) and are only visible to the current connection.

Example of creating and using a local temporary table:

```
CREATE TABLE #TempSales (
    SaleID int,
    SaleDate date,
    Amount decimal(10,2)
);

INSERT INTO #TempSales (SaleID, SaleDate, Amount)
SELECT SaleID, SaleDate, Amount
FROM Sales
WHERE SaleDate >= DATEADD(month, -1, GETDATE());

-- Use the temp table in subsequent queries
SELECT SUM(Amount) AS TotalSales
FROM #TempSales;
```

Global Temporary Tables

Global temporary tables are prefixed with two hashes (##) and are visible to all connections.

Example of a global temporary table:

```
CREATE TABLE ##GlobalTempSales (
    SaleID int,
    SaleDate date,
    Amount decimal(10,2)
);

-- This table can be accessed by other sessions
```

Global temporary tables persist until the session that created them ends and all other sessions stop referencing them.

Table Variables

Table variables are declared using the @variable syntax and have a scope limited to the batch, function, or stored procedure in which they are declared.

Example of using a table variable:

```
DECLARE @RecentSales TABLE (
    SaleID int,
    SaleDate date,
    Amount decimal(10,2)
);

INSERT INTO @RecentSales (SaleID, SaleDate, Amount)
SELECT SaleID, SaleDate, Amount
FROM Sales
WHERE SaleDate >= DATEADD(day, -7, GETDATE());

-- Use the table variable
SELECT AVG(Amount) AS AverageRecentSale
FROM @RecentSales;
```

Comparing Temp Tables and Table Variables

1. **Scope**:

   - Temp tables: Session or connection-wide
   - Table variables: Limited to the batch or procedure

2. **Storage**:

   - Temp tables: Stored in tempdb
   - Table variables: Memory optimized (for small datasets)

3. **Statistics**:

   - Temp tables: Maintain statistics

- Table variables: Do not maintain statistics

4. **Transactions**:

- Temp tables: Can be part of a transaction
- Table variables: Cannot be part of a transaction (except in certain memory-optimized scenarios)

5. **Performance**:

- Temp tables: Generally better for large datasets
- Table variables: Can be more efficient for small datasets

Best Practices and Usage Scenarios

1. Use temp tables for larger datasets or when you need to index the data.
2. Prefer table variables for small datasets or when you need to pass table-valued parameters.
3. Consider using temp tables when you need to update or delete rows frequently.
4. Use global temp tables sparingly, as they can lead to naming conflicts and security issues.
5. Drop temp tables explicitly when no longer needed to free up resources in tempdb.

Example of a complex scenario using both temp tables and table variables:

```
-- Create a temp table for intermediate results
```

```sql
CREATE TABLE #LargeSales (
    SaleID int,
    CustomerID int,
    SaleDate date,
    Amount decimal(10,2)
);

-- Populate the temp table
INSERT INTO #LargeSales (SaleID, CustomerID, SaleDate, Amount)
SELECT SaleID, CustomerID, SaleDate, Amount
FROM Sales
WHERE Amount > 10000;

-- Create an indexed view on the temp table
CREATE UNIQUE CLUSTERED INDEX IX_LargeSales ON #LargeSales
(SaleID);

-- Declare a table variable for customer categorization
DECLARE @CustomerCategories TABLE (
    CustomerID int,
    Category varchar(20)
);

-- Populate the table variable
INSERT INTO @CustomerCategories (CustomerID, Category)
SELECT CustomerID,
       CASE
            WHEN COUNT(*) > 5 THEN 'VIP'
            WHEN COUNT(*) > 2 THEN 'Regular'
            ELSE 'Occasional'
       END AS Category
FROM #LargeSales
GROUP BY CustomerID;

-- Use both the temp table and table variable in a final query
SELECT ls.SaleID, ls.CustomerID, ls.SaleDate, ls.Amount,
cc.Category
FROM #LargeSales ls
JOIN @CustomerCategories cc ON ls.CustomerID = cc.CustomerID
ORDER BY ls.Amount DESC;

-- Clean up
```

```
DROP TABLE #LargeSales;
```

This example demonstrates how temp tables and table variables can be used together to break down a complex analysis into more manageable steps.

Optimizing Large Dataset Operations

When working with large datasets, it's crucial to optimize your operations for performance. Here are some additional techniques and considerations:

Batch Processing

When inserting or updating large amounts of data, use batch processing to reduce the number of transactions and improve overall performance.

Example of batch inserting:

```sql
CREATE TABLE #TempBatch (ID int, Value varchar(50));

-- Populate the temp table with a large dataset

DECLARE @BatchSize int = 1000;
DECLARE @TotalRows int = (SELECT COUNT(*) FROM #TempBatch);
DECLARE @BatchNumber int = 0;

WHILE @BatchNumber * @BatchSize < @TotalRows
BEGIN
    INSERT INTO TargetTable (ID, Value)
    SELECT ID, Value
    FROM #TempBatch
    ORDER BY ID
    OFFSET @BatchNumber * @BatchSize ROWS
    FETCH NEXT @BatchSize ROWS ONLY;

    SET @BatchNumber = @BatchNumber + 1;
```

END

Indexing Strategies

Proper indexing is crucial for large dataset performance. Consider the following:

1. Use clustered indexes on frequently queried columns.
2. Create non-clustered indexes for columns often used in WHERE clauses or joins.
3. Use filtered indexes for specific subsets of data.

Example of creating a filtered index:

```
CREATE NONCLUSTERED INDEX IX_LargeAmountSales
ON Sales (SaleDate)
INCLUDE (Amount)
WHERE Amount > 10000;
```

Parallel Query Execution

SQL Server can execute queries in parallel to improve performance on large datasets. Ensure your server is configured to allow parallel execution and that your queries are written to take advantage of it.

Example of forcing parallel execution:

```
SELECT /*+ PARALLEL(8) */ *
FROM LargeTable
WHERE SomeColumn > 1000;
```

This hint suggests SQL Server use up to 8 parallel threads for the query.

Columnstore Indexes

For data warehouse scenarios with large tables, columnstore indexes can dramatically improve query performance and data compression.

Example of creating a columnstore index:

```
CREATE CLUSTERED COLUMNSTORE INDEX CCI_Sales
ON Sales;
```

Memory-Optimized Tables

For extremely high-performance scenarios, consider using memory-optimized tables, which store data entirely in memory.

Example of creating a memory-optimized table:

```
CREATE TABLE dbo.MemOptSales
(
    SaleID int IDENTITY PRIMARY KEY NONCLUSTERED,
    SaleDate datetime2 NOT NULL,
    Amount decimal(10,2) NOT NULL
)
WITH (MEMORY_OPTIMIZED = ON, DURABILITY = SCHEMA_AND_DATA);
```

Query Optimization Techniques

1. **Use SET NOCOUNT ON**: This reduces network traffic by suppressing messages about the number of rows affected.
2. **Avoid SELECT ***: Always specify only the columns you need.
3. **Use EXISTS instead of IN** for better performance with subqueries.
4. **Consider using UNION ALL instead of UNION** when duplicate rows are acceptable.

5. **Use table-valued parameters** for passing multiple rows to stored procedures.

Example of a table-valued parameter:

```sql
-- Create a user-defined table type
CREATE TYPE SalesTableType AS TABLE
(
    SaleDate datetime2,
    Amount decimal(10,2)
);
GO

-- Create a stored procedure that uses the table-valued parameter
CREATE PROCEDURE BulkInsertSales
    @SalesData SalesTableType READONLY
AS
BEGIN
    INSERT INTO Sales (SaleDate, Amount)
    SELECT SaleDate, Amount FROM @SalesData;
END
GO

-- Use the stored procedure
DECLARE @SalesToInsert SalesTableType;

INSERT INTO @SalesToInsert (SaleDate, Amount)
VALUES ('2023-01-01', 1000), ('2023-01-02', 1500), ('2023-01-03',
2000);

EXEC BulkInsertSales @SalesToInsert;
```

Monitoring and Tuning

Regular monitoring and tuning are essential when working with large datasets:

1. Use Dynamic Management Views (DMVs) to identify performance bottlenecks.
2. Regularly update statistics to ensure the query optimizer has accurate information.
3. Use Query Store to track query performance over time and identify regressions.

Example of using a DMV to find expensive queries:

```
SELECT TOP 10
    qs.total_elapsed_time / qs.execution_count AS
avg_elapsed_time,
    qs.total_logical_reads / qs.execution_count AS
avg_logical_reads,
    qs.execution_count,
    SUBSTRING(qt.text, (qs.statement_start_offset/2)+1,
        ((CASE qs.statement_end_offset
            WHEN -1 THEN DATALENGTH(qt.text)
            ELSE qs.statement_end_offset
        END - qs.statement_start_offset)/2)+1) AS query_text
FROM sys.dm_exec_query_stats qs
CROSS APPLY sys.dm_exec_sql_text(qs.sql_handle) qt
ORDER BY qs.total_elapsed_time / qs.execution_count DESC;
```

Conclusion

Working with large datasets in SQL Server requires a combination of proper database design, efficient querying techniques, and appropriate use of SQL Server features. By leveraging bulk operations, table partitioning, and temporary storage solutions, you can significantly improve the performance and manageability of your large-scale data operations.

Remember that the best approach often depends on your specific use case and data patterns. Always test different strategies with representative data volumes to determine the most effective solution for your particular scenario. Regularly monitor and tune your system to ensure it continues to perform optimally as your data grows and query patterns evolve.

Chapter 17: Real-World Applications

In this chapter, we'll explore practical applications of T-SQL in real-world scenarios. We'll focus on three key areas: building a reporting system, data validation and cleanup, and task automation using scheduled jobs and SQL Agent. These skills are essential for database administrators and developers working with SQL Server in production environments.

Building a Reporting System with T-SQL

Reporting is a crucial aspect of data management and business intelligence. T-SQL provides powerful tools for creating efficient and effective reporting systems. Let's dive into the process of building a comprehensive reporting system using T-SQL.

1. Designing the Report Structure

Before writing any T-SQL code, it's essential to design the structure of your reports. Consider the following aspects:

- Report types (e.g., financial, operational, analytical)
- Data sources and tables required
- Frequency of report generation
- Target audience and their specific needs

- Desired output format (e.g., tables, charts, graphs)

2. Creating Views for Report Data

Views are an excellent way to encapsulate complex queries and provide a consistent data source for reports. Here's an example of creating a view for a sales report:

```
CREATE VIEW vw_SalesReport AS
SELECT
    o.OrderID,
    c.CustomerName,
    p.ProductName,
    od.Quantity,
    od.UnitPrice,
    (od.Quantity * od.UnitPrice) AS TotalAmount,
    o.OrderDate
FROM
    Orders o
    INNER JOIN Customers c ON o.CustomerID = c.CustomerID
    INNER JOIN OrderDetails od ON o.OrderID = od.OrderID
    INNER JOIN Products p ON od.ProductID = p.ProductID;
```

This view combines data from multiple tables to provide a comprehensive overview of sales information.

3. Implementing Stored Procedures for Report Generation

Stored procedures offer a way to encapsulate complex logic and improve performance. Here's an example of a stored procedure that generates a monthly sales report:

```
CREATE PROCEDURE sp_GenerateMonthlySalesReport
    @Year INT,
    @Month INT
```

```
AS
BEGIN
    SET NOCOUNT ON;

    SELECT
        YEAR(OrderDate) AS Year,
        MONTH(OrderDate) AS Month,
        SUM(TotalAmount) AS TotalSales,
        COUNT(DISTINCT OrderID) AS TotalOrders,
        AVG(TotalAmount) AS AverageOrderValue
    FROM
        vw_SalesReport
    WHERE
        YEAR(OrderDate) = @Year
        AND MONTH(OrderDate) = @Month
    GROUP BY
        YEAR(OrderDate), MONTH(OrderDate);
END;
```

To execute this stored procedure and generate a report for a specific month:

```
EXEC sp_GenerateMonthlySalesReport @Year = 2023, @Month = 5;
```

4. Implementing Parameterized Reports

Parameterized reports allow users to customize the output based on specific criteria. Here's an example of a stored procedure that generates a sales report for a specific date range and product category:

```
CREATE PROCEDURE sp_GenerateCustomSalesReport
    @StartDate DATE,
    @EndDate DATE,
    @CategoryID INT = NULL
AS
BEGIN
    SET NOCOUNT ON;

    SELECT
```

```sql
        c.CategoryName,
        p.ProductName,
        SUM(od.Quantity) AS TotalQuantitySold,
        SUM(od.Quantity * od.UnitPrice) AS TotalRevenue
    FROM
        Orders o
        INNER JOIN OrderDetails od ON o.OrderID = od.OrderID
        INNER JOIN Products p ON od.ProductID = p.ProductID
        INNER JOIN Categories c ON p.CategoryID = c.CategoryID
    WHERE
        o.OrderDate BETWEEN @StartDate AND @EndDate
        AND (@CategoryID IS NULL OR c.CategoryID = @CategoryID)
    GROUP BY
        c.CategoryName, p.ProductName
    ORDER BY
        c.CategoryName, TotalRevenue DESC;
END;
```

To execute this stored procedure and generate a custom report:

```sql
EXEC sp_GenerateCustomSalesReport
    @StartDate = '2023-01-01',
    @EndDate = '2023-12-31',
    @CategoryID = 1;
```

5. Implementing Report Caching

For reports that are computationally expensive or frequently accessed, implementing a caching mechanism can significantly improve performance. Here's an example of how to implement report caching using a table:

```sql
-- Create a table to store cached reports
CREATE TABLE CachedReports (
    ReportID INT IDENTITY(1,1) PRIMARY KEY,
    ReportName NVARCHAR(100),
    ReportParameters NVARCHAR(MAX),
    ReportData NVARCHAR(MAX),
    CacheDateTime DATETIME
```

```sql
);

-- Create a stored procedure to get or generate a cached report
CREATE PROCEDURE sp_GetCachedReport
    @ReportName NVARCHAR(100),
    @ReportParameters NVARCHAR(MAX),
    @CacheExpirationMinutes INT = 60
AS
BEGIN
    SET NOCOUNT ON;

    DECLARE @CachedReport NVARCHAR(MAX);
    DECLARE @CacheDateTime DATETIME;

    -- Check if a cached version of the report exists
    SELECT TOP 1
        @CachedReport = ReportData,
        @CacheDateTime = CacheDateTime
    FROM
        CachedReports
    WHERE
        ReportName = @ReportName
        AND ReportParameters = @ReportParameters
    ORDER BY
        CacheDateTime DESC;

    -- If the cached report exists and is not expired, return it
    IF @CachedReport IS NOT NULL AND DATEDIFF(MINUTE,
@CacheDateTime, GETDATE()) <= @CacheExpirationMinutes
    BEGIN
        SELECT @CachedReport AS ReportData;
        RETURN;
    END

    -- Generate the report data (replace this with your actual
report generation logic)
    DECLARE @ReportData NVARCHAR(MAX);
    SET @ReportData = 'Generated report data for ' + @ReportName
+ ' with parameters: ' + @ReportParameters;

    -- Cache the newly generated report
```

```
    INSERT INTO CachedReports (ReportName, ReportParameters,
ReportData, CacheDateTime)
    VALUES (@ReportName, @ReportParameters, @ReportData,
GETDATE());

    -- Return the generated report data
    SELECT @ReportData AS ReportData;
END;
```

To use this cached report system:

```
EXEC sp_GetCachedReport
    @ReportName = 'MonthlySalesReport',
    @ReportParameters = '{"Year": 2023, "Month": 5}',
    @CacheExpirationMinutes = 120;
```

6. Implementing Report Scheduling

To automate report generation and distribution, you can use SQL Server Agent jobs. Here's an example of how to create a job that generates and emails a monthly sales report:

```
-- Create a job to generate and email the monthly sales report
USE msdb;
GO

-- Create the job
EXEC dbo.sp_add_job
    @job_name = N'Generate Monthly Sales Report',
    @enabled = 1,
    @description = N'Generates and emails the monthly sales
report';

-- Add a job step to generate the report
EXEC dbo.sp_add_jobstep
    @job_name = N'Generate Monthly Sales Report',
    @step_name = N'Generate Report',
    @subsystem = N'TSQL',
```

```
    @command = N'
        DECLARE @Year INT = YEAR(GETDATE());
        DECLARE @Month INT = MONTH(GETDATE()) - 1;

        IF @Month = 0
        BEGIN
            SET @Year = @Year - 1;
            SET @Month = 12;
        END

        EXEC sp_GenerateMonthlySalesReport @Year = @Year, @Month
= @Month;
    ';

-- Add a job step to email the report
EXEC dbo.sp_add_jobstep
    @job_name = N'Generate Monthly Sales Report',
    @step_name = N'Email Report',
    @subsystem = N'TSQL',
    @command = N'
        EXEC msdb.dbo.sp_send_dbmail
            @profile_name = ''YourMailProfile'',
            @recipients = ''recipient@example.com'',
            @subject = ''Monthly Sales Report'',
            @body = ''Please find attached the monthly sales
report.'',
            @query = ''EXEC sp_GenerateMonthlySalesReport @Year =
YEAR(GETDATE()), @Month = MONTH(GETDATE()) - 1;'',
            @attach_query_result_as_file = 1,
            @query_attachment_filename =
''MonthlySalesReport.csv'',
            @query_result_header = 1,
            @query_result_width = 32767,
            @query_result_separator = '','''
    ';

-- Set the job schedule (run on the first day of each month)
EXEC dbo.sp_add_schedule
    @schedule_name = N'Monthly Schedule',
    @freq_type = 16,
    @freq_interval = 1,
    @active_start_time = 010000;
```

```
-- Attach the schedule to the job
EXEC sp_attach_schedule
    @job_name = N'Generate Monthly Sales Report',
    @schedule_name = N'Monthly Schedule';
```

This job will run on the first day of each month, generate the previous month's sales report, and email it to the specified recipient.

Data Validation and Cleanup with T-SQL

Data quality is crucial for accurate reporting and analysis. T-SQL provides various tools and techniques for validating and cleaning up data. Let's explore some common scenarios and their solutions.

1. Identifying and Handling Duplicate Data

Duplicate data can skew analysis and reporting. Here's how to identify and remove duplicates:

```
-- Identify duplicate records
WITH DuplicateCTE AS (
    SELECT
        Column1, Column2, Column3,
        ROW_NUMBER() OVER (
            PARTITION BY Column1, Column2, Column3
            ORDER BY (SELECT NULL)
        ) AS RowNum
    FROM
        YourTable
)
SELECT *
FROM DuplicateCTE
```

```
WHERE RowNum > 1;

-- Remove duplicate records
WITH DuplicateCTE AS (
    SELECT
        Column1, Column2, Column3,
        ROW_NUMBER() OVER (
            PARTITION BY Column1, Column2, Column3
            ORDER BY (SELECT NULL)
        ) AS RowNum
    FROM
        YourTable
)
DELETE FROM DuplicateCTE
WHERE RowNum > 1;
```

2. Handling NULL Values

NULL values can cause issues in calculations and reporting. Here's how to handle them:

```
-- Replace NULL values with a default value
UPDATE YourTable
SET Column1 = ISNULL(Column1, 'Default Value')
WHERE Column1 IS NULL;

-- Use COALESCE to handle multiple potential NULL values
SELECT
    COALESCE(Column1, Column2, Column3, 'Default Value') AS
Result
FROM
    YourTable;

-- Exclude NULL values from calculations
SELECT
    AVG(CASE WHEN Column1 IS NOT NULL THEN Column1 END) AS
AverageValue
FROM
```

```
YourTable;
```

3. Data Type Conversion and Validation

Ensuring data is in the correct format is essential for accurate processing:

```
-- Convert string to date
UPDATE YourTable
SET DateColumn = TRY_CONVERT(DATE, StringDateColumn)
WHERE ISDATE(StringDateColumn) = 1;

-- Validate email addresses
UPDATE YourTable
SET IsValidEmail = CASE
    WHEN EmailColumn LIKE '%_@__%.__%'
        AND EmailColumn NOT LIKE '%@%@%'
        AND EmailColumn NOT LIKE '%..%'
        AND LEN(EmailColumn) - LEN(REPLACE(EmailColumn, '@', ''))
= 1
    THEN 1
    ELSE 0
END;

-- Validate phone numbers (assuming a specific format)
UPDATE YourTable
SET IsValidPhone = CASE
    WHEN PhoneColumn LIKE '[0-9][0-9][0-9]-[0-9][0-9][0-9]-[0-9]
[0-9][0-9][0-9]'
    THEN 1
    ELSE 0
END;
```

4. Handling Outliers and Anomalies

Outliers can significantly impact analysis. Here's how to identify and handle them:

```
-- Identify outliers using the Interquartile Range (IQR) method
```

```sql
WITH StatsCTE AS (
    SELECT
        AVG(NumericColumn) AS AvgValue,
        STDEV(NumericColumn) AS StdDevValue,
        PERCENTILE_CONT(0.25) WITHIN GROUP (ORDER BY
NumericColumn) OVER () AS Q1,
        PERCENTILE_CONT(0.75) WITHIN GROUP (ORDER BY
NumericColumn) OVER () AS Q3
    FROM
        YourTable
)
SELECT
    t.*
FROM
    YourTable t
    CROSS JOIN StatsCTE s
WHERE
    t.NumericColumn < (s.Q1 - 1.5 * (s.Q3 - s.Q1))
    OR t.NumericColumn > (s.Q3 + 1.5 * (s.Q3 - s.Q1));

-- Cap outliers at a specific percentile
WITH PercentileCTE AS (
    SELECT
        NumericColumn,
        PERCENTILE_CONT(0.01) WITHIN GROUP (ORDER BY
NumericColumn) OVER () AS LowerBound,
        PERCENTILE_CONT(0.99) WITHIN GROUP (ORDER BY
NumericColumn) OVER () AS UpperBound
    FROM
        YourTable
)
UPDATE p
SET NumericColumn = CASE
    WHEN p.NumericColumn < p.LowerBound THEN p.LowerBound
    WHEN p.NumericColumn > p.UpperBound THEN p.UpperBound
    ELSE p.NumericColumn
END
FROM
    YourTable t
    INNER JOIN PercentileCTE p ON t.ID = p.ID;
```

5. Data Consistency and Referential Integrity

Maintaining data consistency across related tables is crucial:

```sql
-- Identify orphaned records
SELECT c.*
FROM ChildTable c
LEFT JOIN ParentTable p ON c.ParentID = p.ID
WHERE p.ID IS NULL;

-- Delete orphaned records
DELETE c
FROM ChildTable c
LEFT JOIN ParentTable p ON c.ParentID = p.ID
WHERE p.ID IS NULL;

-- Ensure consistent categorization
UPDATE p
SET p.CategoryName = c.CategoryName
FROM ProductTable p
INNER JOIN CategoryTable c ON p.CategoryID = c.CategoryID
WHERE p.CategoryName <> c.CategoryName;
```

6. Data Enrichment and Standardization

Enriching and standardizing data can improve its quality and usefulness:

```sql
-- Standardize address formatting
UPDATE CustomerTable
SET
    Address = UPPER(LTRIM(RTRIM(Address))),
    City = UPPER(LTRIM(RTRIM(City))),
    State = UPPER(LTRIM(RTRIM(State))),
    ZipCode = LTRIM(RTRIM(ZipCode));

-- Enrich data with geolocation information
UPDATE CustomerTable
SET
    Latitude = g.Latitude,
```

```
    Longitude = g.Longitude
FROM
    CustomerTable c
    INNER JOIN GeolocationTable g ON c.ZipCode = g.ZipCode;

-- Standardize product names
UPDATE ProductTable
SET ProductName = REPLACE(REPLACE(REPLACE(ProductName, '  ', '
'), ' - ', '-'), '--', '-');
```

Automating Tasks with Scheduled Jobs and SQL Agent

SQL Server Agent is a powerful tool for automating database maintenance tasks, report generation, and other recurring processes. Let's explore how to leverage SQL Agent for task automation.

1. Creating a Simple Maintenance Job

Here's an example of creating a job to perform regular database maintenance tasks:

```
USE msdb;
GO

-- Create the job
EXEC dbo.sp_add_job
    @job_name = N'Weekly Database Maintenance',
    @enabled = 1,
    @description = N'Performs weekly database maintenance tasks';

-- Add a step to rebuild indexes
EXEC dbo.sp_add_jobstep
    @job_name = N'Weekly Database Maintenance',
```

```
    @step_name = N'Rebuild Indexes',
    @subsystem = N'TSQL',
    @command = N'
        DECLARE @TableName NVARCHAR(128)
        DECLARE @SQL NVARCHAR(MAX)

        DECLARE TableCursor CURSOR FOR
        SELECT TABLE_NAME
        FROM INFORMATION_SCHEMA.TABLES
        WHERE TABLE_TYPE = ''BASE TABLE''

        OPEN TableCursor
        FETCH NEXT FROM TableCursor INTO @TableName

        WHILE @@FETCH_STATUS = 0
        BEGIN
            SET @SQL = N''ALTER INDEX ALL ON '' + @TableName +
N'' REBUILD''
            EXEC sp_executesql @SQL

            FETCH NEXT FROM TableCursor INTO @TableName
        END

        CLOSE TableCursor
        DEALLOCATE TableCursor
    ';

-- Add a step to update statistics
EXEC dbo.sp_add_jobstep
    @job_name = N'Weekly Database Maintenance',
    @step_name = N'Update Statistics',
    @subsystem = N'TSQL',
    @command = N'
        EXEC sp_updatestats;
    ';

-- Set the job schedule (run weekly on Sunday at 1:00 AM)
EXEC dbo.sp_add_schedule
    @schedule_name = N'Weekly Sunday 1AM',
    @freq_type = 8,
    @freq_interval = 1,
    @freq_recurrence_factor = 1,
```

```
    @active_start_time = 010000;

-- Attach the schedule to the job
EXEC sp_attach_schedule
    @job_name = N'Weekly Database Maintenance',
    @schedule_name = N'Weekly Sunday 1AM';
```

2. Implementing a Data Archiving Job

Archiving old data can help maintain database performance. Here's an example of a job that archives old orders:

```
USE msdb;
GO

-- Create the job
EXEC dbo.sp_add_job
    @job_name = N'Archive Old Orders',
    @enabled = 1,
    @description = N'Archives orders older than one year';

-- Add a step to archive old orders
EXEC dbo.sp_add_jobstep
    @job_name = N'Archive Old Orders',
    @step_name = N'Archive Orders',
    @subsystem = N'TSQL',
    @command = N'
        BEGIN TRANSACTION;

        -- Insert old orders into archive table
        INSERT INTO ArchivedOrders (OrderID, CustomerID,
OrderDate, TotalAmount)
        SELECT OrderID, CustomerID, OrderDate, TotalAmount
        FROM Orders
        WHERE OrderDate < DATEADD(YEAR, -1, GETDATE());

        -- Delete archived orders from main table
        DELETE FROM Orders
        WHERE OrderDate < DATEADD(YEAR, -1, GETDATE());
```

```
        COMMIT TRANSACTION;
    ';

-- Set the job schedule (run monthly on the first day at 2:00 AM)
EXEC dbo.sp_add_schedule
    @schedule_name = N'Monthly First Day 2AM',
    @freq_type = 16,
    @freq_interval = 1,
    @active_start_time = 020000;

-- Attach the schedule to the job
EXEC sp_attach_schedule
    @job_name = N'Archive Old Orders',
    @schedule_name = N'Monthly First Day 2AM';
```

3. Implementing a Job to Monitor Database Growth

Monitoring database growth is crucial for capacity planning. Here's a job that tracks database size over time:

```
USE msdb;
GO

-- Create a table to store database size history
USE YourDatabase;
GO

CREATE TABLE DatabaseSizeHistory (
    ID INT IDENTITY(1,1) PRIMARY KEY,
    DatabaseName NVARCHAR(128),
    SizeInMB DECIMAL(10,2),
    RecordDate DATETIME
);
GO

-- Create the job
USE msdb;
GO
```

```sql
EXEC dbo.sp_add_job
    @job_name = N'Monitor Database Growth',
    @enabled = 1,
    @description = N'Records database size daily';

-- Add a step to record database size
EXEC dbo.sp_add_jobstep
    @job_name = N'Monitor Database Growth',
    @step_name = N'Record Size',
    @subsystem = N'TSQL',
    @command = N'
        INSERT INTO YourDatabase.dbo.DatabaseSizeHistory
(DatabaseName, SizeInMB, RecordDate)
        SELECT
            DB_NAME(database_id) AS DatabaseName,
            CAST(SUM(size * 8.0 / 1024) AS DECIMAL(10,2)) AS
SizeInMB,
            GETDATE() AS RecordDate
        FROM
            sys.master_files
        WHERE
            database_id = DB_ID(''YourDatabase'')
        GROUP BY
            database_id;
    ';

-- Set the job schedule (run daily at 3:00 AM)
EXEC dbo.sp_add_schedule
    @schedule_name = N'Daily 3AM',
    @freq_type = 4,
    @freq_interval = 1,
    @active_start_time = 030000;

-- Attach the schedule to the job
EXEC sp_attach_schedule
    @job_name = N'Monitor Database Growth',
    @schedule_name = N'Daily 3AM';
```

4. Implementing a Job for Regular Backups

Regular backups are essential for data protection. Here's a job that performs daily full backups and hourly log backups:

```sql
USE msdb;
GO

-- Create the job for full backups
EXEC dbo.sp_add_job
    @job_name = N'Daily Full Backup',
    @enabled = 1,
    @description = N'Performs daily full backup of the database';

-- Add a step to perform full backup
EXEC dbo.sp_add_jobstep
    @job_name = N'Daily Full Backup',
    @step_name = N'Full Backup',
    @subsystem = N'TSQL',
    @command = N'
        BACKUP DATABASE YourDatabase
        TO DISK = N''C:\Backups\YourDatabase_Full_'' +
CONVERT(NVARCHAR(8), GETDATE(), 112) + N''.bak''
        WITH COMPRESSION, CHECKSUM, INIT
    ';

-- Set the job schedule (run daily at 1:00 AM)
EXEC dbo.sp_add_schedule
    @schedule_name = N'Daily 1AM',
    @freq_type = 4,
    @freq_interval = 1,
    @active_start_time = 010000;

-- Attach the schedule to the job
EXEC sp_attach_schedule
    @job_name = N'Daily Full Backup',
    @schedule_name = N'Daily 1AM';

-- Create the job for log backups
EXEC dbo.sp_add_job
    @job_name = N'Hourly Log Backup',
```

```
@enabled = 1,
@description = N'Performs hourly log backup of the database';

-- Add a step to perform log backup
EXEC dbo.sp_add_jobstep
    @job_name = N'Hourly Log Backup',
    @step_name = N'Log Backup',
    @subsystem = N'TSQL',
    @command = N'
        BACKUP LOG YourDatabase
        TO DISK = N''C:\Backups\YourDatabase_Log_'' +
CONVERT(NVARCHAR(8), GETDATE(), 112) + N''_'' +
REPLACE(CONVERT(NVARCHAR(5), GETDATE(), 108), '':'', '''') +
N''.trn''
        WITH COMPRESSION, CHECKSUM
    ';

-- Set the job schedule (run hourly)
EXEC dbo.sp_add_schedule
    @schedule_name = N'Hourly',
    @freq_type = 4,
    @freq_interval = 1,
    @freq_subday_type = 8,
    @freq_subday_interval = 1,
    @active_start_time = 000000;

-- Attach the schedule to the job
EXEC sp_attach_schedule
    @job_name = N'Hourly Log Backup',
    @schedule_name = N'Hourly';
```

5. Implementing a Job for Data Quality Checks

Regular data quality checks can help maintain data integrity. Here's a job that per-forms various data quality checks and reports issues:

```
USE msdb;
GO
```

```sql
-- Create a table to store data quality issues
USE YourDatabase;
GO

CREATE TABLE DataQualityIssues (
    ID INT IDENTITY(1,1) PRIMARY KEY,
    IssueType NVARCHAR(50),
    TableName NVARCHAR(128),
    ColumnName NVARCHAR(128),
    IssueDescription NVARCHAR(MAX),
    AffectedRows INT,
    DetectedDate DATETIME
);
GO

-- Create the job
USE msdb;
GO

EXEC dbo.sp_add_job
    @job_name = N'Data Quality Check',
    @enabled = 1,
    @description = N'Performs regular data quality checks';

-- Add a step to check for NULL values in important columns
EXEC dbo.sp_add_jobstep
    @job_name = N'Data Quality Check',
    @step_name = N'Check NULL Values',
    @subsystem = N'TSQL',
    @command = N'
        INSERT INTO DataQualityIssues (IssueType, TableName,
ColumnName, IssueDescription, AffectedRows, DetectedDate)
        SELECT
            ''NULL Value'',
            ''Customers'',
            ''Email'',
            ''NULL email addresses found'',
            COUNT(*),
            GETDATE()
        FROM
            Customers
        WHERE
```

```
                    Email IS NULL;
    ';


-- Add a step to check for duplicate records
EXEC dbo.sp_add_jobstep
    @job_name = N'Data Quality Check',
    @step_name = N'Check Duplicates',
    @subsystem = N'TSQL',
    @command = N'
        WITH DuplicateCTE AS (
            SELECT
                Email,
                ROW_NUMBER() OVER (PARTITION BY Email ORDER BY
(SELECT NULL)) AS RowNum
            FROM
                Customers
            WHERE
                Email IS NOT NULL
        )
        INSERT INTO DataQualityIssues (IssueType, TableName,
ColumnName, IssueDescription, AffectedRows, DetectedDate)
        SELECT
            ''Duplicate Record'',
            ''Customers'',
            ''Email'',
            ''Duplicate email addresses found'',
            COUNT(*),
            GETDATE()
        FROM
            DuplicateCTE
        WHERE
            RowNum > 1;
    ';


-- Add a step to check for invalid date values
EXEC dbo.sp_add_jobstep
    @job_name = N'Data Quality Check',
    @step_name = N'Check Invalid Dates',
    @subsystem = N'TSQL',
    @command = N'
        INSERT INTO DataQualityIssues (IssueType, TableName,
ColumnName, IssueDescription, AffectedRows, DetectedDate)
```

```
        SELECT
            ''Invalid Date'',
            ''Orders'',
            ''OrderDate'',
            ''Future order dates found'',
            COUNT(*),
            GETDATE()
        FROM
            Orders
        WHERE
            OrderDate > GETDATE();
    ';

-- Set the job schedule (run daily at 4:00 AM)
EXEC dbo.sp_add_schedule
    @schedule_name = N'Daily 4AM',
    @freq_type = 4,
    @freq_interval = 1,
    @active_start_time = 040000;

-- Attach the schedule to the job
EXEC sp_attach_schedule
    @job_name = N'Data Quality Check',
    @schedule_name = N'Daily 4AM';
```

6. Monitoring and Managing SQL Agent Jobs

To ensure your automated tasks are running smoothly, it's important to monitor and manage SQL Agent jobs effectively. Here are some T-SQL scripts to help with job management:

```
-- View all jobs and their status
SELECT
    j.name AS JobName,
    j.description AS JobDescription,
    CASE j.enabled
        WHEN 1 THEN 'Enabled'
        ELSE 'Disabled'
```

```sql
        END AS JobStatus,
    COALESCE(l.name, 'Not scheduled') AS Schedule,
    COALESCE(
        CONVERT(VARCHAR, DATEADD(S, h.run_time % 86400 / 3600,
DATEADD(MI, h.run_time % 3600 / 60, DATEADD(S, h.run_time % 60,
CONVERT(DATETIME, RTRIM(h.run_date), 112)))), 120),
        'Never'
    ) AS LastRun,
    CASE h.run_status
        WHEN 0 THEN 'Failed'
        WHEN 1 THEN 'Succeeded'
        WHEN 2 THEN 'Retry'
        WHEN 3 THEN 'Canceled'
        ELSE 'Unknown'
    END AS LastRunStatus
FROM
    msdb.dbo.sysjobs j
    LEFT JOIN msdb.dbo.sysjobschedules js ON j.job_id = js.job_id
    LEFT JOIN msdb.dbo.sysschedules l ON js.schedule_id =
l.schedule_id
    LEFT JOIN (
        SELECT
            job_id,
            MAX(instance_id) AS last_instance_id
        FROM
            msdb.dbo.sysjobhistory
        GROUP BY
            job_id
    ) lh ON j.job_id = lh.job_id
    LEFT JOIN msdb.dbo.sysjobhistory h ON lh.job_id = h.job_id
AND lh.last_instance_id = h.instance_id
ORDER BY
    j.name;

-- Enable or disable a job
EXEC msdb.dbo.sp_update_job
    @job_name = N'YourJobName',
    @enabled = 1; -- Set to 0 to disable

-- Start a job
EXEC msdb.dbo.sp_start_job @job_name = N'YourJobName';
```

```sql
-- Stop a running job
EXEC msdb.dbo.sp_stop_job @job_name = N'YourJobName';

-- Delete a job
EXEC msdb.dbo.sp_delete_job @job_name = N'YourJobName',
@delete_unused_schedule = 1;

-- View job history
SELECT
    j.name AS JobName,
    h.step_id AS StepID,
    h.step_name AS StepName,
    CONVERT(VARCHAR, DATEADD(S, h.run_time % 86400 / 3600,
DATEADD(MI, h.run_time % 3600 / 60, DATEADD(S, h.run_time % 60,
CONVERT(DATETIME, RTRIM(h.run_date), 112)))), 120) AS
RunDateTime,
    CASE h.run_status
        WHEN 0 THEN 'Failed'
        WHEN 1 THEN 'Succeeded'
        WHEN 2 THEN 'Retry'
        WHEN 3 THEN 'Canceled'
        ELSE 'Unknown'
    END AS RunStatus,
    h.message AS Message
FROM
    msdb.dbo.sysjobs j
    INNER JOIN msdb.dbo.sysjobhistory h ON j.job_id = h.job_id
WHERE
    j.name = N'YourJobName'
ORDER BY
    h.run_date DESC, h.run_time DESC;
```

These scripts will help you monitor job status, enable or disable jobs, start or stop jobs, delete jobs, and view job history.

In conclusion, this chapter has covered essential real-world applications of T-SQL, including building reporting systems, data validation and cleanup, and task automation using SQL Agent.

Appendix A: T-SQL Reserved Keywords

Introduction to T-SQL Reserved Keywords

T-SQL (Transact-SQL) is Microsoft's proprietary extension to SQL (Structured Query Language) used in SQL Server and Azure SQL Database. It includes a set of reserved keywords that have special meanings and functions within the language. These keywords are fundamental to writing correct and efficient T-SQL code.

Reserved keywords are words that have a predefined meaning in T-SQL and cannot be used as identifiers (such as table names, column names, or variable names) unless they are enclosed in square brackets or quoted. Understanding these keywords is crucial for writing correct and efficient T-SQL code.

Importance of Reserved Keywords

1. **Syntax Structure**: Reserved keywords form the backbone of T-SQL syntax, defining the structure and logic of queries and statements.
2. **Query Optimization**: Proper use of keywords allows the SQL Server query optimizer to understand and optimize queries effectively.

3. **Code Readability**: Familiarity with keywords enhances code readability and maintainability.
4. **Error Prevention**: Knowing reserved keywords helps avoid naming conflicts and syntax errors.

Categories of T-SQL Reserved Keywords

T-SQL reserved keywords can be broadly categorized into several groups based on their functions:

1. **Data Definition Language (DDL) Keywords**
2. **Data Manipulation Language (DML) Keywords**
3. **Data Control Language (DCL) Keywords**
4. **Transaction Control Keywords**
5. **Clause Keywords**
6. **Function Keywords**
7. **Datatype Keywords**
8. **Operator Keywords**
9. **Flow Control Keywords**
10. **Miscellaneous Keywords**

Let's explore each category in detail:

1. Data Definition Language (DDL) Keywords

DDL keywords are used to define, modify, and remove database objects.

CREATE

The CREATE keyword is used to create new database objects such as tables, views, stored procedures, and indexes.

Example:

```
CREATE TABLE Employees (
    EmployeeID INT PRIMARY KEY,
    FirstName VARCHAR(50),
    LastName VARCHAR(50),
    HireDate DATE
);
```

ALTER

ALTER is used to modify the structure of existing database objects.

Example:

```
ALTER TABLE Employees
ADD Email VARCHAR(100);
```

DROP

DROP is used to remove database objects.

Example:

```
DROP TABLE Employees;
```

TRUNCATE

TRUNCATE is used to remove all rows from a table without logging individual row deletions.

Example:

```
TRUNCATE TABLE Employees;
```

2. Data Manipulation Language (DML) Keywords

DML keywords are used to manipulate data within database objects.

SELECT

SELECT is used to retrieve data from one or more tables.

Example:

```
SELECT FirstName, LastName
FROM Employees
WHERE HireDate > '2020-01-01';
```

INSERT

INSERT is used to add new rows of data into a table.

Example:

```
INSERT INTO Employees (EmployeeID, FirstName, LastName, HireDate)
VALUES (1, 'John', 'Doe', '2021-03-15');
```

UPDATE

UPDATE is used to modify existing data in a table.

Example:

```
UPDATE Employees
SET Email = 'john.doe@example.com'
WHERE EmployeeID = 1;
```

DELETE

`DELETE` is used to remove rows from a table.

Example:

```
DELETE FROM Employees
WHERE HireDate < '2019-01-01';
```

MERGE

`MERGE` is used to perform insert, update, or delete operations on a target table based on the results of a join with a source table.

Example:

```
MERGE INTO TargetTable AS Target
USING SourceTable AS Source
ON Target.ID = Source.ID
WHEN MATCHED THEN
    UPDATE SET Target.Column1 = Source.Column1
WHEN NOT MATCHED THEN
    INSERT (ID, Column1) VALUES (Source.ID, Source.Column1);
```

3. Data Control Language (DCL) Keywords

DCL keywords are used to control access to data within the database.

GRANT

`GRANT` is used to give specific privileges to database users.

Example:

```
GRANT SELECT, INSERT ON Employees TO User1;
```

REVOKE

REVOKE is used to remove specific privileges from database users.

Example:

```
REVOKE INSERT ON Employees FROM User1;
```

DENY

DENY is used to explicitly deny specific privileges to database users.

Example:

```
DENY DELETE ON Employees TO User1;
```

4. Transaction Control Keywords

These keywords are used to manage transactions in T-SQL.

BEGIN TRANSACTION

BEGIN TRANSACTION marks the starting point of a transaction.

Example:

```
BEGIN TRANSACTION;
```

COMMIT

COMMIT is used to save the changes made in a transaction.

Example:

```
COMMIT TRANSACTION;
```

ROLLBACK

ROLLBACK is used to undo the changes made in a transaction.

Example:

```
ROLLBACK TRANSACTION;
```

SAVE TRANSACTION

SAVE TRANSACTION creates a savepoint within a transaction.

Example:

```
SAVE TRANSACTION SavePoint1;
```

5. Clause Keywords

Clause keywords are used to define specific parts of a SQL statement.

FROM

FROM specifies the table(s) from which to retrieve data in a SELECT statement.

Example:

```
SELECT * FROM Employees;
```

WHERE

WHERE is used to filter rows based on a specified condition.

Example:

```
SELECT * FROM Employees WHERE Salary > 50000;
```

GROUP BY

GROUP BY is used to group rows that have the same values in specified columns.

Example:

```
SELECT Department, AVG(Salary) AS AvgSalary
FROM Employees
GROUP BY Department;
```

HAVING

HAVING is used to specify a search condition for a group or an aggregate.

Example:

```
SELECT Department, AVG(Salary) AS AvgSalary
FROM Employees
GROUP BY Department
HAVING AVG(Salary) > 60000;
```

ORDER BY

ORDER BY is used to sort the result set in ascending or descending order.

Example:

```
SELECT * FROM Employees
ORDER BY LastName ASC, FirstName DESC;
```

JOIN

JOIN is used to combine rows from two or more tables based on a related column between them.

Example:

```
SELECT e.FirstName, e.LastName, d.DepartmentName
```

```
FROM Employees e
JOIN Departments d ON e.DepartmentID = d.DepartmentID;
```

6. Function Keywords

Function keywords are used to perform calculations, manipulate data, or return system information.

CAST

CAST is used to convert an expression of one data type to another.

Example:

```
SELECT CAST(HireDate AS VARCHAR(10)) AS HireDateString
FROM Employees;
```

CONVERT

CONVERT is similar to CAST but provides more options for date and time conversions.

Example:

```
SELECT CONVERT(VARCHAR(10), HireDate, 101) AS HireDateUS
FROM Employees;
```

COALESCE

COALESCE returns the first non-null expression among its arguments.

Example:

```
SELECT COALESCE(MiddleName, '') AS MiddleName
FROM Employees;
```

ISNULL

`ISNULL` substitutes a specified value when an expression is NULL.

   Example:

```
SELECT ISNULL(PhoneNumber, 'N/A') AS PhoneNumber
FROM Employees;
```

NULLIF

`NULLIF` returns NULL if two specified expressions are equal.

   Example:

```
SELECT NULLIF(Column1, Column2) AS Result
FROM SomeTable;
```

7. Datatype Keywords

Datatype keywords define the type of data that can be stored in a column or variable.

INT

`INT` is used for whole numbers.

   Example:

```
CREATE TABLE Products (
    ProductID INT PRIMARY KEY,
    ProductName VARCHAR(100)
);
```

VARCHAR

VARCHAR is used for variable-length character strings.

Example:

```
CREATE TABLE Customers (
    CustomerID INT PRIMARY KEY,
    CustomerName VARCHAR(100)
);
```

DATETIME

DATETIME is used for date and time values.

Example:

```
CREATE TABLE Orders (
    OrderID INT PRIMARY KEY,
    OrderDate DATETIME
);
```

DECIMAL

DECIMAL is used for fixed-precision and scale numbers.

Example:

```
CREATE TABLE Financials (
    TransactionID INT PRIMARY KEY,
    Amount DECIMAL(10,2)
);
```

8. Operator Keywords

Operator keywords are used in expressions to perform operations on data.

AND

AND is used to combine multiple conditions in a WHERE clause.

Example:

```
SELECT * FROM Employees
WHERE Salary > 50000 AND Department = 'Sales';
```

OR

OR is used to specify multiple alternative conditions.

Example:

```
SELECT * FROM Products
WHERE Category = 'Electronics' OR Price > 1000;
```

IN

IN is used to specify multiple values in a WHERE clause.

Example:

```
SELECT * FROM Customers
WHERE Country IN ('USA', 'Canada', 'Mexico');
```

BETWEEN

BETWEEN is used to select values within a given range.

Example:

```
SELECT * FROM Orders
WHERE OrderDate BETWEEN '2021-01-01' AND '2021-12-31';
```

LIKE

`LIKE` is used for pattern matching with wildcard characters.

Example:

```
SELECT * FROM Employees
WHERE LastName LIKE 'S%';
```

9. Flow Control Keywords

Flow control keywords are used to control the execution flow of SQL statements.

IF...ELSE

`IF...ELSE` is used for conditional execution of SQL statements.

Example:

```
IF (SELECT AVG(Salary) FROM Employees) > 50000
    PRINT 'Average salary is high'
ELSE
    PRINT 'Average salary is low';
```

CASE

`CASE` is used to perform conditional processing in a SELECT statement or elsewhere.

Example:

```
SELECT OrderID,
      CASE
          WHEN TotalAmount > 1000 THEN 'High Value'
          WHEN TotalAmount > 500 THEN 'Medium Value'
          ELSE 'Low Value'
      END AS OrderCategory
```

```
FROM Orders;
```

WHILE

WHILE is used to repeatedly execute a statement or block of statements.

Example:

```
DECLARE @Counter INT = 1;
WHILE @Counter <= 5
BEGIN
    PRINT 'Counter: ' + CAST(@Counter AS VARCHAR);
    SET @Counter = @Counter + 1;
END;
```

BEGIN...END

BEGIN...END is used to group multiple statements into a single block.

Example:

```
BEGIN
    UPDATE Accounts SET Balance = Balance - 100 WHERE AccountID =
1;
    UPDATE Accounts SET Balance = Balance + 100 WHERE AccountID =
2;
END;
```

10. Miscellaneous Keywords

These are additional keywords that don't fit neatly into the above categories but are still important in T-SQL.

GO

GO is a batch separator used to group T-SQL statements into batches.

Example:

```
CREATE TABLE TestTable (ID INT);
GO
INSERT INTO TestTable VALUES (1);
GO
```

SET

SET is used to specify SQL Server options or to assign values to variables.

Example:

```
SET NOCOUNT ON;
```

DECLARE

DECLARE is used to declare variables in T-SQL.

Example:

```
DECLARE @MyVariable INT = 10;
```

WITH

WITH is used to specify named subquery expressions (Common Table Expressions).

Example:

```
WITH CTE AS (
    SELECT CustomerID, COUNT(*) AS OrderCount
    FROM Orders
    GROUP BY CustomerID
```

```
)
SELECT * FROM CTE WHERE OrderCount > 5;
```

Best Practices for Using Reserved Keywords

1. **Avoid Using Reserved Words as Identifiers**: While it's possible to use reserved words as identifiers by enclosing them in square brackets or quotes, it's generally best to avoid this practice to prevent confusion and potential errors.
2. **Use Uppercase for Keywords**: While T-SQL is not case-sensitive, using uppercase for keywords can improve code readability.
3. **Be Aware of Future Reserved Words**: Some words may become reserved in future versions of SQL Server. It's good practice to avoid using these as identifiers as well.
4. **Use Aliases**: When working with complex queries, use aliases to make your code more readable and to avoid potential conflicts with reserved words.
5. **Stay Updated**: Keep yourself informed about any changes to the list of reserved words in new versions of SQL Server.

Conclusion

Understanding T-SQL reserved keywords is crucial for writing efficient and error-free SQL Server code. These keywords form the foundation of T-SQL syntax and are essential for various database operations, from simple queries to complex data manipulations and structural changes.

By mastering these keywords and following best practices, you can write more robust and maintainable T-SQL code. Remember that while this guide covers many important keywords, T-SQL is a rich language with many more features and nuances. Continuous learning and practice are key to becoming proficient in T-SQL programming.

Additional Resources

To further enhance your T-SQL skills, consider exploring the following topics:

1. **Advanced Query Techniques**: Learn about subqueries, correlated subqueries, and derived tables.
2. **Performance Optimization**: Study query execution plans and indexing strategies.
3. **T-SQL Functions**: Explore built-in functions for string manipulation, date/time operations, and mathematical calculations.
4. **Error Handling**: Learn about TRY...CATCH blocks and custom error messages.
5. **Dynamic SQL**: Understand how to generate and execute SQL statements dynamically.
6. **Temporary Tables and Table Variables**: Learn when and how to use these for intermediate result storage.
7. **Stored Procedures and User-Defined Functions**: Explore how to create reusable code modules.

8. **Triggers**: Understand how to create and use triggers for automated actions on data changes.

9. **Transactions and Isolation Levels**: Dive deeper into transaction management and concurrency control.

10. **Security**: Learn about permissions, roles, and encryption in SQL Server.

By continually expanding your knowledge in these areas, you'll be well-equipped to handle a wide range of database programming challenges and optimize your T-SQL code for better performance and maintainability.

Appendix B: Common Error Codes and Troubleshooting

Introduction

When working with T-SQL and SQL Server, encountering errors is a common occurrence. Understanding these errors and knowing how to troubleshoot them is crucial for efficient database development and management. This appendix provides a comprehensive guide to common error codes in SQL Server, along with troubleshooting techniques and best practices.

Error Code Categories

SQL Server error codes are generally categorized into the following groups:

1. Syntax Errors
2. Compilation Errors
3. Runtime Errors
4. Connection Errors
5. Transaction Errors
6. Constraint Violations
7. System Resource Errors
8. Security Errors

Let's explore each category in detail, along with common error codes and their solutions.

1. Syntax Errors

Syntax errors occur when the T-SQL code doesn't conform to the language rules. These errors are typically caught during the parsing phase before execution.

Common Syntax Errors

Error 102: Incorrect Syntax

```
Msg 102, Level 15, State 1, Line X
Incorrect syntax near 'keyword'.
```

This error occurs when there's a syntax mistake in your T-SQL statement. Common causes include:

- Missing or misplaced keywords
- Incorrect use of parentheses
- Misspelled object names

Solution: Carefully review the line indicated in the error message. Check for typos, missing commas, or incorrect placement of clauses.

Error 156: Incorrect Syntax near the Keyword

```
Msg 156, Level 15, State 1, Line X
Incorrect syntax near the keyword 'keyword'.
```

This error is similar to Error 102 but specifically points out a problem near a particular keyword.

Solution: Examine the usage of the mentioned keyword. Ensure it's in the correct position and used appropriately in the context of your statement.

Error 170: Line X: Incorrect Syntax near ')'

```
Msg 170, Level 15, State 1, Line X
Line X: Incorrect syntax near ')'.
```

This error typically occurs when there's a mismatch in parentheses or when a parenthesis is used incorrectly.

Solution: Check for balanced parentheses in your query. Ensure that each opening parenthesis has a corresponding closing parenthesis.

Best Practices for Avoiding Syntax Errors

1. Use an IDE with syntax highlighting and IntelliSense.
2. Format your code consistently for better readability.
3. Break complex queries into smaller, manageable parts.
4. Use comments to explain complex logic or unusual syntax.

2. Compilation Errors

Compilation errors occur when SQL Server cannot compile the T-SQL code due to issues with object references, data types, or other semantic problems.

Common Compilation Errors

Error 207: Invalid Column Name

```
Msg 207, Level 16, State 1, Line X
Invalid column name 'column_name'.
```

This error occurs when you reference a column that doesn't exist in the table or view you're querying.

Solution:

- Double-check the spelling of the column name.
- Verify that the column exists in the table or view.
- If using aliases, ensure they are correctly defined and referenced.

Error 208: Invalid Object Name

```
Msg 208, Level 16, State 1, Line X
Invalid object name 'object_name'.
```

This error happens when you reference a table, view, or other database object that doesn't exist in the current database or schema.

Solution:

- Check the spelling of the object name.
- Verify that the object exists in the current database and schema.
- If the object is in a different schema, use the fully qualified name (schema.object).

Error 245: Conversion Failed

```
Msg 245, Level 16, State 1, Line X
Conversion failed when converting the varchar value 'value' to
data type int.
```

This error occurs when trying to convert a value from one data type to another in-compatible type.

Solution:

- Ensure that the data you're trying to convert is compatible with the target data type.
- Use appropriate conversion functions (e.g., CAST or CONVERT) with error handling.
- Consider using TRY_CAST or TRY_CONVERT for safer conversions.

Best Practices for Avoiding Compilation Errors

1. Use schema-qualified object names to avoid ambiguity.
2. Implement a naming convention for database objects.
3. Regularly update statistics and rebuild indexes to ensure optimal query plans.
4. Use appropriate data types for columns and variables.

3. Runtime Errors

Runtime errors occur during the execution of T-SQL code. These can be caused by various factors, including data inconsistencies, resource constraints, or unexpected conditions.

Common Runtime Errors

Error 8134: Divide by Zero

```
Msg 8134, Level 16, State 1, Line X
Divide by zero error encountered.
```

This error occurs when attempting to divide a number by zero.

Solution:

- Use NULLIF to handle potential zero divisors:

```
SELECT column1 / NULLIF(column2, 0) AS result
```

- Implement error handling to catch and manage divide-by-zero scenarios.

Error 512: Subquery Returned More Than One Value

```
Msg 512, Level 16, State 1, Line X
Subquery returned more than 1 value. This is not permitted when
the subquery follows =, !=, <, <= , >, >= or when the subquery is
used as an expression.
```

This error occurs when a subquery that should return a single value returns multiple rows.

Solution:

- Modify the subquery to ensure it returns only one value.
- Use aggregate functions (e.g., MAX, MIN) to reduce multiple rows to a single value.
- Consider using EXISTS instead of a comparison operator if checking for the existence of rows.

Error 547: The INSERT Statement Conflicted with the FOREIGN KEY Constraint

```
Msg 547, Level 16, State 0, Line X
The INSERT statement conflicted with the FOREIGN KEY constraint
"FK_name". The conflict occurred in database "db_name", table
"table_name", column 'column_name'.
```

This error occurs when trying to insert a value into a foreign key column that doesn't have a corresponding value in the referenced table.

Solution:

- Ensure that the value you're inserting exists in the referenced table.
- If necessary, insert the required data into the referenced table first.
- Consider using cascading referential integrity constraints for automatic updates/deletes.

Best Practices for Handling Runtime Errors

1. Implement proper error handling using TRY...CATCH blocks.
2. Use transaction management to ensure data consistency.
3. Validate input data before processing.
4. Log errors for analysis and troubleshooting.

4. Connection Errors

Connection errors occur when there are issues establishing or maintaining a connection to the SQL Server instance.

Common Connection Errors

Error 18456: Login Failed

```
Msg 18456, Level 14, State 1, Line X
Login failed for user 'username'.
```

This error occurs when the provided credentials are incorrect or the account is locked or disabled.

Solution:

- Verify the username and password.
- Check if the account is locked or disabled in SQL Server.
- Ensure the user has the necessary permissions to connect to the database.

Error 53: Unable to Connect

```
A network-related or instance-specific error occurred while
establishing a connection to SQL Server. The server was not found
or was not accessible. Verify that the instance name is correct
and that SQL Server is configured to allow remote connections.
(provider: Named Pipes Provider, error: 40 - Could not open a
connection to SQL Server)
```

This error typically occurs when there are network issues or the SQL Server instance is not running.

Solution:

- Verify that the SQL Server service is running.
- Check network connectivity between the client and server.
- Ensure that the SQL Server Browser service is running if using named instances.
- Verify that the firewall is not blocking the connection.

Error 4060: Cannot Open Database

```
Msg 4060, Level 11, State 1, Line X
Cannot open database "database_name" requested by the login. The
login failed.
```

This error occurs when the user doesn't have permission to access the specified database.

Solution:

- Grant the user appropriate permissions on the database.
- Verify that the database exists and is online.
- Check if the user is mapped to the correct database role.

Best Practices for Avoiding Connection Errors

1. Use Windows Authentication when possible for better security.
2. Implement connection pooling to improve performance and reduce connection-related issues.
3. Use a dedicated service account for application connections.
4. Regularly audit and review user permissions.

5. Transaction Errors

Transaction errors occur when there are issues with the management of transactions in SQL Server.

Common Transaction Errors

Error 1205: Transaction (Process ID) was deadlocked

```
Msg 1205, Level 13, State 51, Line X
Transaction (Process ID X) was deadlocked on {resource} resources
with another process and has been chosen as the deadlock victim.
Rerun the transaction.
```

This error occurs when two or more processes are waiting for each other to release resources, creating a deadlock.

Solution:

- Analyze the deadlock graph to identify the resources involved.
- Optimize queries to reduce lock duration.

- Consider using READCOMMITTEDLOCK hint for critical transactions.
- Implement retry logic in your application to handle deadlocks.

Error 3930: The current transaction cannot be committed and cannot support operations that write to the log file

```
Msg 3930, Level 16, State 1, Line X
The current transaction cannot be committed and cannot support
operations that write to the log file. Roll back the transaction.
```

This error typically occurs when attempting to perform a write operation within a read-only transaction.

Solution:

- Ensure that the transaction is not marked as read-only if write operations are required.
- Review the transaction isolation level and adjust if necessary.
- Separate read and write operations into different transactions if possible.

Error 3902: The COMMIT TRANSACTION request has no corresponding BEGIN TRANSACTION

```
Msg 3902, Level 16, State 1, Line X
The COMMIT TRANSACTION request has no corresponding BEGIN
TRANSACTION.
```

This error occurs when there's an attempt to commit a transaction that hasn't been explicitly started.

Solution:

- Ensure that each COMMIT TRANSACTION statement has a corresponding BEGIN TRANSACTION.
- Review the transaction management logic in your code.
- Consider using TRY...CATCH blocks to handle transaction errors.

Best Practices for Transaction Management

1. Keep transactions as short as possible to reduce lock contention.
2. Use appropriate isolation levels based on your concurrency requirements.
3. Implement error handling and rollback mechanisms for failed transactions.
4. Avoid mixing implicit and explicit transaction management.

6. Constraint Violations

Constraint violations occur when an operation violates the defined constraints on a table or column.

Common Constraint Violations

Error 2627: Violation of UNIQUE KEY constraint

```
Msg 2627, Level 14, State 1, Line X
```

```
Violation of UNIQUE KEY constraint 'constraint_name'. Cannot
insert duplicate key in object 'table_name'. The duplicate key
value is (column_value).
```

This error occurs when attempting to insert or update a value that already exists in a column with a unique constraint.

Solution:

- Check for existing values before inserting or updating.
- Implement MERGE statements for upsert operations.
- Consider using a TRY...CATCH block to handle potential duplicates gracefully.

Error 547: The INSERT statement conflicted with the CHECK constraint

```
Msg 547, Level 16, State 0, Line X
The INSERT statement conflicted with the CHECK constraint
"constraint_name". The conflict occurred in database "db_name",
table "table_name", column 'column_name'.
```

This error occurs when the inserted or updated value doesn't meet the conditions specified in a CHECK constraint.

Solution:

- Review the CHECK constraint definition and ensure the data meets the specified conditions.
- Validate input data before attempting to insert or update.
- Consider modifying the constraint if it's too restrictive for valid business scenarios.

Error 515: Cannot insert the value NULL into column

```
Msg 515, Level 16, State 2, Line X
Cannot insert the value NULL into column 'column_name', table
'table_name'; column does not allow nulls. INSERT fails.
```

This error occurs when attempting to insert a NULL value into a column defined as NOT NULL.

Solution:

- Provide a non-NULL value for the column.
- If NULL values are valid for the business scenario, consider altering the column to allow NULLs.
- Use ISNULL or COALESCE to provide default values for potentially NULL inputs.

Best Practices for Handling Constraint Violations

1. Validate data at the application level before sending it to the database.
2. Use appropriate constraints (UNIQUE, CHECK, FOREIGN KEY) to enforce data integrity.
3. Implement error handling to provide meaningful messages for constraint violations.
4. Regularly review and update constraints to align with changing business rules.

7. System Resource Errors

System resource errors occur when the SQL Server instance or the underlying hardware lacks the necessary resources to complete an operation.

Common System Resource Errors

Error 701: There is insufficient system memory to run this query

```
Msg 701, Level 17, State 123, Line X
There is insufficient system memory to run this query.
```

This error occurs when SQL Server cannot allocate enough memory to execute a query.

Solution:

- Optimize the query to reduce memory usage.
- Increase the maximum server memory configuration.
- Consider scaling up the hardware or using a more powerful instance.
- Implement query hints like OPTION (RECOMPILE) for memory-intensive queries.

Error 1204: The instance of the SQL Server Database Engine cannot obtain a LOCK resource

```
Msg 1204, Level 19, State 1, Line X
The instance of the SQL Server Database Engine cannot obtain a
LOCK resource at this time. Rerun your statement when there are
fewer active users. Ask the database administrator to check the
```

```
lock and memory configuration for this instance, or to check for
long-running transactions.
```

This error occurs when SQL Server cannot allocate additional lock resources due to excessive concurrent activity.

Solution:

- Review and optimize long-running transactions.
- Increase the 'locks' configuration option if necessary.
- Implement application-level connection pooling.
- Consider using snapshot isolation to reduce lock contention.

Error 9002: The transaction log for database is full

```
Msg 9002, Level 17, State 2, Line X
The transaction log for database 'database_name' is full due to
'ACTIVE_TRANSACTION'.
```

This error occurs when the transaction log has reached its maximum size and cannot grow further.

Solution:

- Perform a log backup to free up space in the log file.
- Enable auto-growth for the log file if it's not already configured.
- Consider switching to SIMPLE recovery model if full logging is not required.
- Review and optimize long-running transactions that may be preventing log truncation.

Best Practices for Managing System Resources

1. Regularly monitor system resource usage (CPU, memory, disk I/O).
2. Implement a performance baseline and track deviations.
3. Use Resource Governor to manage resource allocation for different workloads.
4. Optimize queries and indexes to reduce resource consumption.

8. Security Errors

Security errors occur when there are issues related to permissions, authentication, or other security mechanisms in SQL Server.

Common Security Errors

Error 229: The SELECT permission was denied

```
Msg 229, Level 14, State 5, Line X
The SELECT permission was denied on the object 'object_name',
database 'database_name', schema 'schema_name'.
```

This error occurs when the user doesn't have the necessary permissions to perform a SELECT operation on the specified object.

Solution:

- Grant the appropriate SELECT permissions to the user or role.
- Verify that the user is a member of the correct database role.

- Use EXECUTE AS to temporarily elevate permissions if necessary.

Error 916: The server principal is not able to access the database under the current security context

```
Msg 916, Level 14, State 1, Line X
The server principal "principal_name" is not able to access the
database "database_name" under the current security context.
```

This error occurs when a login doesn't have permission to access a specific database.

Solution:

- Grant the login access to the database using CREATE USER or sp_adduser.
- Ensure the login is mapped to a user in the database.
- Verify that the database is not in single-user mode or restricted access.

Error 15151: Cannot find the symmetric key 'key_name', because it does not exist or you do not have permission

```
Msg 15151, Level 16, State 1, Line X
Cannot find the symmetric key 'key_name', because it does not
have permission.
```

This error occurs when attempting to use a symmetric key without the necessary permissions.

Solution:

- Grant the appropriate permissions on the symmetric key to the user.
- Verify that the key exists in the database.

- Ensure that the user has the necessary permissions to use encryption functions.

Best Practices for SQL Server Security

1. Follow the principle of least privilege when granting permissions.
2. Use Windows Authentication when possible for better security.
3. Regularly audit and review user permissions and access.
4. Implement row-level security and dynamic data masking for sensitive data.
5. Use Always Encrypted for sensitive columns that require end-to-end encryption.

Troubleshooting Techniques

When encountering errors in SQL Server, follow these general troubleshooting steps:

1. **Analyze the Error Message:**

- Read the error message carefully, noting the error number, severity level, and any specific details provided.
- Look up the error code in SQL Server documentation or online resources for additional context.

2. **Check SQL Server Logs:**

- Review the SQL Server Error Log for additional information about the error.
- Use SQL Server Management Studio or system stored procedures like sp_readerrorlog to access log files.

3. Isolate the Problem:

- If the error occurs in a complex script or stored procedure, try to reproduce it with a simplified version.
- Use commenting to isolate specific sections of code that may be causing the issue.

4. Use Debugging Techniques:

- Implement PRINT or RAISERROR statements to output variable values and execution flow.
- Use SQL Server Profiler or Extended Events to capture detailed information about query execution.

5. Check System Resources:

- Monitor CPU, memory, and disk usage to ensure the server has sufficient resources.
- Review wait statistics to identify potential bottlenecks.

6. Verify Object Existence and Permissions:

- Use system views like sys.objects and sys.database_permissions to check object existence and user permissions.

7. Review Recent Changes:

- If the error started occurring recently, review any changes made to the database schema, code, or server configuration.

8. Consult Documentation and Community Resources:

- Refer to official Microsoft documentation for detailed information on error messages and troubleshooting steps.
- Search online forums and community sites for similar issues and potential solutions.

9. Implement Error Handling:

- Use TRY...CATCH blocks to catch and handle errors gracefully.
- Implement custom error logging to capture detailed information about errors for analysis.

10. Consider Server-Level Issues:

- Check for any server-level configuration changes or maintenance activities that might impact database operations.
- Review SQL Server Agent jobs and other scheduled tasks that might interfere with normal operations.

Advanced Troubleshooting Tools

For complex issues, consider using these advanced troubleshooting tools:

1. **SQL Server Profiler:**

   - Captures detailed information about query execution, including duration, resource usage, and error events.
   - Useful for identifying performance bottlenecks and tracing the source of errors.

2. **Extended Events:**

   - A more lightweight and flexible alternative to SQL Server Profiler.
   - Allows for targeted capture of specific events with minimal performance impact.

3. **Database Engine Tuning Advisor:**

   - Analyzes workloads and provides recommendations for index and partition strategies.
   - Helpful in identifying missing indexes that may cause performance issues.

4. **System Dynamic Management Views (DMVs):**

   - Provide detailed information about server state, resource usage, and query performance.

- Examples include sys.dm_exec_requests, sys.dm_os_wait_stats, and sys.dm_db_index_usage_stats.

5. **Query Store:**

- Captures query execution plans and runtime statistics over time.
- Useful for identifying query plan regressions and performance variations.

6. **Data Collection Sets:**

- Allows for scheduled collection of performance data and custom reports.
- Helpful in establishing baselines and tracking performance trends over time.

7. **SQL Server Management Studio Reports:**

- Provides pre-built reports for various aspects of database and server performance.
- Includes reports on disk usage, query statistics, and index recommendations.

Conclusion

Effectively troubleshooting errors in SQL Server requires a combination of understanding common error codes, following best practices, and utilizing appropriate tools and techniques. By familiarizing yourself with the error categories and solutions presented in this appendix, you'll be better equipped to diagnose and resolve issues quickly, ensuring the smooth operation of your SQL Server databases.

Remember that prevention is often the best cure. Implementing robust coding practices, regular maintenance routines, and proactive monitoring can help you avoid many common errors before they occur. When errors do arise, approach them methodically, leveraging the wealth of information provided by SQL Server's error messages and diagnostic tools.

As you gain experience, you'll develop intuition for quickly identifying the root causes of errors and implementing effective solutions. Keep learning, stay updated with the latest SQL Server features and best practices, and don't hesitate to seek help from the vibrant SQL Server community when faced with challenging issues.

Appendix C: Glossary of Terms

A

ACID

Definition: An acronym for Atomicity, Consistency, Isolation, and Durability, which are the four key properties that guarantee reliable processing of database transactions.

Explanation: ACID properties ensure that database transactions are processed reliably, even in the event of errors, power failures, or other issues.

- **Atomicity:** Ensures that all operations within a transaction are completed successfully, or none of them are applied.
- **Consistency:** Guarantees that a transaction brings the database from one valid state to another valid state.
- **Isolation:** Ensures that concurrent execution of transactions leaves the database in the same state as if the transactions were executed sequentially.
- **Durability:** Guarantees that once a transaction has been committed, it will remain committed even in the case of system failure.

Aggregate Function

Definition: A function that performs a calculation on a set of values and returns a single result.

Explanation: Aggregate functions operate on multiple rows and return a single value. Common aggregate functions include:

- SUM: Calculates the sum of a set of values
- AVG: Calculates the average of a set of values
- COUNT: Counts the number of rows or non-null values
- MAX: Returns the maximum value in a set
- MIN: Returns the minimum value in a set

Example:

```
SELECT AVG(Salary) AS AverageSalary
FROM Employees;
```

ALTER Statement

Definition: A SQL statement used to modify the structure of an existing database object.

Explanation: The ALTER statement is used to change the structure of tables, views, indexes, and other database objects. It can be used to:

- Add, modify, or drop columns in a table
- Add or remove constraints
- Modify data types
- Rename objects

Example:

```
ALTER TABLE Customers
ADD Email VARCHAR(100);
```

ANSI SQL

Definition: The standard form of SQL (Structured Query Language) as defined by the American National Standards Institute (ANSI).

Explanation: ANSI SQL provides a standardized syntax for database operations, ensuring compatibility across different database management systems. While most database systems support ANSI SQL, they may also include proprietary extensions.

Alias

Definition: A temporary name assigned to a table, column, or expression in a SQL query.

Explanation: Aliases are used to:

- Simplify complex queries
- Provide more meaningful names for columns or expressions
- Disambiguate column names when joining tables

Example:

```
SELECT e.FirstName, e.LastName, d.DepartmentName
FROM Employees e
JOIN Departments d ON e.DepartmentID = d.DepartmentID;
```

APPLY Operator

Definition: An operator in T-SQL that allows you to join a table-valued expression with a table.

Explanation: There are two types of APPLY operators:

1. CROSS APPLY: Returns only matching rows
2. OUTER APPLY: Returns all rows from the left table, similar to a LEFT OUTER JOIN

APPLY is particularly useful when working with table-valued functions or subqueries that depend on values from the outer table.

Example:

```
SELECT c.CustomerID, c.CustomerName, o.OrderID, o.OrderDate
FROM Customers c
CROSS APPLY (
    SELECT TOP 3 OrderID, OrderDate
    FROM Orders
    WHERE CustomerID = c.CustomerID
    ORDER BY OrderDate DESC
) o;
```

B

Backup

Definition: A copy of data from a database that can be used to reconstruct data in the event of data loss.

Explanation: Regular backups are crucial for data protection and disaster recovery. SQL Server supports various types of backups:

- Full backup: A complete copy of the entire database
- Differential backup: A copy of all changes made since the last full backup
- Transaction log backup: A copy of the transaction log, containing all transactions since the last log backup

Example:

```
BACKUP DATABASE AdventureWorks
TO DISK = 'C:\Backups\AdventureWorks.bak'
WITH FORMAT, COMPRESSION;
```

Batch

Definition: A group of one or more T-SQL statements submitted to SQL Server as a single unit for execution.

Explanation: Batches are separated by the GO statement in T-SQL. They are useful for:

- Organizing and structuring code
- Controlling the scope of variables and temporary objects
- Improving performance by reducing network traffic

Example:

```
CREATE TABLE #TempTable (ID INT, Name VARCHAR(50));
GO

INSERT INTO #TempTable (ID, Name) VALUES (1, 'John');
GO
```

```
SELECT * FROM #TempTable;
GO
```

BEGIN...END

Definition: Keywords used to define a block of T-SQL statements that are executed as a unit.

Explanation: BEGIN...END blocks are used to group multiple statements together, particularly in control-of-flow language elements like IF...ELSE statements, stored procedures, and functions.

Example:

```
IF EXISTS (SELECT 1 FROM Customers WHERE CustomerID = 1)
BEGIN
    UPDATE Customers SET CustomerName = 'New Name' WHERE
CustomerID = 1;
    PRINT 'Customer updated successfully';
END
ELSE
BEGIN
    PRINT 'Customer not found';
END
```

Bulk Insert

Definition: A feature in SQL Server that allows for efficient loading of large amounts of data from external files into database tables.

Explanation: Bulk Insert is optimized for performance and is particularly useful when importing large datasets. It supports various file formats and offers options for data transformation and error handling.

Example:

```
BULK INSERT Customers
FROM 'C:\Data\customers.csv'
WITH (
    FIELDTERMINATOR = ',',
    ROWTERMINATOR = '\n',
    FIRSTROW = 2
);
```

C

Cardinality

Definition: The number of unique values in a column relative to the total number of rows in a table.

Explanation: Cardinality is an important concept in database design and query optimization. It can be:

- High cardinality: Many unique values (e.g., a primary key column)
- Low cardinality: Few unique values (e.g., a boolean column)

Understanding cardinality helps in creating effective indexes and optimizing query performance.

Cascading Actions

Definition: Automatic actions that occur on related tables when a primary key is updated or deleted.

Explanation: Cascading actions are defined as part of foreign key constraints and can include:

- CASCADE: Automatically update or delete related rows
- SET NULL: Set the foreign key to NULL when the referenced row is deleted
- SET DEFAULT: Set the foreign key to its default value when the referenced row is deleted

Example:

```
CREATE TABLE Orders (
    OrderID INT PRIMARY KEY,
    CustomerID INT,
    FOREIGN KEY (CustomerID) REFERENCES Customers(CustomerID)
    ON DELETE CASCADE
    ON UPDATE CASCADE
);
```

CASE Statement

Definition: A conditional expression in T-SQL that returns a value based on specified conditions.

Explanation: The CASE statement can be used in SELECT, UPDATE, DELETE, and SET statements to perform conditional processing. There are two forms:

1. Simple CASE: Compares an expression to a set of simple expressions
2. Searched CASE: Evaluates a set of Boolean expressions

Example:

```
SELECT OrderID, OrderTotal,
    CASE
        WHEN OrderTotal < 100 THEN 'Small Order'
        WHEN OrderTotal BETWEEN 100 AND 1000 THEN 'Medium Order'
        ELSE 'Large Order'
    END AS OrderSize
```

```
FROM Orders;
```

Checkpoint

Definition: A process that writes all modified pages in the buffer cache to disk.

Explanation: Checkpoints help reduce recovery time by ensuring that modified data is periodically written to disk. They can be:

- Automatic: Performed by SQL Server based on various factors
- Manual: Initiated by executing the CHECKPOINT command

Example:

```
CHECKPOINT;
```

Clustered Index

Definition: An index that determines the physical order of data in a table.

Explanation: A clustered index stores the actual data rows in the leaf nodes of the index structure. Key characteristics include:

- Only one clustered index per table
- Typically created on the primary key
- Faster for range queries and sorting operations

Example:

```
CREATE CLUSTERED INDEX IX_Customers_CustomerID
ON Customers (CustomerID);
```

Collation

Definition: A set of rules that determine how character data is sorted and compared.

Explanation: Collations define:

- Character set
- Sort order
- Case sensitivity
- Accent sensitivity

Collations can be set at the server, database, column, or expression level.

Example:

```
CREATE TABLE Employees (
    EmployeeID INT PRIMARY KEY,
    LastName NVARCHAR(50) COLLATE SQL_Latin1_General_CP1_CI_AS
);
```

Common Table Expression (CTE)

Definition: A named temporary result set that exists within the scope of a single SELECT, INSERT, UPDATE, DELETE, or MERGE statement.

Explanation: CTEs are useful for:

- Simplifying complex queries
- Writing recursive queries
- Improving query readability

Example:

```
WITH EmployeeCTE AS (
    SELECT EmployeeID, FirstName, LastName, ManagerID
```

```
  FROM Employees
)
SELECT e.FirstName, e.LastName, m.FirstName AS ManagerFirstName,
m.LastName AS ManagerLastName
FROM EmployeeCTE e
LEFT JOIN EmployeeCTE m ON e.ManagerID = m.EmployeeID;
```

Computed Column

Definition: A column in a table whose value is calculated from an expression that uses other columns in the same table.

Explanation: Computed columns can be:

- Persisted: Stored physically in the table
- Non-persisted: Calculated when referenced

They are useful for storing derived values and simplifying queries.

Example:

```
CREATE TABLE Products (
    ProductID INT PRIMARY KEY,
    UnitPrice DECIMAL(10,2),
    Quantity INT,
    TotalValue AS (UnitPrice * Quantity) PERSISTED
);
```

Concurrency

Definition: The ability of multiple users or processes to access and modify shared data simultaneously.

Explanation: Concurrency control is crucial for maintaining data integrity in multi-user environments. SQL Server uses various mechanisms to manage concurrency, including:

- Locks
- Isolation levels
- Optimistic concurrency control

Constraint

Definition: A rule that enforces data integrity in a table.

Explanation: Common types of constraints include:

- PRIMARY KEY: Ensures uniqueness and non-null values
- FOREIGN KEY: Enforces referential integrity between tables
- UNIQUE: Ensures uniqueness of values in a column or combination of columns
- CHECK: Enforces domain integrity by limiting the values that can be entered into a column

Example:

```
CREATE TABLE Orders (
    OrderID INT PRIMARY KEY,
    CustomerID INT,
    OrderDate DATE,
    TotalAmount DECIMAL(10,2),
    CONSTRAINT FK_Orders_Customers FOREIGN KEY (CustomerID)
REFERENCES Customers(CustomerID),
    CONSTRAINT CHK_TotalAmount CHECK (TotalAmount > 0)
);
```

Correlated Subquery

Definition: A subquery that depends on the outer query for its values.

Explanation: Correlated subqueries are executed once for each row processed by the outer query. They can be used in SELECT, UPDATE, DELETE, and MERGE statements.

Example:

```
SELECT e.EmployeeID, e.FirstName, e.LastName,
    (SELECT COUNT(*) FROM Orders o WHERE o.EmployeeID =
e.EmployeeID) AS OrderCount
FROM Employees e;
```

Cursor

Definition: A database object that allows row-by-row processing of a result set.

Explanation: Cursors provide a way to iterate through a result set and perform operations on individual rows. While they can be useful for certain tasks, they are generally less efficient than set-based operations.

Example:

```
DECLARE @CustomerID INT, @CustomerName NVARCHAR(100);

DECLARE customer_cursor CURSOR FOR
SELECT CustomerID, CustomerName FROM Customers;

OPEN customer_cursor;

FETCH NEXT FROM customer_cursor INTO @CustomerID, @CustomerName;

WHILE @@FETCH_STATUS = 0
BEGIN
    PRINT 'Processing customer: ' + @CustomerName;
    -- Perform operations on the current customer
```

```
     FETCH NEXT FROM customer_cursor INTO @CustomerID,
@CustomerName;
END

CLOSE customer_cursor;
DEALLOCATE customer_cursor;
```

D

Data Definition Language (DDL)

Definition: A subset of SQL used to define and modify the structure of database objects.

Explanation: Common DDL statements include:

- CREATE: Creates new database objects

- ALTER: Modifies existing database objects

- DROP: Removes database objects

- TRUNCATE: Removes all rows from a table

Example:

```
CREATE TABLE Customers (
    CustomerID INT PRIMARY KEY,
    CustomerName NVARCHAR(100),
    Email NVARCHAR(100)
);

ALTER TABLE Customers
ADD PhoneNumber NVARCHAR(20);

DROP TABLE Customers;
```

Data Manipulation Language (DML)

Definition: A subset of SQL used to retrieve, insert, update, and delete data in a database.

Explanation: Common DML statements include:

- SELECT: Retrieves data from one or more tables
- INSERT: Adds new rows to a table
- UPDATE: Modifies existing rows in a table
- DELETE: Removes rows from a table
- MERGE: Performs insert, update, or delete operations based on a join condition

Example:

```
INSERT INTO Customers (CustomerID, CustomerName, Email)
VALUES (1, 'John Doe', 'john@example.com');

UPDATE Customers
SET Email = 'johndoe@example.com'
WHERE CustomerID = 1;

DELETE FROM Customers
WHERE CustomerID = 1;
```

Data Control Language (DCL)

Definition: A subset of SQL used to control access to data within the database.

Explanation: Common DCL statements include:

- GRANT: Gives specific privileges to users or roles
- REVOKE: Removes specific privileges from users or roles

- DENY: Explicitly prevents a user from performing specific actions

Example:

```
GRANT SELECT, INSERT ON Customers TO SalesRole;

REVOKE INSERT ON Customers FROM SalesRole;

DENY DELETE ON Customers TO SalesRole;
```

Database Diagram

Definition: A visual representation of the tables in a database and their relationships.

Explanation: Database diagrams help in:

- Understanding the structure of a database
- Identifying relationships between tables
- Planning database changes
- Documenting database design

Deadlock

Definition: A situation where two or more transactions are waiting for each other to release locks, resulting in a circular dependency.

Explanation: Deadlocks can occur when:

- Transactions acquire locks in different orders
- Long-running transactions hold locks for extended periods

SQL Server automatically detects and resolves deadlocks by choosing a deadlock victim to roll back.

Declarative Referential Integrity (DRI)

Definition: A method of enforcing data integrity through the use of constraints defined in the database schema.

Explanation: DRI is implemented using:

- PRIMARY KEY constraints
- FOREIGN KEY constraints
- UNIQUE constraints
- CHECK constraints

DRI ensures that relationships between tables are maintained and that only valid data is entered into the database.

Default Constraint

Definition: A constraint that specifies a default value for a column when no value is explicitly provided during an insert operation.

Explanation: Default constraints are useful for:

- Providing meaningful default values
- Reducing the need for explicit values in INSERT statements
- Ensuring consistency in data entry

Example:

```
CREATE TABLE Orders (
    OrderID INT PRIMARY KEY,
```

```
    OrderDate DATE DEFAULT GETDATE(),
    Status NVARCHAR(20) DEFAULT 'Pending'
);
```

Derived Table

Definition: A subquery that returns a result set and is used in the FROM clause of an outer query.

Explanation: Derived tables are useful for:

- Breaking down complex queries into simpler parts
- Creating temporary result sets for further processing
- Applying aggregations or filters before joining with other tables

Example:

```
SELECT dt.CategoryName, AVG(dt.ProductCount) AS AvgProductCount
FROM (
    SELECT c.CategoryName, COUNT(*) AS ProductCount
    FROM Categories c
    JOIN Products p ON c.CategoryID = p.CategoryID
    GROUP BY c.CategoryID, c.CategoryName
) AS dt
GROUP BY dt.CategoryName;
```

Dynamic SQL

Definition: SQL statements that are constructed and executed at runtime.

Explanation: Dynamic SQL allows for:

- Creating flexible queries based on runtime conditions

- Executing SQL statements stored in variables or generated by the application

- Performing operations on database objects whose names are not known until runtime

Example:

```
DECLARE @TableName NVARCHAR(100) = 'Customers';
DECLARE @SQL NVARCHAR(MAX);

SET @SQL = 'SELECT * FROM ' + @TableName;

EXEC sp_executesql @SQL;
```

E

Execution Plan

Definition: A representation of the steps SQL Server takes to execute a query.

Explanation: Execution plans provide information about:

- The order of operations

- Indexes used

- Join algorithms

- Estimated and actual row counts

Analyzing execution plans is crucial for query optimization and performance tuning.

EXISTS

Definition: A subquery operator that tests for the existence of rows that satisfy the subquery.

Explanation: EXISTS is often more efficient than IN when working with large datasets. It stops processing as soon as a match is found.

Example:

```sql
SELECT CustomerID, CustomerName
FROM Customers c
WHERE EXISTS (
    SELECT 1
    FROM Orders o
    WHERE o.CustomerID = c.CustomerID
);
```

Extended Events

Definition: A lightweight, highly scalable system for collecting diagnostic information in SQL Server.

Explanation: Extended Events are used for:

- Performance monitoring
- Troubleshooting
- Auditing database activity

They offer more flexibility and lower overhead compared to SQL Trace.

Example:

```sql
CREATE EVENT SESSION [MonitorDeadlocks] ON SERVER
ADD EVENT sqlserver.xml_deadlock_report
ADD TARGET package0.event_file(SET filename=N'C:
\Logs\Deadlocks.xel')
```

```
WITH (MAX_MEMORY=4096
KB,EVENT_RETENTION_MODE=ALLOW_SINGLE_EVENT_LOSS,
MAX_DISPATCH_LATENCY=30 SECONDS,MAX_EVENT_SIZE=0
KB,MEMORY_PARTITION_MODE=NONE,
TRACK_CAUSALITY=OFF,STARTUP_STATE=OFF)
GO

ALTER EVENT SESSION [MonitorDeadlocks] ON SERVER STATE = START;
```

F

File Group

Definition: A logical container for file allocation and administration in SQL Server databases.

Explanation: File groups allow for:

- Distributing data across multiple files and disks
- Improving I/O performance
- Simplifying database administration

Every database has at least one file group (the PRIMARY file group).

Full-Text Search

Definition: A feature in SQL Server that allows for efficient searching of character-based data in database tables.

Explanation: Full-text search provides:

- Language-aware searching

- Inflectional and thesaurus matching

- Relevance ranking

- Support for proximity searches

Example:

```
CREATE FULLTEXT CATALOG ft_catalog AS DEFAULT;

CREATE FULLTEXT INDEX ON Products(Description)
KEY INDEX PK_Products
ON ft_catalog;

SELECT ProductID, ProductName
FROM Products
WHERE CONTAINS(Description, 'comfortable AND chair');
```

Function

Definition: A reusable block of T-SQL code that returns a value.

Explanation: SQL Server supports several types of functions:

- Scalar functions: Return a single value

- Table-valued functions: Return a table result set

- Aggregate functions: Perform calculations across a set of rows

Example (Scalar function):

```
CREATE FUNCTION dbo.CalculateAge
(
    @BirthDate DATE
)
RETURNS INT
AS
BEGIN
    RETURN DATEDIFF(YEAR, @BirthDate, GETDATE()) -
        CASE
```

```
            WHEN (MONTH(@BirthDate) > MONTH(GETDATE())) OR
                 (MONTH(@BirthDate) = MONTH(GETDATE()) AND
DAY(@BirthDate) > DAY(GETDATE()))
              THEN 1
              ELSE 0
         END
END;
```

G

GUID (Globally Unique Identifier)

Definition: A 128-bit integer used to identify database objects.

Explanation: GUIDs (also known as UUIDs) are useful for:

- Generating unique identifiers across distributed systems

- Merging data from multiple sources

- Creating surrogate keys

In SQL Server, GUIDs are represented by the UNIQUEIDENTIFIER data type.

Example:

```
CREATE TABLE Documents (
    DocumentID UNIQUEIDENTIFIER PRIMARY KEY DEFAULT NEWID(),
    Title NVARCHAR(100),
    Content NVARCHAR(MAX)
);

INSERT INTO Documents (Title, Content)
VALUES ('Sample Document', 'This is the content of the sample
document.');
```

H

Hash Join

Definition: A join algorithm that uses a hash table to match rows from two tables.

Explanation: Hash joins are often used for equi-joins on large tables. The process involves:

1. Building a hash table from the smaller table
2. Probing the hash table with rows from the larger table

Hash joins are generally more efficient than nested loops joins for large datasets.

Hierarchyid

Definition: A data type in SQL Server used to represent hierarchical data.

Explanation: Hierarchyid provides:

- Efficient storage of tree structures
- Built-in methods for traversing and manipulating hierarchies
- Support for common hierarchical operations (e.g., finding ancestors, descendants)

Example:

```
CREATE TABLE Employees (
    EmployeeID INT PRIMARY KEY,
    Name NVARCHAR(100),
    Position HIERARCHYID
);

INSERT INTO Employees (EmployeeID, Name, Position)
```

```
VALUES
(1, 'John Doe', hierarchyid::GetRoot()),
(2, 'Jane Smith', hierarchyid::GetRoot().GetDescendant(NULL,
NULL)),
(3, 'Bob Johnson', hierarchyid::GetRoot().GetDescendant(NULL,
NULL));

UPDATE Employees
SET Position = hierarchyid::GetRoot().GetDescendant(NULL, NULL)
WHERE EmployeeID = 2;

SELECT EmployeeID, Name, Position.ToString() AS HierarchyString
FROM Employees;
```

I

Identity Column

Definition: A column in a table that automatically generates unique numeric values.

Explanation: Identity columns are commonly used for:

- Creating surrogate primary keys
- Generating sequential numbers

The IDENTITY property specifies the seed (starting value) and increment for the column.

Example:

```
CREATE TABLE Orders (
    OrderID INT IDENTITY(1000, 1) PRIMARY KEY,
    CustomerID INT,
    OrderDate DATE
```

```
) ;
```

Index

Definition: A database object that improves the speed of data retrieval operations on database tables.

Explanation: Indexes can be:

- Clustered: Determines the physical order of data in a table (one per table)
- Non-clustered: Creates a separate structure for faster data lookups (multiple per table)

Proper indexing is crucial for query performance optimization.

Example:

```
CREATE NONCLUSTERED INDEX IX_Customers_LastName
ON Customers (LastName);
```

INSTEAD OF Trigger

Definition: A trigger that executes instead of the triggering action (INSERT, UPDATE, or DELETE).

Explanation: INSTEAD OF triggers are useful for:

- Implementing complex business rules
- Modifying or preventing the original operation
- Handling operations on views that cannot be directly updated

Example:

```
CREATE TRIGGER tr_InsteadOfInsertCustomers
ON Customers
INSTEAD OF INSERT
AS
BEGIN
    SET NOCOUNT ON;

    INSERT INTO Customers (CustomerName, Email)
    SELECT CustomerName, LOWER(Email)
    FROM inserted
    WHERE NOT EXISTS (SELECT 1 FROM Customers WHERE Email =
inserted.Email);
END;
```

Isolation Level

Definition: A setting that determines how transaction integrity is enforced.

Explanation: SQL Server supports several isolation levels:

- READ UNCOMMITTED: Allows dirty reads

- READ COMMITTED: Prevents dirty reads (default)

- REPEATABLE READ: Prevents dirty reads and non-repeatable reads

- SERIALIZABLE: Prevents dirty reads, non-repeatable reads, and phantom reads

- SNAPSHOT: Provides statement-level read consistency

Isolation levels balance data consistency with concurrency and performance.

Example:

```
SET TRANSACTION ISOLATION LEVEL READ COMMITTED;

BEGIN TRANSACTION;

-- Perform database operations
```

```
COMMIT TRANSACTION;
```

J

Join

Definition: An operation that combines rows from two or more tables based on a related column between them.

Explanation: Common types of joins include:

- INNER JOIN: Returns only matching rows
- LEFT JOIN: Returns all rows from the left table and matching rows from the right table
- RIGHT JOIN: Returns all rows from the right table and matching rows from the left table
- FULL OUTER JOIN: Returns all rows when there is a match in either table
- CROSS JOIN: Returns the Cartesian product of both tables

Example:

```
SELECT o.OrderID, c.CustomerName, o.OrderDate
FROM Orders o
INNER JOIN Customers c ON o.CustomerID = c.CustomerID;
```

K

Key

Definition: A column or set of columns used to identify rows in a table or establish relationships between tables.

Explanation: Types of keys include:

- Primary Key: Uniquely identifies each row in a table
- Foreign Key: Establishes a link between two tables
- Candidate Key: A minimal set of columns that could serve as a primary key
- Composite Key: A key that consists of two or more columns

Example:

```
CREATE TABLE Orders (
    OrderID INT PRIMARY KEY,
    CustomerID INT,
    OrderDate DATE,
    FOREIGN KEY (CustomerID) REFERENCES Customers(CustomerID)
);
```

L

Locking

Definition: A mechanism used to control concurrent access to shared resources in a database.

    Explanation: SQL Server uses various types of locks:

- Shared (S) locks: Used for read operations
- Exclusive (X) locks: Used for write operations
- Update (U) locks: Used to prevent deadlocks in update scenarios
- Intent locks: Used to establish a lock hierarchy

Proper lock management is crucial for maintaining data integrity and optimizing concurrency.

Log Shipping

Definition: A high-availability solution that maintains one or more secondary databases for a primary database.

    Explanation: Log shipping involves:

1. Backing up the transaction log on the primary server
2. Copying the log backup to one or more secondary servers
3. Restoring the log backup on each secondary server

Log shipping provides a disaster recovery solution with minimal data loss.

M

Materialized View

Definition: A database object that contains the results of a query, stored as a physical table.

Explanation: In SQL Server, materialized views are implemented as indexed views. They offer:

- Improved query performance for complex aggregations
- Data redundancy for frequently accessed data
- Support for distributed queries

Example:

```
CREATE VIEW vw_OrderSummary
WITH SCHEMABINDING
AS
SELECT o.CustomerID, COUNT_BIG(*) AS OrderCount, SUM(od.Quantity
* od.UnitPrice) AS TotalAmount
FROM dbo.Orders o
JOIN dbo.OrderDetails od ON o.OrderID = od.OrderID
GROUP BY o.CustomerID;

CREATE UNIQUE CLUSTERED INDEX IX_vw_OrderSummary
ON vw_OrderSummary (CustomerID);
```

Merge Statement

Definition: A T-SQL statement that performs insert, update, and delete operations in a single statement.

Explanation: MERGE is useful for:

- Synchronizing data between tables

- Implementing upsert operations

- Performing complex data integration tasks

Example:

```
MERGE INTO TargetTable AS target
USING SourceTable AS source
ON (target.ID = source.ID)
WHEN MATCHED THEN
    UPDATE SET target.Column1 = source.Column1, target.Column2 =
source.Column2
WHEN NOT MATCHED BY TARGET THEN
    INSERT (ID, Column1, Column2)
    VALUES (source.ID, source.Column1, source.Column2)
WHEN NOT MATCHED BY SOURCE THEN
    DELETE;
```

N

Normalization

Definition: The process of organizing data in a database to reduce redundancy and improve data integrity.

Explanation: Common normal forms include:

- First Normal Form (1NF): Eliminate repeating groups

- Second Normal Form (2NF): Remove partial dependencies

- Third Normal Form (3NF): Remove transitive dependencies

Normalization helps prevent update anomalies and ensures data consistency.

NOLOCK Hint

Definition: A table hint that specifies that no shared locks are issued against the table or view.

Explanation: NOLOCK (equivalent to READ UNCOMMITTED) allows:

- Dirty reads (reading uncommitted data)
- Non-repeatable reads
- Phantom reads

While it can improve concurrency, it should be used with caution due to potential data inconsistencies.

Example:

```
SELECT * FROM Orders WITH (NOLOCK)
WHERE OrderDate >= '2023-01-01';
```

O

Optimistic Concurrency

Definition: A concurrency control method that allows multiple users to access data simultaneously without locking.

Explanation: Optimistic concurrency:

- Assumes conflicts are rare
- Checks for conflicts at the time of update
- Uses timestamps or version numbers to detect changes

It can improve performance in scenarios with low contention.

Output Clause

Definition: A clause in T-SQL that returns data from the modified rows in INSERT, UPDATE, DELETE, and MERGE statements.

Explanation: The OUTPUT clause is useful for:

- Capturing the results of data modification operations
- Auditing changes
- Performing additional operations based on the modified data

Example:

```
UPDATE Employees
SET Salary = Salary * 1.1
OUTPUT inserted.EmployeeID, deleted.Salary AS OldSalary,
inserted.Salary AS NewSalary
WHERE Department = 'Sales';
```

P

Partition

Definition: A division of a table or index into smaller, more manageable units.

Explanation: Partitioning offers several benefits:

- Improved query performance through partition elimination
- Easier data archiving and maintenance

- Enhanced scalability for very large tables

Example:

```
CREATE PARTITION FUNCTION PF_OrderDate (DATE)
AS RANGE RIGHT FOR VALUES ('2022-01-01', '2023-01-01',
'2024-01-01');

CREATE PARTITION SCHEME PS_OrderDate
AS PARTITION PF_OrderDate
TO (FG1, FG2, FG3, FG4);

CREATE TABLE Orders (
    OrderID INT,
    OrderDate DATE,
    CustomerID INT,
    TotalAmount DECIMAL(10,2)
) ON PS_OrderDate(OrderDate);
```

Pivot

Definition: An operation that converts rows into columns, typically used for generating crosstab reports.

Explanation: PIVOT is useful for:

- Creating summary reports
- Transforming normalized data into a more readable format
- Performing complex aggregations

Example:

```
SELECT *
FROM (
    SELECT Category, YEAR(OrderDate) AS Year, TotalAmount
    FROM Orders
) AS SourceTable
```

```
PIVOT (
    SUM(TotalAmount)
    FOR Year IN ([2021], [2022], [2023])
) AS PivotTable;
```

Primary Key

Definition: A column or set of columns that uniquely identifies each row in a table.

Explanation: Primary keys:

- Ensure data integrity

- Provide a natural way to reference rows

- Are often used as the target of foreign key relationships

Example:

```
CREATE TABLE Customers (
    CustomerID INT PRIMARY KEY,
    CustomerName NVARCHAR(100),
    Email NVARCHAR(100)
);
```

Procedure (Stored Procedure)

Definition: A named collection of T-SQL statements stored in the database.

Explanation: Stored procedures offer several advantages:

- Code reusability

- Improved security through encapsulation

- Reduced network traffic

- Better performance through execution plan caching

Example:

```
CREATE PROCEDURE usp_GetCustomerOrders
    @CustomerID INT
AS
BEGIN
    SET NOCOUNT ON;

    SELECT o.OrderID, o.OrderDate, o.TotalAmount
    FROM Orders o
    WHERE o.CustomerID = @CustomerID
    ORDER BY o.OrderDate DESC;
END;

-- Execute the stored procedure
EXEC usp_GetCustomerOrders @CustomerID = 1001;
```

Q

Query Hint

Definition: An instruction to the query optimizer that affects how a query is executed.

Explanation: Query hints can be used to:

- Force a specific join order
- Specify a particular index
- Control parallelism

While hints can be useful for troubleshooting, they should be used sparingly as they can prevent the optimizer from choosing the best execution plan.

Example:

```
SELECT c.CustomerID, c.CustomerName, o.OrderID, o.OrderDate
FROM Customers c
INNER LOOP JOIN Orders o ON c.CustomerID = o.CustomerID
OPTION (FORCE ORDER, LOOP JOIN);
```

Query Plan Cache

Definition: A memory area in SQL Server that stores execution plans for reuse.

Explanation: The query plan cache:

- Improves query performance by avoiding repeated compilation
- Stores plans based on the exact text of the query
- Can be monitored and managed to optimize server performance

R

RAISERROR

Definition: A T-SQL statement used to generate error messages and initiate error processing.

Explanation: RAISERROR allows you to:

- Generate custom error messages
- Control the severity and state of the error
- Trigger error handling in applications

Example:

```
RAISERROR ('An error occurred: %s', 16, 1, 'Custom error
message');
```

Ranking Function

Definition: A type of window function that assigns a rank to each row within a partition of a result set.

Explanation: Common ranking functions include:

- ROW_NUMBER(): Assigns unique sequential integers
- RANK(): Assigns ranks with gaps for ties
- DENSE_RANK(): Assigns ranks without gaps for ties

Example:

```
SELECT
    ProductName,
    Category,
    Price,
    ROW_NUMBER() OVER (PARTITION BY Category ORDER BY Price DESC)
AS PriceRank
FROM Products;
```

Recovery Model

Definition: A database property that controls how transactions are logged, whether the transaction log requires backing up, and what kinds of restore operations are available.

Explanation: SQL Server offers three recovery models:

1. Simple: No log backups, minimal logging for bulk operations
2. Full: Requires log backups, full point-in-time recovery

3. Bulk-logged: Minimal logging for bulk operations, requires log backups

Recursive CTE

Definition: A common table expression that references itself, used for querying hierarchical or graph-structured data.

Explanation: Recursive CTEs consist of:

- An anchor member: The initial query that forms the base result set
- A recursive member: The part that references the CTE itself

Example (Employee hierarchy):

```
WITH EmployeeHierarchy AS (
    -- Anchor member
    SELECT EmployeeID, FirstName, LastName, ManagerID, 0 AS Level
    FROM Employees
    WHERE ManagerID IS NULL

    UNION ALL

    -- Recursive member
    SELECT e.EmployeeID, e.FirstName, e.LastName, e.ManagerID,
eh.Level + 1
    FROM Employees e
    INNER JOIN EmployeeHierarchy eh ON e.ManagerID =
eh.EmployeeID
)
SELECT * FROM EmployeeHierarchy
ORDER BY Level, EmployeeID;
```

Replication

Definition: A set of technologies for copying and distributing data and database objects from one database to another, then synchronizing between databases to maintain consistency.

Explanation: SQL Server supports several types of replication:

- Snapshot replication: Distributes data exactly as it appears at a specific moment in time
- Transactional replication: Propagates changes to subscribers in near real-time
- Merge replication: Allows both the publisher and subscribers to make updates

Rollback

Definition: A statement that undoes all the data modifications made in the current transaction.

Explanation: ROLLBACK is used to:

- Maintain data consistency in case of errors
- Implement transaction control in applications
- Undo changes in a transaction that should not be committed

Example:

```
BEGIN TRANSACTION;

UPDATE Accounts SET Balance = Balance - 1000 WHERE AccountID = 1;
UPDATE Accounts SET Balance = Balance + 1000 WHERE AccountID = 2;

IF @@ERROR <> 0
```

```
    ROLLBACK TRANSACTION;
ELSE
    COMMIT TRANSACTION;
```

S

Scalar Function

Definition: A user-defined function that returns a single value.

Explanation: Scalar functions:

- Can be used in SELECT statements, WHERE clauses, and computed columns
- Accept parameters and perform calculations
- Are useful for encapsulating complex logic

Example:

```
CREATE FUNCTION dbo.CalculateDiscount
(
    @Price DECIMAL(10,2),
    @DiscountPercentage DECIMAL(5,2)
)
RETURNS DECIMAL(10,2)
AS
BEGIN
    RETURN @Price * (1 - @DiscountPercentage / 100);
END;

-- Usage
SELECT ProductName, Price, dbo.CalculateDiscount(Price, 10) AS
DiscountedPrice
```

```
FROM Products;
```

Schema

Definition: A named container for database objects such as tables, views, and stored procedures.

Explanation: Schemas provide:

- Logical grouping of database objects
- A way to manage security and permissions
- Namespace separation to avoid naming conflicts

Example:

```
CREATE SCHEMA Sales;
GO

CREATE TABLE Sales.Customers (
    CustomerID INT PRIMARY KEY,
    CustomerName NVARCHAR(100)
);
```

Sequence

Definition: A schema-bound object that generates a sequence of numeric values according to the specified parameters.

Explanation: Sequences offer advantages over identity columns:

- Can be shared across multiple tables
- Allow for more control over the generated values
- Support cycling and custom increments

Example:

```
CREATE SEQUENCE dbo.OrderNumberSequence
    AS INT
    START WITH 1000
    INCREMENT BY 1
    MINVALUE 1000
    MAXVALUE 999999
    CYCLE;

-- Usage
INSERT INTO Orders (OrderID, CustomerID, OrderDate)
VALUES (NEXT VALUE FOR dbo.OrderNumberSequence, 1001, GETDATE());
```

Service Broker

Definition: A feature in SQL Server that provides native support for messaging and queuing applications.

Explanation: Service Broker enables:

- Asynchronous processing
- Reliable message delivery
- Scalable application design

It's particularly useful for building distributed and decoupled applications.

Snapshot Isolation

Definition: A transaction isolation level that allows transactions to read data as it existed at the start of the transaction, without acquiring locks.

Explanation: Snapshot isolation:

- Reduces blocking and deadlocks

- Provides statement-level read consistency

- Uses row versioning to maintain data consistency

To enable snapshot isolation:

```
ALTER DATABASE YourDatabase
SET ALLOW_SNAPSHOT_ISOLATION ON;

-- Usage
SET TRANSACTION ISOLATION LEVEL SNAPSHOT;
BEGIN TRANSACTION;
-- Perform operations
COMMIT TRANSACTION;
```

Sparse Column

Definition: A column that is optimized for storing null values.

Explanation: Sparse columns:

- Reduce storage space for tables with many null values

- Are transparent to applications

- Have some limitations (e.g., cannot be used in clustered indexes)

Example:

```
CREATE TABLE Employees (
    EmployeeID INT PRIMARY KEY,
    FirstName NVARCHAR(50),
    LastName NVARCHAR(50),
    MiddleName NVARCHAR(50) SPARSE NULL,
    SecondaryEmail NVARCHAR(100) SPARSE NULL
);
```

Statistics

Definition: Objects that contain statistical information about the distribution of values in one or more columns of a table or indexed view.

Explanation: Statistics are used by the query optimizer to:

- Estimate the cost of different query plans
- Choose the most efficient execution plan
- Improve query performance

SQL Server can create and update statistics automatically, but manual management is sometimes necessary for optimal performance.

Example:

```
-- Create statistics
CREATE STATISTICS Stats_LastName ON Employees(LastName);

-- Update statistics
UPDATE STATISTICS Employees Stats_LastName WITH FULLSCAN;
```

Synonym

Definition: A database object that serves as an alternative name for another database object.

Explanation: Synonyms are useful for:

- Providing a layer of abstraction
- Simplifying access to objects in different schemas or databases
- Easing the transition when refactoring database objects

Example:

```
CREATE SYNONYM dbo.Customers FOR Sales.Customers;
```

```
-- Usage
SELECT * FROM dbo.Customers;
```

T

Table Variable

Definition: A variable that can hold a table-like result set in memory.

Explanation: Table variables:

- Have a scope limited to the batch, function, or stored procedure in which they are declared
- Are useful for storing temporary results
- Can have indexes, but statistics are not maintained

Example:

```
DECLARE @TopCustomers TABLE (
    CustomerID INT,
    CustomerName NVARCHAR(100),
    TotalPurchases DECIMAL(10,2)
);

INSERT INTO @TopCustomers (CustomerID, CustomerName,
TotalPurchases)
SELECT TOP 10 c.CustomerID, c.CustomerName, SUM(o.TotalAmount) AS
TotalPurchases
FROM Customers c
JOIN Orders o ON c.CustomerID = o.CustomerID
GROUP BY c.CustomerID, c.CustomerName
ORDER BY TotalPurchases DESC;
```

```
-- Use the table variable
SELECT * FROM @TopCustomers;
```

Temporal Tables

Definition: A feature in SQL Server that provides built-in support for maintaining a history of data changes.

Explanation: Temporal tables:

- Automatically maintain historical data
- Allow for querying data as it existed at any point in time
- Simplify auditing and point-in-time analysis

Example:

```
CREATE TABLE Products (
    ProductID INT PRIMARY KEY,
    ProductName NVARCHAR(100),
    Price DECIMAL(10,2),
    ValidFrom DATETIME2 GENERATED ALWAYS AS ROW START,
    ValidTo DATETIME2 GENERATED ALWAYS AS ROW END,
    PERIOD FOR SYSTEM_TIME (ValidFrom, ValidTo)
)
WITH (SYSTEM_VERSIONING = ON);

-- Query data as of a specific point in time
SELECT * FROM Products
FOR SYSTEM_TIME AS OF '2023-01-01 12:00:00';
```

Transaction

Definition: A sequence of database operations that are treated as a single unit of work.

Explanation: Transactions ensure:

- Atomicity: All operations succeed or all fail
- Consistency: The database remains in a consistent state
- Isolation: Transactions are isolated from each other
- Durability: Committed changes are permanent

Example:

```
BEGIN TRANSACTION;

UPDATE Accounts SET Balance = Balance - 100 WHERE AccountID = 1;
UPDATE Accounts SET Balance = Balance + 100 WHERE AccountID = 2;

IF @@ERROR = 0
    COMMIT TRANSACTION;
ELSE
    ROLLBACK TRANSACTION;
```

Trigger

Definition: A special type of stored procedure that automatically executes when a specified event occurs in the database.

Explanation: Types of triggers:

- DML triggers: Respond to INSERT, UPDATE, or DELETE operations
- DDL triggers: Respond to CREATE, ALTER, or DROP statements
- Logon triggers: Execute in response to LOGON events

Triggers are useful for enforcing business rules, maintaining data integrity, and auditing changes.

Example (DML Trigger):

```
CREATE TRIGGER tr_UpdateOrderTotal
ON OrderDetails
AFTER INSERT, UPDATE, DELETE
AS
BEGIN
    SET NOCOUNT ON;

    UPDATE o
    SET TotalAmount = (SELECT SUM(Quantity * UnitPrice) FROM
OrderDetails WHERE OrderID = o.OrderID)
    FROM Orders o
    JOIN (
        SELECT DISTINCT OrderID FROM inserted
        UNION
        SELECT DISTINCT OrderID FROM deleted
    ) AS affected ON o.OrderID = affected.OrderID;
END;
```

U

Union

Definition: A set operator that combines the result sets of two or more SELECT statements.

Explanation: UNION:

- Removes duplicate rows by default (use UNION ALL to keep duplicates)
- Requires that all SELECT statements have the same number of columns
- Matches columns based on their position, not their names

Example:

```
SELECT CustomerID, CustomerName, 'Customer' AS Type
```

```
FROM Customers
UNION
SELECT SupplierID, SupplierName, 'Supplier' AS Type
FROM Suppliers
ORDER BY Type, CustomerName;
```

User-Defined Data Type

Definition: A custom data type created by a user based on an existing SQL Server system data type.

Explanation: User-defined data types:

- Enhance data consistency across tables
- Improve code readability
- Can include constraints and default values

Example:

```
CREATE TYPE PhoneNumber
FROM NVARCHAR(20) NOT NULL;

CREATE TABLE Contacts (
    ContactID INT PRIMARY KEY,
    FirstName NVARCHAR(50),
    LastName NVARCHAR(50),
    Phone PhoneNumber
);
```

User-Defined Table Type

Definition: A user-defined type that represents a table structure.

Explanation: User-defined table types:

- Can be used as parameters for stored procedures and functions

- Allow for passing multiple rows of data in a single parameter

- Improve performance when working with large sets of data

Example:

```sql
CREATE TYPE OrderDetailsType AS TABLE (
    ProductID INT,
    Quantity INT,
    UnitPrice DECIMAL(10,2)
);

CREATE PROCEDURE usp_CreateOrder
    @CustomerID INT,
    @OrderDate DATE,
    @OrderDetails OrderDetailsType READONLY
AS
BEGIN
    -- Create the order
    INSERT INTO Orders (CustomerID, OrderDate)
    VALUES (@CustomerID, @OrderDate);

    DECLARE @OrderID INT = SCOPE_IDENTITY();

    -- Insert order details
    INSERT INTO OrderDetails (OrderID, ProductID, Quantity,
UnitPrice)
    SELECT @OrderID, ProductID, Quantity, UnitPrice
    FROM @OrderDetails;
END;

-- Usage
DECLARE @Details OrderDetailsType;
INSERT INTO @Details VALUES (1, 5, 10.00), (2, 3, 15.00);

EXEC usp_CreateOrder @CustomerID = 1001, @OrderDate =
'2023-05-01', @OrderDetails = @Details;
```

V

View

Definition: A virtual table based on the result set of a SELECT statement.

Explanation: Views provide:

- A way to simplify complex queries
- A security layer by restricting access to underlying tables
- A mechanism for presenting data in a format that's different from the physical storage

Example:

```sql
CREATE VIEW vw_CustomerOrders AS
SELECT
    c.CustomerID,
    c.CustomerName,
    o.OrderID,
    o.OrderDate,
    od.ProductID,
    p.ProductName,
    od.Quantity,
    od.UnitPrice,
    (od.Quantity * od.UnitPrice) AS TotalAmount
FROM Customers c
JOIN Orders o ON c.CustomerID = o.CustomerID
JOIN OrderDetails od ON o.OrderID = od.OrderID
JOIN Products p ON od.ProductID = p.ProductID;

-- Usage
SELECT * FROM vw_CustomerOrders
WHERE CustomerID = 1001;
```

W

Window Function

Definition: A function that performs calculations across a set of rows that are related to the current row.

Explanation: Window functions:

- Allow for complex analytical queries
- Can be used for ranking, running totals, and moving averages
- Are processed after the WHERE clause but before the final SELECT list

Common window functions include ROW_NUMBER(), RANK(), DENSE_RANK(), LAG(), LEAD(), and aggregates with OVER clause.

Example:

```
SELECT
    OrderID,
    OrderDate,
    TotalAmount,
    SUM(TotalAmount) OVER (ORDER BY OrderDate) AS RunningTotal,
    AVG(TotalAmount) OVER (ORDER BY OrderDate ROWS BETWEEN 2
PRECEDING AND CURRENT ROW) AS MovingAverage
FROM Orders;
```

X

XML

Definition: A data type in SQL Server used to store and manipulate XML data.

Explanation: XML support in SQL Server includes:

- Storage of XML documents and fragments
- Querying XML data using XQuery
- Indexing XML columns for improved performance
- Shredding XML data into relational format

Example:

```
CREATE TABLE Documents (
    DocumentID INT PRIMARY KEY,
    DocumentData XML
);

INSERT INTO Documents (DocumentID, DocumentData)
VALUES (1, '<Document><Title>Sample Document</Title><Author>John
Doe</Author></Document>');

-- Query XML data
SELECT
    DocumentID,
    DocumentData.value('(/Document/Title)[1]', 'NVARCHAR(100)')
AS Title,
    DocumentData.value('(/Document/Author)[1]', 'NVARCHAR(100)')
AS Author
FROM Documents;
```

This glossary covers a wide range of terms and concepts related to T-SQL and SQL Server programming. It provides definitions, explanations, and examples to help users understand and apply these concepts in their database development and administration tasks.

Made in United States
Troutdale, OR
01/03/2025

27502909R00244